# The Spinner's Turn

# The Spinner's Turn

## PATRICK MURPHY
### Foreword by G.O.Allen

J. M. Dent & Sons Ltd
London   Melbourne   Toronto

First published 1982
© Patrick Murphy 1982

This book is set in 11/13 VIP Sabon by
D. P. Media Limited, Hitchin, Hertfordshire
Printed in Great Britain by
The Alden Press Ltd, Oxford, for
J. M. Dent & Sons Ltd
Aldine House, 33 Welbeck Street, London W1


British Library Cataloguing in Publication Data

Murphy, Patrick
    The spinner's turn.
    1. Cricket — Bowling
    I. Title
    796.35′822        GV917

ISBN 0-460-04552-0

# Contents

Acknowledgements *vi*
Foreword by G. O. Allen CBE *vii*
Preface *ix*

1 **What Hope For Spin?** *1*
2 **The Characters** *11*
3 **The Artists** *51*
4 **The Psychology of Spin** *99*
5 **Captaining Slow Bowlers** *111*

**FOUR GREAT TEST MATCHES** *119*

6 **Batting Against Spin** *147*
7 **Keeping Against Spin** *159*
8 **Spin in Limited-Over Cricket** *169*
9 **Portents from the 1981 Season** *179*
10 **How to Revive Spin Bowling** *183*

Statistical Appendix *197*
Index *203*

## Acknowledgments

The author and publisher wish to thank the following for their kind permission to reproduce the photographs as listed below:

Birmingham Gazette: p. 23
Central Press Photos Ltd: p. 31, 129, 136, 142
Patrick Eagar: frontispiece, p. 118, 156
Ken Kelly: p. 32, 44, 65, 71, 73, 74, 80, 82, 85, 91, 94, 100, 105, 108–9, 113, 114, 117, 152, 153, 154, 155, 157, 165, 176
S & G Press Agency Ltd: p. 12, 35, 41, 53, 54, 57, 62, 120, 163


The jacket photograph is of John Emburey bowling in the last Test at the Oval, 1981, England v. Australia, and is reproduced by courtesy of Ken Kelly.

# Foreword by G.O.Allen CBE

This book should be read by all lovers of cricket and, more importantly, should be studied carefully by all administrators of the game. I urge this because it deals, as the title suggests, with one of cricket's major problems, one which has become even more important in the last ten or fifteen years.

The gradual dominance of fast and seam bowling which has contributed to the virtual demise of the leg-spinner and slow left-armer is, in my judgement, a tragedy. Quite apart from the pleasure of watching a slow bowler in action and of appreciating the immense skill his art requires, the game without a fair ration of spin must inevitably lack variety – surely one of its greatest charms.

My only regret about this book is that it was not published some years ago. Indeed my one fear for it is its timing. Following close upon an exciting home Test series against Australia with record gate receipts, I sense that complacency is rampant. Money is, of course, very important but, if the game is not right, I for one do not believe the public will support it indefinitely. I suggest to those who are happy with the present state of affairs that they give thought to what the receipts last summer might have been had Ian Botham not made those two thrilling match-winning centuries.

This book has been energetically researched and written with the zest of someone who earnestly believes in his crusade. The anecdotes, too, are superbly told and I found them highly amusing. I have been somewhat surprised to find there are so many who share the author's view – and indeed mine – that something must be put in motion now with a view to helping the spinners. Lip-service, of which regrettably there is plenty, achieves nothing.

I warmly commend this book to all those who really care about the future of the game of cricket.

# Preface

This book is not designed to be a textbook on the art of spin. Therefore I have assumed that those who read it will not need explanations of terms like 'googly', 'chinaman', 'off-break', 'leg-break' and so on.

What I have tried to do instead is to advance arguments for the revival of spin bowling in modern, top-class cricket. Statistics over the last twenty years show the extent to which slow bowling has declined in the face of medium-pace, and, more recently, fast, short-pitched bowling. Yet at the same time the statistics show just how useful – and potentially important – spin bowling can be, at both Test and County level.

Many people wring their hands and say 'something must be done' to revive spin bowling. I have attempted to show what *can* be done – and what is in danger of being lost for ever if it is *not* done. To that end I am enormously grateful to the scores of past and present first-class cricketers who willingly gave me their time to discuss the subject. Many of the arguments for the revival of spin bowling will be found in their words, as much as in mine, in this book. Between us, I hope we can jog the minds and hearts of the legislators and administrators of the game, who alone have the power to change the rules for the benefit of not only the spinner, but, above all, the spectator.

My thanks are also due to Ken Kelly for his original suggestion and photographs, to John Stockwell and Charles Heward for specific statistical research, and to Robert Brooke for overall statistical assistance.

Patrick Murphy
November 1981

# 1. What Hope For Spin?

'God gave us memory so we could have roses in December', wrote J. M. Barrie, and for all those lovers of spin bowling, it now must seem like December every day. When analysing the modern decline in the use of spin bowling, it is perhaps easy to don rose-tinted spectacles and convince oneself that, in the past, every day of first-class cricket was chockful of men round the bat on a 'turner', with the ball being tossed generously up in the air for a hard-driving batsman to take his chance. Having conceded that point, there is still no doubt in my mind that first-class cricket has become a stereotyped exercise in England – and the lack of high-class spinners in regular use is a major contributing factor.

Despite the proliferation of world-class cricketers in English cricket, the first-class game in this country lacks variety. Slow bowling once offered that variety. The game used to have interesting phases – the fast men would start the attack, then, with the shine off the ball, the spinner would come on long before lunch. He might operate in tandem with a stock bowler at the other end who would provide solidity, while the spinner plied his more imaginative trade. Regularly two spinners would operate in harness – say an orthodox slow left-armer at one end and an offspinner at the other. Leg-spin was used to attack batsmen. When the second new ball was imminent, the batsmen would do their best to carry the attack to the spinners – especially if they realised that the opening bowlers were high-class performers. There was variety, a regular change in tempo and varying challenges to the batsmen.

No captain of any status used to think of going into a match without a balanced attack – and that usually included at least two spinners of different styles. Now the strategy revolves around a group of seam bowlers who are encouraged to run long distances, bowl short of a length and rely on wickets of uneven bounce to do their work for them. That fine batsman, John Hampshire, has a typically pithy response to the tactic – 'I get bored to bloody tears waiting for them to come in. Time just seems to stand still.' In Test cricket it is now

1

accepted that the batsman has to make the running and the fewer balls he gets, so much the better for the fielding side. As Colin Cowdrey puts it, 'The dot ball has become the Holy Grail. If I came back today as a young batsman, I wouldn't enjoy having to face just seamers hour after hour.'

Nor do the public. Hard-headed professionals tell me: 'The public are happy as long as England win, they don't care if the over-rate is 12 or 20 an hour', yet I feel that is just reaction to the fact that if the best team in the world – the West Indies – do not bother about such considerations, why should other Test sides? On the 1980 tour of England, the West Indies cynically exploited their advantage of having four high-class seam bowlers of varying types. In the absence of official censure or penalties, they simply bowled as few balls as possible and a full day's play would result in less than 20 overs apiece from Roberts, Holding, Croft and Garner. Their manager, Clyde Walcott, remained unconcerned about over-rates, contenting himself with the bleak forecast that the way the 1980 West Indies side played was the shape of things to come for all Test cricket. Just a couple of statistics underline the spectacular decline in over-rates in the last quarter of a century. At the Oval in 1980, the West Indies sent down 75 balls an hour – in the First Test against South Africa at Trent Bridge in 1947, the total was 141 an hour, with the daily average for that Test series 127 an hour. At Trent Bridge in 1957, the England attack included just one spinner – Jim Laker. He bowled 105 overs in the match, Statham and Trueman a total of 135 and yet the England over rate averaged 111 in a six-hour a day!

Although the West Indies are currently the masters at the 'percentage' form of out-cricket, other countries are following suit. After all, runs the argument, Test cricketers are a pragmatic breed of men and if the world champions can get away with robbing the public of at least an hour's cricket every day, why should other Test teams perform differently? The 85 balls per hour that were delivered on average in the Ashes series of 1981 only underlines the fact that Clyde Walcott's philosophy is continuing to triumph, and no amount of pious statements from the International Cricket Conference will make the slightest difference.

So where does all this leave the spinner? The answer – in danger of being classified as an endangered species. The influence of Test cricket percolates down through to all levels of cricket and the attitudes of the captains, the tactical formulae and bowling strategies are copied.

G. O. Allen, a man associated with first-class cricket for sixty years, underlined the crisis when he told me, 'All kids are mimics. But who in their right mind would think of becoming a leg-spinner these days? There are hardly any of them around, so where would a young lad actually see a leggie in action to be inspired enough to want to emulate him?' On the village green, in club cricket, in the leagues, through to county cricket, the pattern is becoming depressingly familiar – strong, fit bowlers running far too many yards to deliver medium-pace to a defensive field. Limited-over cricket is the vogue in all branches of the English game – David Allen, an off-spinner good enough to take more than a hundred wickets for England, still plays club cricket in Bristol and he told me, 'The field placings are just like those in the John Player League. The captains have seen how the modern game's being played by the professionals and they think that's the right way. It certainly isn't for the poor spinner, because he doesn't get a look in.'

Nowhere is this more of a problem than in Yorkshire, the spiritual home of slow bowling for decades. The county that produced Peel, Rhodes, Verity and Wardle cannot find a good enough spinner to hold down a regular first-team place. Their manager, Ray Illingworth – himself a great slow bowler for the county – sums up the dilemma: 'Thirty years ago, you could get a dozen slow left arm bowlers from the Bradford League who could do a good job for Yorkshire, and perhaps one of them might have turned out to be a great bowler. Today, I can't find one that is good enough for county cricket – and the same applies to offspinners. Mind you, in those days, we didn't have league cricketers sitting around watching the John Player League on TV, picking up all the tips. At fifty overs, the Bradford League is just an extension of the John Player, which doesn't produce any spinners – just containment bowlers. The situation for slow bowling is the worst I've ever known and what frightens me is – where the hell are we going to find them?'

So if Yorkshire – with its resources, tradition and sheer volume of cricketers – cannot find top-class young spinners, who can? One-day cricket has harmed the cause of the slow bowler, spawning not only a negative form of bowling to defensive fields, but also the 'utility' player, the 'bits and pieces' man who is jack of no trade, but competent enough in at least two aspects of the game. He is the man who comes on with the ball still shiny, bowls short of a length at medium pace on green wickets that give him too much assistance and ends up with 2 for 30 in his allotted 8 overs in the Sunday League. He fields superbly –

saving an average of ten runs in a forty-over innings – and when he bats, he can slog a quick twenty. A specialist slow bowler, on the other hand, is not really required to unveil his art in limited-over cricket; his captain's priority is to keep things quiet, rather than look to his slow bowler's subtleties to dismiss batsmen. That might be expensive and in the limited-over game, 2 for 30 beats 4 for 45 every time. No wonder the slow bowler fires the ball in on the leg-stump, forgets about the principles of flight and counts himself down to the end of his stint. No wonder Surrey's Pat Pocock says, 'To be a specialist spin bowler these days, you have to be rather special. You have to compromise so much.' Like the winger in soccer, the class spin bowler who relies on the same principles as Rhodes, Laker or any of the greats is now a rare breed. In both cricket and soccer, the 'keep-it-tight' philosophy is now the received wisdom, the Holy Writ of the coaches and managers. The utility player – the footballer who runs around in midfield, winning the ball by guts and then not knowing what to do with it, or the cricketer who bowls and bats a bit – he is prospering while the winger or slow bowler plays in the second team. Derek Underwood put his finger on the prospects for the spinner as we sat watching Kent pile up a big score on a flat Derby wicket where the medium pacers toiled *ad nauseam* – 'Can you name a specialist spinner in the side purely for his bowling?' he asked. We came up with a handful – Childs of Gloucestershire, Cook of Leicestershire, Surrey's Pocock, Acfield of Essex, Worcestershire's Gifford, Emburey of Middlesex and, of course, Underwood himself. Robin Hobbs, the last leg-spinner to play for England, has an even bleaker opinion of the specialist slow bowler's relevance to modern first-class cricket: 'I honestly think that on a good wicket, a slow bowler is only brought on these days to improve the over rate to avoid the county getting fined, or as cannon-fodder on the last morning to give the batsmen a chance of quick runs for an early declaration.' That may seem too sardonic a remark from a man leaving the game after entertaining many spectators for two decades, but one can see what Hobbs means. Too often the slow bowler *is* brought on as a last resort; the batsmen are well set, the captain is in a negative frame of mind and he baulks at the idea of using the close-in fielders that any top-class spinner needs. Come the third morning of a county match, however, and the captain, with his eye on a run chase at five o'clock is happy to toss the ball to any spinner. He will bowl a lot of overs in a couple of hours and the runs will come, especially as the fielders realise there is no pressing need to give the spinner too much of their zealous expertise to stem the tide of runs. Yet a spinner should be used to attack. The weapons in his armoury – flight, turn, change of pace and angle of delivery – are designed to bowl sides out, not as sacrificial gestures to relentless batsmen. Many modern captains seem to forget that you can win games by bowling sides out, rather than in a frantic slog against the clock. 'The great skill in cricket is getting a side out that wants to stay in', says Tony Brown, a man associated with the fortunes of Gloucestershire for nearly three decades. 'What worries me about the modern game is that the actual art of taking wickets has become incidental to bowling for under three an over.'

Spinners just do not bowl enough in English first-class cricket any more, even though there are now fewer championship games. In 1979, Phil Edmonds was 28, an England slow left-arm bowler of classical style and emerging influence. He bowled 564 overs in first-class cricket that year. At the same age, in 1950, Johnny Wardle bowled 1,628 overs of slow left-arm. In another example from the 1979 season, Geoff Miller bowled 452 overs of off-spin (he was an England bowler at the time, incidentally), while at the same age, in 1950, Jim Laker delivered 1,400 overs of off-breaks.

Agreed it is vital to bring on a spinner at the right time, but how can he develop let alone maintain his skills when he does not bowl in a match? The captains say that the wickets do not favour their spinners. Certainly the wickets in England are getting lower and slower, benefiting the accumulator of runs rather than the stroke maker, and the medium-pacer rather than the spinner who relies on bounce. Derek Underwood underlined the frustration of the spinner on a slow wicket: 'It's heartbreaking to beat a batsman by skill, then see the edge fail to carry to slip or watch him have the time to adjust his shot as the ball turns slowly. The spinner should be rewarded for beating the batsman, not left to curse the groundsman as he stands at third man, watching the seamers bowl all day.'

While researching this book, the question of wickets cropped up in every discussion I had with a slow bowler. The majority of cricketers I talked to who had played for more than a decade agreed that wickets in England have deteriorated. Those from a different generation felt that the wickets had started to change in character from the late 1950s onwards. Hardly anyone disagreed with the view that hard, fast, dry wickets with even bounce are a thing of the past in England. Doug Insole, the former Essex captain, now the influential chairman of the Test and County Cricket Board's Cricket Committee at Lord's, agrees that something must be done about English wickets. 'We need wickets where every skill is involved. Groundsmen have a definite fear that they'll be reported if they take off the grass, thereby nullifying the effectiveness of the seamer. We have to overcome that fear.' Reassuring words for the spinner, but it remains to be seen whether the county groundsmen take more notice of Lord's than of the wishes of their captains. The captain and his committee are the ones who hire and fire groundsmen, not the sincere, well-intentioned men of Lord's and if a captain has an attack dominated by seamers, he will not wish to see too many dry wickets that turn on the second evening of a three-day match.

An analysis of the twenty leading wicket-takers in English first-class cricket over the last thirty years only confirms how dramatic the move away from slow bowling has been. Take seasons 1950 and 1980 for example:

1950 – 16 slow bowlers (82.89%): 4 fast/fast-medium bowlers (17.11%)
1980 – 7 slow bowlers (35.46%): 13 fast/fast-medium bowlers (64.54%)

(The percentage figure quoted is that of the total number of wickets taken by the first twenty wicket-takers.)

Statistically the decline in the use of slow bowlers started about 1960 and over the most recent seasons in England, that decline has accelerated. In the 1981 English first-class season, the spinners bowled 36.49% of the deliveries – a quarter of a century earlier in 1956, they had claimed over half, 51.61% (See Appendix A). Was Colin Cowdrey really being over-sentimental when he told me: 'Day after day, we played some magnificent cricket in the 'fifties. With a great leg-spinner like Doug Wright in the Kent side, everyone was on tenterhooks – the crowd, the wicket-keeper, the fielders, the batsmen, even the umpires'? Nobody would call Les Ames an incurable romantic, but he maintains: 'More than anyone, the spinner brought entertainment into the game' – this from a man who's been an England player, Test selector and manager of Kent, in a career that has kept him in close contact with an evolving game. Nor is Geoff Boycott the kind of man to luxuriate in misty-eyed nostalgia, yet he deplores the eclipse of slow bowling: 'When one section of the game disappears, part of cricket's attraction also goes. I can't see the spinners coming back as a force at the moment, even though I feel that this is a game of cycles. There is nothing wrong with genuine fast bowlers, they're a great sight – but I'm sorry to see a lot of grace and skill going out of cricket with the decline of the spinner.'

Boycott is right about the need for balance in cricket but the tragedy about the modern attitude to slow bowling is that two facets are harmed. The art of wicket-keeping has slipped as well; the lack of bowlers who can spin the ball away from the bat means a stumping is a rare event in modern first-class cricket. In the last twenty years, the ratio of catches to stumpings by a wicket-keeper has remained stable at about 86:14, compared with 60:40 for a decade after the Second World War. Wicket-keepers and class slow bowlers work in tandem and they become more proficient in their respective crafts when a spinner is regularly used. The late Hugo Yarnold would agree; in 1949, he made 48 stumpings for Worcestershire and the bulk of his days were spent standing up to the left-arm slow of Dick Howarth (117 wickets) and the leg-breaks of 'Roley' Jenkins (183 wickets). Both bowlers regularly beat the right-hand batsman on the outside edge, making Yarnold's job easier because he could see the turning ball all the way, rather than be obscured by the batsman while trying to follow the off-break. The memory of that golden summer's achievements warmed Hugo Yarnold for the rest of his life – I wonder how his successor at Worcester will view his tally of stumpings for the 1981 season? David Humphries picked up fourteen stumpings because he stood up to the spin of Norman Gifford and Dipak Patel for long periods, yet even that modest amount of stumpings would have been drastically reduced if his county had possessed a fully-fit Hartley Alleyne and an equally hostile opening partner. A whole generation of wicket-keepers is emerging with a cursory knowledge of how to stand up to slow bowling, but examination of the very highest level of the game – Test Cricket – only underlines that such skills may as well remain dormant. Rodney Marsh has been an acrobatic wicket-keeper for more than a decade in the Australian team, yet his tally of stumpings stands at eleven. Alan Knott, great performer that he undoubtedly is, could only manage nineteen in a glorious Test career that lasted from 1969 to 1981. Yet Godfrey Evans took 46 stumpings for England between 1946 and 1959. *Autres temps, autres moeurs . . .*

Knott is honest about the way the game has changed in his lifetime: 'Cricket is nowhere near as entertaining to watch as it was but as professionals, we think it's better. I appreciate we are slightly hidden from the realities, because we sit in the dressing-room, trying to work out how to play the game.' He is well aware that modern tactics mean that he does not get many chances to stand up to the stumps, hour after hour, every day, and he takes steps to get round that with his customary dedication: 'Every morning now I practise standing up to the stumps because I can't be sure I'll get all that much work at it during the day's play.' If Alan Knott, one of the greatest wicket-keepers of all time, who gets at least some chance to stand up to the stumps in a game for Kent, when Underwood and Johnson are bowling, has to practise standing up to the spinners, what hope has a lesser man got in a county side that lacks Kent's tradition of slow bowling? The 'stopper' behind the stumps will wax while the fortunes of the slow bowler continue to wane.

So two of the basic arts of cricket are on the downward slope. How many really care? The overwhelming majority of past and present cricketers I interviewed seem genuinely to care; some of them would grope around for panaceas after finishing the ritual of deploring the decline of spin. In the end, they would content themselves with a condemnation of the standard of wickets. Some, like Ray Illingworth were grimly pessimistic: 'In five years' time, I can envisage cricket involving nothing but four quickies all the time. That would drive me away from the game.' Mike Brearley was far from sanguine, too: 'Quick bowlers have got bigger, stronger and better and I don't see why their dominance will stop. The balance of the game should be consciously shifted back towards the spinner.' Tony Brown – player, captain and administrator with Gloucestershire since 1953 – has seen the game change drastically in tactics and philosophy during that period and he does not particularly like the modern version: 'We should look after spin in the way we do everything else in the game. We've allowed it to drift away. In the end, you can't beat skill and you don't need to crack people on the head to get them out.' Pat Pocock – one of the few slow bowling artists still playing in England – has no doubts about where the responsibility lies: 'As things stand, spin won't come back by itself. The door has to be kicked open by force.'

At Lord's, one man is particularly scathing about the way spinners have been eclipsed. G. O. ('Gubby') Allen speaks with the authority of one who, for almost two decades, was the most influential man in English cricket. 'I am very unhappy', he says, 'at the modern attitude to slow bowlers. Everyone gives lip-service to helping them but no one seems willing to sit down and really try to think out what could be done'. 'Gubby' Allen is clear-sighted enough to avoid platitudes about the exciting 1981 series between England and Australia. He rightly points out that two exciting finishes in one series should not justify complacency on the part of the game's administrators: 'The standard of batting was poor but of course, some of the pitches did not help. That series certainly did little for the slow bowler, especially after the Australians refused to have anything to do with improving the over-rate. What causes me particular concern is the lack of variety in Test matches and I don't believe the public will stand for this state of affairs indefinitely. We need to create conditions helpful to spinners and by that I don't mean by the preparation of pitches. With the present predominance of fast bowlers, all a batsman needs to do to be rated as top-class is to play speed and seam extremely well. There was a time when a great batsman also had to pit his wits against the wrist and finger spinner.'

So which view will prevail? The disinterested one of 'Gubby' Allen that the alarm bells are clanging because of cricket's lack of contrast? Or Clyde Walcott's opinion that low over rates are the concern of the cricket theorists and not of the general public? Walcott believes that the best bowlers should be picked to represent a country and for that reason only a truly great spin bowler can be considered because the bulk of the bowling is preordained to be done by the speed merchants. Judged by the performances of recent West Indian sides, one can understand Walcott's preference for such a strategy – and several England players have told me they do not blame him for a moment, that England would play it the same way given similar firepower. That begs the question that Test cricket will continue to be played on wickets of uneven bounce, with the main features being intimidation backed up by an appalling over rate.

I believe that the character of Test cricket must change and with it, the way all cricket is played. Unless a stand is taken, unless something is done to legislate the spinner back into the mainstream of the game, cricket will lose its most subtle and delightful art. The record books are crammed with the deeds of the slow bowler, whether the career total of Wilfred Rhodes, Jim Laker's 19 for 90, Hedley Verity's 10 for 10 or the 309 Test wickets of Lance Gibbs. Slow bowlers have ennobled cricket and in an era where helmets have made it permissible for fast bowlers to pitch the ball in their half of the wicket and not be censured, it is clear that the administrators have unconsciously allowed the fast men to dominate the game. When will they officially acknowledge that an undiluted supply of seam bowling is boring to watch, tedious to bat against and monotonous for the fielders and the wicket-keeper?

No one would deny the manifest qualities of a Holding, a Lillee or a Willis but how often do we see a youngster impersonating an Emburey or a Bedi in the streets and in the parks? Cricket owes it to future generations to put variety back into the game – by law if necessary. The saddest story about slow bowling I heard during my work on this book came from Glamorgan's Alan Jones, that fine batsman who has adorned the county scene for nearly three decades. He was playing for Glamorgan at Bath when his old friend, David Allen, popped into the dressing-room for a chat. They reminisced for a time about the days when Jones would be playing Allen through the covers from a long way down the wicket and the times when Allen would deceive Jones in the air and leave the wicket-keeper to pick up the stumping. After a mellow half-hour, David Allen took his amiable personality off in search of more cricketing friends. Then one of the younger Glamorgan players asked Alan Jones the identity of his friend: after a moment or two, Jones was asked the devastating question: 'Oh really, who did he play for?' As he recounted the story to me, Alan Jones shook his head sadly: 'Imagine it, he'd never heard of the partnership of Allen and Mortimore, didn't know a thing about the fun of playing on turning wickets against great spinners. And the lad was playing first-class cricket!'

I share Alan Jones' sadness that the name of David Allen meant nothing to a young first-class cricketer, just fifteen years after he took his 122nd and last wicket for England, and less than a decade after he spun his last off-break for Gloucestershire. I wonder if the name Freddie Titmus meant much to that young player? Or Johnny Wardle? Jim Laker? Bruce Dooland? Something must be done to re-forge the chain of respect for the slow bowler, to let future generations realise there is more to bowling than simply moving the ball around off the seam or getting the batsman to fend off a short-pitched delivery to the bat-pad position. Ray Illingworth, the arch-realist, the epitome of the shrewd, analytical professional cricketer, encapsulated the charm of spin to me: 'There is no finer sight in cricket than seeing two good spinners bowling at a class batsman on a wicket that gives some help to both. It's a battle of wits, rather than a question of ducking and weaving.' Will Illingworth be consigned to the pejorative status of a 'cricket purist' by the pragmatists? Or could it be that the purists, the theorists, the idealists – call us what you will – have a conception of a great game that goes beyond the single-minded pursuit of a trophy?

# 2. The Characters

As a breed, slow bowlers are good company. To meet the mental demands of such a difficult sphere of the game, they have to be equable and philosophical. By their personalities they have enriched the public's appreciation of the game, quite apart from their skills with the ball. In this appreciation of nine spinners, what seems to me to be most appealing about them is their imprint on the game's tapestry, which I find more important than their statistical achievements, impressive though they are, too. That is why I have called this chapter 'Characters.'

**Brian 'Bomber' Wells** was one of the real originals of post-war English cricket. He played from 1951 to 1965 and only Fred Trueman has gathered more stories about him in that period, and unlike the great FST, most of the 'Bomber' stories were rooted in fact. In any conversation with an old cricketer, mention of 'Bomber' Wells usually evokes a spontaneous chuckle, a twinkle of the eyes and a comment along the lines of: 'Dear old Bomber, there was a character if ever there was one.'

The nickname 'Bomber' came from the deeds of the famous Bombadier Billy Wells, but any resemblance between the pugilistic instincts of the latter and the genial Gloucestershire off-spinner was completely fanciful. Enjoyment was the key note of 'Bomber's' attitude to the game he loved – whether it was in his bowling, his clowning on the field, or his complete inability to run sensibly between the wickets. He was an old-fashioned cricketer par excellence; a chubby man with no pretensions to athleticism, he merely wanted to bowl. He had no interest in field-setting when he bowled; he would leave that to his captain. His fielding, apart from a very strong throw, was ponderous and he never really made any effort to improve it; and his batting was based on the principle that the less time he spent at the crease, the happier he would be. 'I used to get bored to tears with batting,' he recalls, 'all I ever wanted to do was bowl. I had one shot – the slog –

B. D. ('Bomber') Wells, unathletic off-spinner and number eleven batsman for Gloucestershire and Nottinghamshire, who took 998 wickets in his first-class career

and if I hit it, the ball went a long way and the crowd and I were happy. If I missed it, well I was that much nearer to bowling. When I batted, I used to run on the sound – my eyes would usually be closed at the moment of impact and if the shot sounded promising, I'd start running.'

Yet though his attitude to cricket was light years away from the ultra-professional school of thought, 'Bomber' was a fine bowler. He had very small hands and he would spin the ball from his palm, rather than the first two fingers. He had a fast arm action and many a class batsman was fatally trapped by him on the back foot. His flight was deceptive, as his former team-mate Arthur Milton recalls: 'He was the only bowler I've seen that made the ball pitch further up to you than it looked. After all, flight is about making the ball pitch shorter than it looks. He had such a quick arm action that the ball would be on you, half a yard further up than you thought.'

One aspect of his bowling was remarkable – his run to the wicket. On a cold day, 'Bomber' would run two paces, and when it was hot, he would cut it down to one. The list of batsmen who were kidded out by 'Bomber' before they were ready to take guard is long and amusingly impressive; 'Bomber' felt comfortable with a short run and as he always wanted to bowl, he saw no reason to curtail his pleasure. When he first came into county cricket, he delivered the ball off one pace until his captain, George Emmett, told him, 'You'll have to take more than one step, you're making the game look ridiculous'. The bewildered bowler responded by coming off two paces. After a match or two, the county grapevine reported on this remarkable young off-spinner in the Gloucestershire side and the umpires soon decided to ensure he took no unfair advantages by bowling at the batsman before he was ready. 'Bomber' would circumvent that by standing beside the umpire with his hand in the delivery position waiting for the umpire's arm to drop, signifying that the batsman was ready – then 'Bomber' would release the ball from where he stood! Arthur Milton vividly remembers a match that 'Bomber' won using this method: 'The last pair were together and 'Bomber' was bowling. There was a quick single to cover, the ball came whistling back and, typically, 'Bomber' wasn't behind the stumps. Serve him right, the ball clattered him on the shin and he started hobbling around. The captain, George Emmett, asked him if he could finish the over, so he put one foot either side of the wicket and asked the batsman if he was ready. With the first delivery, he bowled him and we'd won. Typical 'Bomber' – he even told us he'd planned that.'

The venerable John Langridge could never come to terms with this remarkable approach to the wicket. The Sussex opener had played for twenty-five years before he first encountered 'Bomber' and in that period he had developed a series of mannerisms that had to be completed before he could take delivery. They included touching his cap, his abdominal protector, his pads, then looking up at the bowler, down again at his feet, then finally up again at the bowler. With 'Bomber' standing beside the umpire waiting to bowl, and the umpire's arm going up and down like a traffic policeman, it made a bizarre sight. Finally, 'Bomber' managed to bowl at Langridge, whose serenity was by now completely disturbed. He was out soon after. As Langridge stumped off, the umpire apologised. Came the reply, 'I might have been looking at you, but I wasn't ready!'

Rightly, 'Bomber' never saw any reason why he should alter his style of bowling for county cricket – bowling from one pace got him enough wickets for Gloucester City, so why change for Peter May or Len Hutton? As a boy, he started bowling with a wooden ball, then some friendly American serviceman left him a baseball before going off to the 'D' Day landings. He liked the feel of the ball in his hand, and from that day he decided to bowl slow – to the recurring delight of hundreds of cricketers, thousands of spectators, endless cricket dinners and of course, Brian Douglas Wells.

If 'Bomber' ever had any doubts about his bowling technique he never showed them. Perhaps a conversation early in his county career with the legendary C. W. L. Parker reassured him. 'Charlie told me there was a lot of rubbish talked about run-ups. He said you could do handstands and somersaults on your way to the wicket, but it was what you did *at* the wicket that was important. He spun enough men out for Gloucestershire to convince me I was doing nothing wrong.'

Everything seemed to be larger than life about 'Bomber', not least of all his ample girth. 'I was always rather large,' he grins, 'and looking at all these lads running around today in their tracksuits, I'm convinced I wouldn't have been fit to bowl. All this sprinting would have done me for the rest of the game.'

Even his debut for Gloucestershire was typically Wells. How many county cricketers have made their debut because an England bowler has fallen on a packet of mints? That was the fate which befell Sam Cook, as he was running up to bowl; he slipped, fell over and split the webbing of his hand as he fell on his packet of mints in his pocket. With Tom Goddard out with pleurisy, the Gloucestershire side needed a spinner in the summer of 1951. One balmy Friday evening, 'Bomber' was taking his usual leisurely stroll down Park End Road, Gloucester, with his fiancée for company. His destination – the fish-and-chip shop (he was a dedicated athlete even in those days). A car drew up in front of him and Tom Goddard shouted, 'You 'Bomber' Wells? Well, you're playing for the county tomorrow against Sussex. Be at the county ground at half-ten,' and the great bowler was gone. 'Bomber' took it all in his stride in his customary fashion and his family cobbled together enough kit to make him at least *look* like a county cricketer.

Most young cricketers making their county debut would ease their way into the proceedings, getting the feel of the atmosphere, drinking in every word of advice from the grizzled old pros, and only speaking when asked to do so, Not 'Bomber'. In the first over of the match, he found himself at gully, chasing a cut from John Langridge that 'Bomber' turned from a casual two into an all-run four! 'Bomber' found himself re-stationed at short leg. As George Lambert ran in to bowl, 'Bomber' felt he should demonstrate he was still concentrating hard. He spat on his hands and brought them together loudly – Langridge jumped out of the way, Lambert pulled up and umpire Alex Skelding tried hard to keep a straight face. This was to be no ordinary debut . . .

When he bowled, he took 6 for 47, and with the bat he made the first of many noughts for the county. The top brass at Bristol did not really know what to make of him, but he could certainly bowl. Early on, it was clear that 'Bomber' would make few concessions to the grim realities of first-class cricket. In one match in his debut season, the opposition were struggling desperately for a few more runs for first-innings lead, and bonus points. 'Bomber' was bowling, he was played to mid-off, our athletic hero stuck out a foot, managed to intercept the ball, turned and shied it at the wicket. If he had hit the stumps, the batsman would have been out, but the ball went for four overthrows. His captain was livid, yet stunned by a classic Wells reply: 'Sorry skipper, it hit an air-pocket!'

Soon crowds all round the country perked up at the sight of 'Bomber'. Not only was he a funny man, but he was demonstrably funny; the crowd loved his big hitting, his low-key attitude to fielding, the maiden over that took less than a minute to bowl and his accident-prone nature. Once at Rushden, he began his usual forlorn chase after an on-drive, hoping desperately that the ball would soon reach the boundary so he could call a halt to this sprinting lark. Unfortunately for 'Bomber' the ball stopped short, he continued lumbering after it and then, just inside the boundary rope, an empty lemonade bottle made a decisive intervention. 'Bomber' slipped on the bottle, was catapulted through the air, over the rope and fell into a chicken coop. 'Bomber' picked himself out of it with all the dignity he could muster, despite the feathers and chicken droppings that

15

festooned his ample proportions. The crowd loved it, and just as 'Bomber' thought the hilarity was subsiding, his captain clapped him over the boundary and told him to bowl. Reluctantly, 'Bomber' walked to the middle, still disentangling himself from feathers and other more unpleasant offerings. As he reached the stumps, a voice from the crowd rang out, 'Bloody hell, he doesn't bowl as well does he? What's his next trick, a white rabbit?'

His inability to judge a run was awesome. Time after time, a conversation at the wicket between 'Bomber' and his fellow-spinner, Sam Cook, would proceed along the following lines:

Cook:  (after failing to receive a call from the other end for a single): 'Can't you say anything?
Wells:  (on seeing the run-out possibility becoming a reality): 'Goodbye!'
*or*
Cook:  'Can't you bloody well call?'
Wells:  'How about tails?'

Sam Cook remembers the time when Wells not only ran himself out, he lay down and offered up his wicket. 'It was against Sussex and I actually managed to hit one to the covers. I told 'Bomber' to stay where he was and Jim Parks threw into the bowler. The ball was bouncing easily enough towards the stumps at the bowler's end and 'Bomber' was out of his crease, but his bat inside. What does 'Bomber' do? He sees the ball coming towards him, lifts his bat up and the ball hits the stumps, and he's run out. Bloody fool!'

Once 'Bomber' contrived the difficult feat of being run out at the bowler's end by a man at backward short leg, who had ran all the way up the wicket with the ball in his hand! This was after 'Bomber' had been threatened with a fine by his captain if he was run out again that season. It happened against Derbyshire and Sam Cook was keeping 'Bomber' company in the usual tenuous fashion.

Cliff Gladwin bowled an enormous inswinger at 'Bomber', it struck him painfully on the toe and he hopped around from one foot to the other. Meanwhile Sam for some reason, felt a quick single was a real possibility. The conversation from the non-striker's end was of the usual 'yes, no' variety, so Derek Morgan calmly picked up the ball in the leg-trap and trotted up to run out 'Bomber'. The aggrieved 'Bomber', suddenly remembering the threatened fine, asked Morgan why he hadn't run out Sam instead. Came the reply, 'I needed the exercise, Bomber. I haven't touched the ball the whole session.'

Eventually, 'Bomber' tried concentrating to avoid run-outs. He mentioned his reforming instinct to the Middlesex fast bowler, Alan Moss. 'I shan't get run out this game, Mossy,' he said, 'Let's have a bet on it.' They shook hands on a bet and, next day, Moss ran out Wells.

Only 'Bomber' could see the funny side of all those laughable run-outs. Only he could brag about using only one bat throughout his career. Who else would think of bringing a portable gramophone and a copy of 'The Peanut Vendor' by Stan Kenton to county matches and getting it played over the public address system? It was the 1954 season and 'Bomber' had become addicted to 'The Peanut Vendor': he not only played it in the dressing-room, but at five consecutive games persuaded the ground authorities to foist it on the unwilling public just before play started. Luckily for the morale of the Gloucestershire dressing-room sabotage was close at hand. . .

He was an absolutely natural cricketer when he first played for Gloucestershire, with no knowledge of the game or the illustrious players he would face. When he first bowled at Laurie Fishlock, that fine batsman for Surrey and England, 'Bomber' asked who he was and which way round did he bat. When his team mates told him he was a left-hander, he said, 'Right, I'll do him with the leg-break, then.' Fishlock soon padded up and was bowled round his legs.

Despite his eccentricities, he was highly respected as a slow bowler by all players of that era. Both Tom Graveney and Tony Brown consider that if he were allowed to bowl the same way today (a big 'if' admittedly), he would be very close to the England side, and Brown feels that his deceptive speed through the air would be invaluable in limited-over cricket. 'Bomber' feels that he mastered the basics of slow bowling early and they stood him in good stead: 'Charlie Parker told me never to allow the batsman to see the top of the ball. He should always be looking up, so he can't judge its length. Make the batsman come down the wicket and keep it in the air.' This mastery of first principles was invaluable to 'Bomber' when sadly, he had to leave his beloved Gloucestershire and test his talents on the flat Trent Bridge wicket for Nottinghamshire. By the end of the 1950s, David Allen and John Mortimore, the established England off-spinners, were in the Gloucestershire side, and they could bat and field far better than the rotund Wells. He accepted the situation and went to Trent Bridge because it represented a challenge. He did not fail himself or Notting-

17

hamshire; in five full seasons, he took over 400 first-class wickets. Somehow it seemed appropriate for this individualistic man to end his county career with 998 wickets, just two short of the coveted round figure.

He still plays – in the local amateur league in Nottingham. When I last saw him, he was chuckling at the way he made his side hustle through 45 overs in 72 minutes to get bonus points. He bowled 23 of them and told the other spinners simply to stand at the stumps and deliver the ball, just as he had done in his early days. He is only sad when he talks about today's tactics: 'I wouldn't get in a county side because my captain wouldn't trust me. I'd bowl my overs too quickly. If we're not careful, cricket will end up like soccer, where the coaches and theorists have moulded the game to their own satisfaction, irrespective of the public's needs.'

No one could ever accuse 'Bomber' Wells of ignoring the lighter side of the game. To him cricket has always been more than a theoretical exercise.

---

**Sam Cook** was another man who readily saw the funny side of cricket. Like his Gloucestershire team-mate, 'Bomber' Wells, there was never any doubt about his bowling ability, only about his aptitude to get his bat on the ball or to avoid being run out. A career batting average of 5.40 and a top score of 35 not out only hint at the hilarity of a stand between Wells and Cook, each one vying with the other to devise new ways of being dismissed. The Gloucestershire batsmen – Graveney, Milton, Emmett and the others – would look forward to such a moment when the situation of the game permitted it. Otherwise, the captain would declare earlier to save Cook and Wells for their specialist job – bowling.

Like 'Bomber', Sam was very much a man of Gloucestershire. He was born in Tetbury and still lives there. That soft Gloucestershire burr makes him compulsive listening, especially when he whimsically denigrates his batting and fielding. 'Cook and Wells were the worst number ten and eleven in the game for years. I was a mediocre fielder, I agree, but 'Bomber' was worse than me – he needed a bloody scooter to get round!'

When Sam started playing for Gloucestershire in 1946, he often used to walk up to seven miles to his home after being in the field all day. The last bus to Tetbury left Bristol at 6.35, so Sam had to rely on spectators for lifts to anywhere near Tetbury. Such physical resilience helped Sam become such a fine bowler, he regularly bowled fifty overs in a day, a master of accuracy. He was never the biggest spinner of the ball, but he complemented the off-spin of Goddard and then Wells. Tony Brown, who played in the same side with him for more than a decade says, 'Sam was just about the most accurate bowler over a long period that I've ever seen. After a winter's break, he'd come to the nets in April and pitch the first one on the spot. Batsmen were always looking to drive him, but they couldn't.'

Sam always loved his pint. When he first started in county cricket, Tom Goddard asked him if he wanted some lunch. Sam declined and Goddard replied, 'Wise lad – what you want is a pint.' Sam recalls, 'That was no hardship. I'd have a big breakfast in the morning, three pints of beer for lunch and a meal in the evening. When B. O. Allen was captain, he'd send for a whisky for me if I'd been bowling a long spell.' Sam's fondness for a beer was never more apparent one day at Trent Bridge. He was injured and doing twelfth man duties; that was not exactly to his tastes, so he slipped a few bob to the Nottinghamshire twelfth man and settled down to enjoy the day. 'Bomber' Wells noticed him: 'I had to bowl about fifty overs on the flattest Trent Bridge wicket you've ever seen. My bowling partner, meanwhile, had lined up all his empty glasses in front of him and every time I turned round to start a new over, he'd stand up and toast me.'

On another occasion, Sam managed to hoodwink his captain to have a tipple. 'We were playing at Ashby-de-la-Zouche against Leicestershire and I wasn't bowling. I kept crossing from fine leg to fine leg at the end of every over and I got more and more bored. I thought, "I might as well be back in the pub", and I told my captain I had terrible stomach pains. He looked concerned and told me to go off and have a port and brandy on his expenses. When they came off at close of play, I was drunk on the captain's expenses!'

He always managed to set up a new umpire with a little trick. When it was Sam's turn to bat, he would saunter out, trailing his bat reluctantly behind him like a schoolboy on the beach. By the time he had reached the crease, the umpire would be worrying about the march of time; Sam would look around him, saying 'Good Morning' to anyone who cared to look his way, all the time deliberately neglecting to ask for a guard. Eventually the umpire would say: 'What would you like?' and Same would reply: 'That's very kind of you, I'll have a gin and tonic, please.'

Once Sam found himself in the unaccustomed position of gully. He was just wondering what he had done to deserve this when a square cut hit him straight in the eye. Down he went, and a few seconds later, he heard some comforting words from his captain, George Emmett – 'get up, you're holding up the bloody game' – and the even more reassuring solace from Arthur Milton: 'That's not blood coming down your face, Sam, it's Worthington "E"!'

Although Sam only just managed to score more runs in his career than take wickets, he has always insisted that he could bat. None of his team-mates would believe Sam, but he swears he used to get hundreds in wartime Rhodesia with the RAF. 'It all changed when I got to Bristol. They told me to forget about my batting, that all I was going to do was bowl. That was good enough for me – especially as Wally Hammond used to get enough runs for us!'

Arthur Milton never really believed Sam's tales about wartime hundreds. 'Sam was a close contender to "Bomber" as our worst batsman. To see him batting against Doug Wright's leg-breaks was unbelieveable. He'd get the googly to third man and the leggie to long leg – great fun.'

As a bowler and a team man, Sam was loyal, strong and blessed with an iron constitution – but he saw no sense in being a batting hero when the fast men were pawing the ground with the new ball. Frank Tyson scared the life out of Sam when he came to Bristol early in his career. Tyson was busy earning the soubriquet of 'Typhoon' as he terrorised better batsmen than Cook and Wells up and down the land. Even the sandy Bristol wicket did not dampen his fire and he was still firing on all cylinders at the end of the Gloucestershire innings. Enter Wells to join Cook, each one eyeing the figure of Tyson anxiously as he scented a final, cheap wicket. 'Nobby' Clark, the ageing pace bowler, bowled the last ball of his over to Sam, who top-edged one down to the vacant third man area. 'Bomber' trotted up to the other end for a routine single, only to find an immovable Sam. The conversation went as follows:

Wells: 'One there, Sam.'
Cook: 'I don't think so.'
Wells: 'There must be, because I'm standing here talking to you and there isn't anybody near the ball.'
Cook: 'Go back or you'll be run out – again.'

'Bomber' ignored the implied insult in the last word and he walked back to his end, bewildered. Then it dawned on him: that was the last ball of the over and he had to face Tyson. As Sam tried hard to see through the tears of laughter, 'Bomber' closed his eyes and swung at the first ball. It was so quick that it knocked the bat out of his hand and it sailed away towards square leg. Sam was still on top of things, however; he noticed that the ball had dollied up in the direction of mid-off. He shouted to the nearest fielder to 'catch it', which he duly did. His ordeal over, Sam had the telling phrase to hand – 'Thank God for that, let's all go and have a beer!'

Sam did have a Test trial – on his honeymoon. He had already postponed his wedding twice and he was determined not to put it off again just for a Test trial. Sam admits that he bowled badly on a wicket that should have helped him and Wally Hammond was of the same opinion: 'On your honeymoon are you? Spent too many nights in the bloody saddle, you have!' Sam then played for England just once – 1947, within a year of his first-class debut. It was at Trent Bridge on a perfect batting wicket against the powerful South African batsmen. His spinning partner, Tom Goddard, had a mordant piece of advice for him . . . 'If I were you, I'd go sick.' Doug Wright was twelfth man for the Test and after shaking hands with Sam, he said: Good luck, Sam, I'm glad it's you and not me.' Hardly an encouraging omen for young Cook and sure enough Tom Goddard's shrewd assessment was spot on the mark. Sam took 0 for 127 and he never played for England again, despite his consistency.

With realists like Goddard and Hammond around, there was no chance of any prima donna antics from the young Gloucestershire players. Sam still has his England blazer – hanging up in the garden shed for use when he potters around in the vegetable patch. His prize possession is Wally Hammond's blazer – 'When I was capped by Gloucestershire, I had no blazer for the team photo, so Wally loaned me one of his. The shoulders came half-way down my arms, but that didn't bother me. I idolized Wally Hammond.'

Despite his endearing eccentricities, Sam Cook was first and foremost a fine slow bowler. The sandy pitches at Cheltenham, Bristol and Stroud favoured him, but you have to take a lot of wickets away from home to gather a hundred a season nine times. His left arm orthodox was the perfect foil to the more ambitious right-arm off-breaks of Wells, Allen and Mortimore. When the ball turned, his accuracy and the ability to spin the ball just enough were deadly weapons, and on good wickets his change of pace and nagging flight meant that he could afford to have only three men on the legside. As Tom Graveney put it, 'Sam was a modern bowler in the sense that he could shut one end up. On a bad wicket, he wasn't that much slower than Underwood.'

A happy man, Sam Cook. A man at peace with his environment and his choice of career. It was inevitable he would continue his love affair with cricket after he retired as a player at the age of 44. He became an umpire, and although he now finds the legal nitpickings of the first-class game more of a headache, he can still find something to amuse him. Sam has never lost contact with the grass-roots of cricket in his beloved Gloucestershire – nor his fondness for a pint, a cigarette and a warm-hearted chat. He is convinced he played cricket at the right time; 'It was a better era for variety and for fun. I wouldn't want to play now, it's sometimes difficult to get a smile out of some of the players.'

A man who could not share a happy moment with Sam Cook is an unfortunate fellow.

---

'I never tried to bowl a maiden. Every time I played, I wanted a wicket every ball.' Anyone who has known Roland Jenkins will have none of the scepticism usually elicited by such a remark. For **'Roley' Jenkins** was the epitome of the attacking leg-break bowler – he was proud to be known as the 'the millionaire bowler'. Doug Wright was a faster leg-break bowler, but nobody spun it more than 'Roley' or used the air more imaginatively. If ever a nickname suited a man's cricketing style, it was 'Roley': it summed up his sailor's walk and his warmth of personality.

'Roley' was that rarity among cricketing characters; he was both clown and ready quipper. Some manage to communicate their style of humour to the crowd, others amuse the players on the field with a flash of wit. 'Roley' was adept at both. Once at Cheltenham, George Emmett took him apart; four times in a row, he hit 'Roley' to the boundary. The large crowd loved it and cheered Emmett to the echo. 'Roley' – sensing the comic potential while genuinely admiring Emmett's virtuoso display – stood in the middle of the pitch till the roar subsided, looked straight at the batsman and his words echoed round the cosy, small ground: 'George, if you don't like me, say so –

Roley Jenkins – 'I bowled like a millionaire even though my childhood was so poor that knives and forks were like jewellery.'

but for Christ's sake don't keep taking it out on the bloody ball!' Those who cheered Emmett laughed with Jenkins.

Once at Bristol, 'Roley' was not happy. He had come down with the Worcestershire side, but the sandy conditions nullified his style of bowling. 'Roley' was not too impressed with the Bristol wicket and when he saw the aristocratic figure of the Gloucester-shire secretary, Colonel Henson, he decided to get his own back. Colonel Henson greeted him urbanely and asked after his health.

23

'Fine, thank you, Colonel,' came the reply. 'In fact if I'd known there was going to be so much sand on the wicket, I'd have brought down the caravan, the wife, kids, a couple of deck-chairs and made a weekend out of it'. Nobody talked to Colonel Henson like that and the players out in the middle still talk about the booming retort.

Norman Gifford will never forget the first time he played with 'Roley'. The young Gifford was in a scratch Worcestershire side, playing a friendly at Birmingham University. 'I was at mid-off as 'Roley' came in to bowl. All of a sudden, there was a terrific bang and he dropped down like a sack of potatoes. I thought he'd been shot, but he'd just set the new lads up – there was a rifle range on the University and 'Roley' was just waiting for his chance.'

In a game against Scotland, even the equanimity of 'Roley' was ruffled by some bad luck and dubious umpiring decisions. After a series of LBW appeals were turned down, 'Roley' said to the umpire: 'I'm very sorry for those appeals, I forgot we were playing under Scottish Law'. Yet his frustration was still boiling over as the Rev. J. Aitchison continued to play and miss at him. At the end of the over, 'Roley' ambled his bandy-legged way down the wicket and said to the fortunate batsman: 'I understand you're a parson.' And on receiving affirmation, added the killing thrust, 'With your bloody luck, you'll soon be Archbishop of Canterbury!' Shortly afterwards the umpire who had displeased 'Roley' asked about the state of his spinning finger. Like lightning, 'Roley' fired back: 'Lend me the one you're not using.'

Yet there was no malice in 'Roley' Jenkins. His sportsmanship was admired throughout the game. George Lambert, that fine Gloucestershire opening bowler, achieved his only hundred because of 'Roley'. George had played very well to reach 88 not out when the number ten batsman joined him – 'Bomber' Wells. The Wells inadequacy with the bat was now legendary on the county circuit, so there was little chance of George reaching three figures for the first time. 'Roley' greeted Wells in his usual cheery fashion: 'Are you in good nick, then, "Bomber"?' and proceeded to bowl two full tosses and a half volley in a row. They went for fourteen runs, and Lambert got his century.

Tom Dollery, the former Warwickshire captain, remembers the generous Jenkins nature with great affection. The year was 1949, Dollery's benefit season and, as usual, the beneficiary was cajoling big-name players to play for him in a benefit match. 'Roley' heard

24

about the game and offered to play before anyone else, refusing all offers of expenses. At the start of the match, he told Dollery: 'I'll give the crowd some entertainment at lunch and tea, leave it all to me.' During both intervals, 'Roley' walked across the ground on his hands and warmed the day for the crowd.

Perhaps the experience of his first wicket in county cricket shaped his principles. It was at Bradford in 1938 and 'Roley' was bowling at Maurice Leyland, a man who had been a legend to the young leg spinner for years. 'I clean-bowled him almost straight away and to my surprise, I saw Maurice walk up the wicket towards me, instead of turning round and walking back to the pavillion. I wondered what was happening until he stopped halfway and shouted to me "Very well bowled, sonny!" He'd heard that I was new and there was the great Leyland encouraging me. Marvellous!'

'Roley' was not only naturally amusing, he was unconsciously funny. Every season, a crisis point would arrive for him – 'I've lost my mechanics, they're just not working,' he'd tell his team-mates. This would be the signal for 'Roley' to go off to the nets and bowl even longer on his own and later he would be seen walking down the street, muttering again, 'I've lost my mechanics'. He was dedicated to practice even when in form – Tom Graveney recalls seeing 'Roley' in the nets on his own one afternoon with a box of balls, hour after hour, in a season when he had easily topped the hundred wicket mark. 'Roley' himself remembers the time when he bowled for no less than fourteen hours in the nets at Oxford during a three-day game, and still played in the match.

A worrier by nature, 'Roley' always dreaded the day when his great gifts would desert him for good. In 1949, he did the 'double' after a very successful England tour of South Africa – yet he admits he was close to a nervous breakdown by the end of that season. He even paid his own fare to go down to Kent and visit the great 'Tich' Freeman to check out his bowling; to this day 'Roley' maintains 'Tich' helped him spin the ball even more and that he became a better bowler as a result of the trip to Maidstone. But 'Roley' refused to wear his England blazer again until he had sorted out his 'mechanics'.

He lived and loved cricket and the ironies it reflects. He performed the 'hat-trick' three times – all against Surrey, two of them in the same match – yet the only wicket of those nine that gave him any pleasure came after a disagreement with his captain, R. E. S. Wyatt. He was bowling at M. R. Barton, a batsman who used the bottom hand a great deal to punch the ball through the on-side. For a time, Barton refused to play a shot through the off-side and 'Roley', always a man to want some action, was getting bored. He asked Wyatt to leave a huge gap on the offside between deep mid-off and square cover. Wyatt considered that a bizarre field for a leg-spinner bowling to a right-hander, but 'Roley' eventually got his way. 'I ran up and bowled an absolute dolly, right up in the air and kept on running out to extra cover, where I caught and bowled him. At last I'd tempted him to play on the off-side!'

'Roley' prided himself on his fielding. Hand on heart, he swears that he never dropped an authentic chance in ten successive years of first-class cricket – 'I know that sounds arrogant, but I don't mean to be. I was conscious during all that period that I never missed one I felt I should have taken. Mind you, once the spell was broken, I shelled out a few!' Certainly, the contemporaries of 'Roley' testify to his brilliance as a fielder. As Tom Graveney puts it, 'He would dive under a bus for a catch.'

His crablike action may have displeased the purists, but 'Roley' had all the attributes of the great slow bowlers, including the priceless ability to take punishment. 'I was a 3½ runs an over man, whereas Dick Howarth, my spin partner, was the craftsman, a slow left-armer going for 2½ runs an over. But I preferred it my way, I loved to experiment and get the batsman looking up in the sun for the ball.' He thrived on hard work and remembers with amusement the day he bowled at Jack Robertson when he hit 331 not out on a perfect Worcester wicket. Jenkins had 0 for 153 off 30 overs 'and do you know, to this day, there are still some people who swear it was me who let down Jack's tyres that night in the car park!' The day after his honeymoon ended, he bowled 49 overs in a day, which prompted a remark from his captain that still amuses 'Roley' – 'either you've had a bloody awful honeymoon, or you've had them before'.

He was still playing in the Birmingham League at the age of 55 (taking 7 for 51) and still remains close to cricket. He watches Worcestershire whenever possible, helps out in Duncan Fearnley's bat-making factory and coaches and umpires at a local village club. A voracious reader, a dabbler in poetry and an inveterate coiner of literary aphorisms, the name of 'Roley' Jenkins always brings a smile to the face of men like Tom Graveney: 'I remember once at Worcester when 'Roley' was trying to kid me out. I kept playing him down to deep mid-on for singles and I could see he was getting agitated. Finally, he shouted out, "Tom, you're an England player and they haven't come here to see you do that. The crowd wants to see you hit me through the covers!" It was always fun to play in the same match as 'Roley', something was always happening when he was around.'

Even an arch perfectionist like R. O. Jenkins would settle for a tribute like that.

---

If 'Roley' Jenkins was the supreme all-round entertainer, his great friend **Eric Hollies** was no less popular with both players and spectators. Eric's sense of humour was quieter, less susceptible to flights of fancy and mock tragedy, but the crowd loved him just as much. When he walked out to bat for Warwickshire at Edgbaston, he would get the warmest applause of the day; to those who had never met him, he seemed such a nice, kind person, a man to whom cricket was still just a game. To his friends and team-mates, he was quite simply the little lad from the Black Country who never forgot his roots, his sense of humour and proportion, nor the people who helped him along the way to deserved eminence as a cricketer.

Eric was a specialist slow bowler, one of those players who took more wickets than scored runs in their first-class career. He was a natural number eleven, a fact which seemed to escape the attention of the children who would jump up and down with excitement whenever he ambled out to the wicket. He must be the only man to use a bat with a nail in it during a modern-day Test; all the Warwickshire team had used it during the season of 1947, so Eric thought he would see if some expertise would rub off on him. To his amusement, he managed to take part in a stand of 51 with Kent's Jack Martin against the South Africans.

If necessary, Eric could keep an end up while an established batsman would blaze away, but in the main, he felt his job was to bowl. Once against Derbyshire, he was waiting to go in to face Cliff Gladwin, one of the best pace bowlers in England at that time. Eric, not surprisingly, viewed his chances of survival as something less than nil, yet he was happy to listen to some advice from Warwickshire's opening batsman, Norman Horner. A cigarette packet was utilised, a pencil procured and Horner drew Eric a list of alternative deliveries from the fearsome Gladwin and how to play them – inswinger, outswinger, yorker, the straight one, the short-pitched one that goes for the throat and so on. Just as Horner was going through the extensive list, a wicket fell and it was Eric's big moment. Snatching the cigarette packet, he walked out to the wicket, and handed it to Gladwin with the immortal words: 'There you are, Cliff, bowl them in that order and we'll see how I get on!'

Eric's stonewalling technique once saved the day for the professionals in a Gents v Players match. Trevor Bailey was bowling well and he crowded Eric who watched the scene with detached amusement. As Bailey assembled his close-in fielders with a punctilious air, the humour of the situation was too tempting for Eric: 'And where would you like me, Trevor?' he asked.

Sometimes Eric's dry humour would spill over into something more extrovert. Just after the War, he had to do a tremendous amount of bowling and one day at Edgbaston he felt a little weary as the clock edged towards close of play. Eric decided to come in for his final over in a rather unconventional way – by bicycle. He borrowed the groundsman's bike, pedalled in from fine leg and told the bemused umpire, 'Hang onto that till the end of the over.'

His practical joking was legendary. With the help of Charlie Harris, the eccentric Nottinghamshire batsman, he duped Tom Pritchard at the start of his Warwickshire career. Pritchard had just come over from New Zealand and Eric persuaded Charlie Harris to pose as a journalist to interview the new fast bowling hope. He borrowed a bowler hat and raincoat, gave Harris a pencil and notebook and told him the questions to ask. After an interview lasting thirty minutes, Pritchard thanked the pressman for his interest and asked him to remember to send him a copy of the article for the folks back home. A few minutes later, Warwickshire went out to field, young Pritchard organised his run-up, looked down the wicket at the opening batsman . . . and spotted the journalist minus his props!

Don Taylor, another New Zealander, felt the full impact of the Hollies poker face. In his first season with Warwickshire, Eric convinced Taylor that a passport was vital for the trip to Wales to play Glamorgan. The callow Taylor was only informed of the alleged regulation as the coach neared the Welsh border. Luckily, Eric had the solution – Taylor was told to lie under the seat under the cover of the players' kit for the next twenty miles before the border was successfully negotiated.

Yet it was impossible to feel angry at the leg-pulling of so affable a man. It was far easier to admire the quick wit behind remarks to men like Horace Hazell, of Somerset, who took an inordinately long time to take guard, then looked round the field before taking strike. The exasperated Hollies roared: 'Come on Horace, you take longer to get ready than my missus.'

For some reason, the undergraduates of Oxford and Cambridge always irritated Eric. He called them 'jazzhats' and could never see why any of them should be called first-class cricketers. Once he dismissed an Oxford batsman with a typically deft piece of artistry. 'Good ball,' the batsman said sportingly on the way out. 'Wasted on thee,' was Eric's dismissive reply.

'Roley' Jenkins loved him like a brother and when they played against each other in the Birmingham League, it was a privilege to be part of a stroll down memory lane with two such great raconteurs. One story from 'Roley' underlines the genuine rapport between the two men and also the spirit in which county cricket used to be played. It was a derby match at Edgbaston between Warwickshire and Worcestershire and things were very tight at the finish. Worcestershire needed three to win in the last over with several wickets in hand – but Eric, that most accurate of leg-spinners, was bowling. 'Roley' put an end to all speculation by hitting him for six into the pavillion. As the ball sailed over the boundary, Eric's first action was to walk up to 'Roley', shake his hand and say 'Well done mate, I didn't give you that.'

'Roley', in common with everyone who ever knew Eric, was stunned by his sudden death from a heart attack in 1981. Tom Dollery, his former captain at Warwickshire took it very badly. 'Eric was a perfect example of how to behave oneself on and off the field,' says Dollery. 'He was the ideal senior pro and in our twenty years together we only ever had words when I wanted to take him off!'

Tom called Eric 'the toothache bowler' because of his remarkable accuracy: 'He didn't know how to bowl a bad ball. In a space of ten years, I couldn't remember seeing Eric bowl a full toss. Even the great Denis Compton would struggle against him – Eric would watch his feet as he ran up to bowl and make sure the ball followed Denis. He was such a reliable bowler that a captain could plan his strategy around him. He just sealed up an end all day.'

Eric must have been the most consistently accurate leg-spinner the game has known. Nearly a third of his overs in his 26-year career were maidens. Off a brief, bustling run, he bowled with a brisk turn of the arm, dealing mainly with top spin, the occasional googly and leg-spin that was slight but enough to find the edge of the bat. He was more like a right-handed Sam Cook than a flighty leg-break bowler, relying on variation of the arc rather than giving the ball air. This pragmatic method was shaped in the early days of Eric's career by the great Wally Hammond. His slow, tossed-up leg-spin was cruelly treated by Hammond to the tune of nearly ten an over.

Eric was heartbroken but on the train journey home, he resolved to sort out his style. He went to the nets next morning at the Old Hill ground where he first played League cricket and he worked and worked at his flight; he decided he had been giving the ball too much air. Henceforth, the quick-footed batsman would not find the time to get down the pitch to smash Hollies. The following season Eric had his revenge when he took eight wickets against Gloucestershire – including that of Hammond.

Despite Eric's tremendous record (and only 'Tich' Freeman among leg-spinners took more first-class wickets), his fame rests upon a single ball at the Oval in August, 1948. He bowled Don Bradman for nought second ball, to deprive the great man of the chance of reaching a Test average of a hundred in his last game. Eric always remained amused at the fuss over that dismissal and the irony of it all was that he never saw the ball hit the stumps. Bradman had lunged over to play a supposed leg-break, but the ball was a googly, it turned back into the wicket and Bradman's body deprived Eric of the sight that established his fame in non-Midland eyes. So Eric was the hero of the hour, yet few realized that he had to be talked into playing by Tom Dollery and the Warwickshire secretary, Leslie Deakins. When he was selected by England, Eric felt there was little point in playing; the series had been decided and surely he would be more use to his county in the next two matches? Reason prevailed and before he left for the Oval, Eric had a talk with Dollery. A few weeks earlier, he had bowled magnificently for the county against the Australians; he had bowled Bradman with a top-spinner in the first innings and the great man paid Eric the ultimate compliment by coming out to bat in the second knock when there was no need for it. Dollery felt that was purely because he wanted to look at Eric, with an eye on the next Test. Australia only needed a few runs to win, so Eric followed Dollery's advice and did not bowl the googly at Bradman. Nevertheless Dollery was convinced that Bradman had not spotted the googly in the first innings and he told Eric: 'At the Oval he'll be looking for the googly first ball. Bowl it second ball.'

When Bradman came out to play his last Test innings, the England captain, Norman Yardley, led the cheers, then turned to Eric: 'That's

Bradman goes for a duck in the final Test at the Oval in 1948. It was Bradman's last Test innings and he admitted that Eric Hollies' googly was the perfect ball

all we're giving him.' It was in the middle of a Hollies over and Bradman pushed forward to the first ball. A leg-break. Forward defensive. The second was the googly which hit the middle and off stumps. Later Bradman admitted it was the perfect ball and Eric rang up his captain that night and said: 'He never spotted it, Tom.'

The sequel to that immortal wicket was pure Hollies. Leslie Deakins recalls that he was sitting in his office at Edgbaston the day after the Test ended when Eric popped his head round the door. His first words were: 'Did you notice who was left not out?' In the face of the Lindwall/Miller onslaught he had made two noughts, but one of them an undefeated nought. That seemed far more important to Eric than any swollen-headed nonsense about 'the hand that bowled Bradman'.

Nothing really surprised Eric, he took it all in his easy-paced stride. When he took all ten Nottinghamshire wickets in an innings without the help of the field (seven clean bowled and three LBW), he was more concerned that Warwickshire lost the match by seven wickets. He never showed any resentment at the way he was denied his home Test

At the end of the 1957 season Eric Hollies retired – seen here with some of the trophies from his long career, during which he took 2323 first-class wickets

debut in 1935 at Leeds when he was just 23. Just before the Test, Warwickshire were playing Glamorgan at Swansea and, late at night, one of Eric's team-mates entered his room by mistake and flopped on his bed. Unfortunately, Eric was asleep in the bed, and he was left with a ricked neck and had to drop out of the Leeds Test. Sir Pelham Warner, the chairman of the England selectors, demanded an inquiry but Eric refused to name the player involved. As far as he was concerned it was a genuine accident. The fact that he had to wait until 1947 before his Test debut in England may have annoyed him, but he never showed any resentment at the Swansea incident.

Eric could always see the comic potential in most situations. In 1953, Warwickshire had the Australians on the rack on a wicket made for him. Only the captain, Lindsay Hassett, stood between Eric and defeat for the tourists; Hassett played a masterly defensive innings that hardly endeared him to the partisan Edgbaston crowd. After all, their hero was being denied his true deserts. At one stage the mood of the crowd became rather ugly and it actually looked as if they would flood onto the pitch. Hassett surveyed the unruly scene and announced: 'The first one that comes for me, I shall wrap this bat handle round his head,' Eric gave him his most winning smile and replied: 'Yes, but what about the one after him – then the next one?'

He retired in 1957 from first-class cricket, walking off the pitch at Edgbaston with an endearingly bemused air as he noticed tears in the eyes of both players and spectators. They still talk about Eric at Edgbaston – middle-aged men who remember that he would always sign their inky autograph books, his pals from the Black Country to whom he remained so close, his former team-mates who close their eyes, concentrate hard and always fail to think of anyone with a bad word for him. It was fitting that, in his last season, Eric should bowl more overs than anyone else in the country, and take his usual crop of a hundred wickets. And all this at the age of 45. Eric was not the man to hang around and wait for the secretary to have a quiet word about calling it a day.

Tom Dollery maintains that Eric was never happy after he retired, despite his successes in the Birmingham League (playing till he was 63), the attentions of a loving, devoted family, the diversions of watercolour painting and racing pigeons. He would play in occasional benefit matches and try just as hard as ever. For several years, Eric's cheery presence was missing from Edgbaston; there had been a mis-understanding over a coaching position and Eric had sworn never to set foot on the County Ground again. Happily, the differences were resolved and Eric would be there on Sundays in the 1980 season, intently watching Warwickshire winning the John Player League, no doubt wondering if there would have been a place for his supremely accurate spin.

At Easter 1981 he was gone. The heart that had sustained him through a long and happy career gave out while he and his wife were looking after their grandchildren in Derbyshire. Late in the summer, his ashes were scattered on the ground at Edgbaston – on the very wicket where he took all ten against Nottinghamshire. If you stand on that spot and listen very closely, you may just hear Eric's familiar, warm chuckle; 'Ay and we still bloody lost by seven wickets!'

---

**Johnny Wardle** may have lacked the personal warmth of a Hollies or a Jenkins, but he was just as big a darling of the crowd. Wardle had the gift of timing, not only in his cricket but also in his comic touch. His clowning – mostly improvised – usually guaranteed that there would be something happening when he was involved in the game, whether he was batting, fielding or bowling.

Once in a Roses Match at Sheffield, Cyril Washbrook was advancing towards a hundred with measured tread. The atmosphere was of the 'tha Sootherners know nowt about it' variety, with grim concentration on both sides of the boundary. Washbrook went for his favourite hook shot and it was caught at short fine leg by Wardle with one hand. Wardle made a point of looking around for the ball and Washbrook was only informed that he was out when he was completing his second run. Washbrook was not amused – these things do not happen in Roses Matches – but the crowd took Wardle to their hearts.

One of his party pieces was to deceive both batsmen and spectators into thinking there were some overthrows going begging. He would stand at the bowler's end, and if a wild throw came in and Wardle could gather it, he would take it one-handed, pretend he had missed it and go running after the ball, even though it was nestling snugly in his hand. The crowd would be roaring 'go on, overthrows,' the batsmen would be totally confused and Wardle would be relishing the role of ringmaster.

As befits a man good enough to sign professional forms for Wolves, Wardle's footwork with a cricket ball was brilliant. Another of his party pieces was to flick up the ball with his boot, knee it over his head and catch it behind his back with one hand. Sometimes, when the proceedings had gone a little dull, he would make a spurious appeal for LBW; he would stay crouched low in best Dennis Lillee fashion, wait for the ball to be lobbed back, and then catch it one-handed after it had passed his shoulder.

Although he had a routine of tricks, his clowning was spontaneous and geared to the state of the game. Never was his innate sense of timing more valuable than in the West Indies in 1953–4. Len Hutton, the England captain, should have struck a special medal for Wardle for averting a riot in the Guyana Test; as bottles started raining onto the pitch in protest at some umpiring decisions, Hutton told Wardle to go down to fine leg, where the worst of the rioting was taking place. Wardle reminded his captain he had a wife and children back home, but he went with as much good grace as he could muster. Hutton was determined to stay on the field and as the bottles still came over onto the pitch, Wardle delivered his masterstroke. He picked up a bottle, pretended to drink from it, then staggered around like a drunken sailor on shore leave. It worked. The crowd fell around at such knockabout humour, Wardle kept them amused with his antics for the rest of the session and England stayed on the field.

'The clowning was merely to relieve the tension during a match,' he says. 'There's a lot that goes on in the middle that the spectators don't know about and by mid-season, I could have been a nervous wreck if I hadn't tried to have a laugh. But it never affected my cricket.'

Wardle's batting can best be summed up in his proud statement: 'I've had the ball out of the ground on three sides of Lord's, but never middled one over the Pavillion. God knows, I tried enough but I could never quite get hold of it.' He was a tremendous hitter, a glorious member of the trinity of numbers 9, 10 and 11, who all tried to smash the ball out of the ground in those days – 'We used to love having a go

Johnny Wardle, a great slow left-arm bowler with the ability to bowl chinamen and googlies at will, plus the priceless knack of entertaining the crowd

35

at the ball. None of this playing down the line stuff you see today. Mind you, there were plenty of slow bowlers around in those days and we used to relish the chance to diddle each other out with flight and cunning.'

Perhaps Wardle never really did himself justice with the bat; he was far more than a tail-end slogger. Fred Trueman, who played in the same Yorkshire side, considers Wardle should have scored several first-class hundreds. He was so naturally talented that he seemed to be able to turn his hand to all aspects of cricket.

His bowling strategy was of the type that the crowd would welcome; he would bowl a long hop or a full toss if he thought it would get him a wicket. In a Roses Match, he kidded out Alan Wharton with a tactic that was Chaplinesque. He made a point of moving a fieldsman round to deep square leg and decided to bowl a slow long-hop, 'But I knew Alan wouldn't fall for just any old long-hop, so I decided to fall down as I bowled. I shouted in pain as I fell over, the ball came out a really slow one, Alan's eyes lit up and he hit it straight to deep square leg!'

He once deceived Keith Miller with a classical piece of slow bowling in a Lord's Test. Australia had eased past 200 for the loss of just two wickets and Wardle decided to trust to Miller's attacking instincts and throw one up to him. 'I bowled it a little bit slower and higher and he hit it in the air and the catch was dropped – by a bloke on the second balcony in the Father Time Stand. Len Hutton, the captain, told me to cut that rubbish out, but as I ran up to bowl the next one, I gave it another go. I held it back a bit more, Keith went for the same shot and I bowled him. That's what happens sometimes when you disobey orders!'

Although he loved a close rapport with the crowd, slow bowling was a serious business to Johnny Wardle. He was always acutely conscious of the slow left-arm heritage of Yorkshire. He saw Hedley Verity bowl for Yorkshire before the War, and, as a youngster, he would drink in the stories about Rhodes, Peel and Verity. He wanted to be a worthy successor to such great names. 'When I got in the first team, I'd sit with Wilfred Rhodes at Bradford and Scarborough and listen to him. Although blind, he could tell me if the batsman had played the cut or the drive. He gave me some invaluable advice – "never let them cut you, Johnny, over pitch, rather than under pitch." How right he was.'

Wardle carried that precept through is career. He would train hard during the winter, come to the nets in the spring and bowl and bowl. He thrived on hard work and loved to have a ball in his hand even when there was no bowling to be done. He just liked the feel of a cricket ball, spinning it, turning it over. He would set his fielding front of the wicket and insist on his best fielders in key positions for the left-hander – in the covers and at mid-off. His accuracy was phenomenal, the product of hard, unyielding work in the nets, and if he bowled a long hop it was for a purpose. 'I used to bowl four or five overs in advance, working out a strategy against a good player. That's why I wanted good fielders in certain positions, to stop him getting a single and escaping from me. I remember getting John Waite in a Test in South Africa. I gave him three fours in an over just to lull him. I over-pitched, he was a good player and he drove me away easily enough. At the end of the over, Peter May wanted to take me off and I was furious. I pleaded with him, said "he's mine next over, skipper", and so I stayed on. Next over, I held one back and he was caught at mid-off.'

He had a tremendous command of the chinaman and googly. At school, he had mastered the chinaman to supplement his medium-pace bowling, and in his early seasons with Yorkshire, he just concentrated on becoming an orthodox slow left-armer. In the second half of his career, his ability to bowl the chinaman and googly at will made him the best of his type on good wickets. Doug Insole recalls a Test at Cape Town on the 1956–7 tour, when Wardle took twelve wickets in the match. 'I had been ill the night before, so I sat on the balcony watching him diddle them out, the ball going one way and the bat the other. It was the best piece of bowling I've ever seen.'

Ray Illingworth recalls: 'He could go for weeks without bowling the funny stuff. Then one day, he'd decide the conditions were right and he'd drop it on the spot straight away, and spin it. He was tremendously talented.' Yet Wardle was never really encouraged to bowl his 'funny stuff' by Yorkshire; it was felt to be too risky, even though Wardle was shrewd enough to avoid bowling it if he thought the conditions were not favourable.

In 1958, Johnny Wardle was at the peak of his powers; he was, in effect, two bowlers in one, a highly-respected Test Match bowler, and senior professional at Yorkshire. At the end of July, he was sacked by Yorkshire. No official reason was given to the public. Wardle then contributed to a series of newspaper articles that put Yorkshire in a rather unflattering light – particularly their new captain, Ronnie

Burnet. After the articles were published, the MCC withdrew their invitation to Wardle to go on the England tour to Australia that winter. Finally, Yorkshire issued a statement which alleged that Wardle had been a bad influence in the dressing-room for some seasons and that his general behaviour left much to be desired. Wardle was finished with first-class cricket. He was just thirty-five.

Today Wardle remains unrepentant. He says that he had never been warned by the committee about his behaviour. He admits differences of opinion with the captain – 'but I was senior pro at the time and surely entitled to express my opinion, especially as I was working so hard on the field to get things right. I always made sure we were alone when we had our arguments.' He was approached by several counties but could not face playing for any other side but Yorkshire. He played in the Lancashire League for a decade, then for Cambridgeshire. 'It was a soul-destroying time. I had ten good years left in me and I could have ended my career with over 3000 wickets. I've turned the events of 1958 over in my mind so many times but I still feel I was wronged.'

He admits that he could be a difficult man. The public who adored him never saw the bitter side of Johnny Wardle when things went wrong for him – a point that the autobiographies of Fred Trueman, Brian Close and Ray Illingworth have emphasized. Yet his departure from the game was a tragedy for Yorkshire, England and all lovers of high-class slow bowling.

Perhaps his occasionally abrupt manner stemmed from his rivalry with Tony Lock for the slow left-armer's place in the England side. For several years, Lock's action was distinctly dubious; everyone knew that, including the England selectors, yet Lock normally played ahead of Wardle, a situation that embittered the Yorkshireman. 'I had a chip on my shoulder over Locky,' he agrees, 'But I reckon anyone else would. He was throwing it and keeping me out of Tests. To me it was the biggest mystery of all time that he could play first-class cricket with that action, never mind Tests.' He now tends the cricket ground at Doncaster Town CC with all the attention to detail he displayed when bowling. Golf is now his major passion and he admits he gets more nervous standing on the first tee in a big match than he ever did in a Test Match. He is sorry for today's spinners – 'I'd bowl more overs by the end of May than these lads do in a season'. Perhaps he has mellowed over the years, perhaps his bark was always worse than his bite. He remains compulsive listening on cricket and philosophical on his career – 'God's been good to me in many ways, even though he gave me some stick in 1958.'

---

**Tony Lock**, Johnny Wardle's rival for an England place in the 'fifties, was a character on several levels. It took enormous character to remodel his bowling action after its illegality was blatantly demonstrated. All through his career, he was one of the greatest triers the game has known – his sense of commitment transmitted itself to the crowd, who relished the battle. With the bat, he was generally of the swashbuckling fraternity; he was one of the best close fielders of all time; ultimately he became a successful captain of style and panache.

His bowling career went through three phases: slow (very slow) left-arm; medium-fast (with the illegal quicker ball); and finally, the classical, orthodox style with generous spin that was a joy to behold. Tom Graveney remembers phase one with amusement: 'It was in the late 'forties and I played against this soft, gentle little floater. It was a case of "down the wicket and help yourself". I never thought he would amount to much.' For a couple of seasons, Lock could not spin the ball and the contrast with his new spinning partner, Jim Laker, was particularly marked on rain-affected wickets. Laker would run through the sides with his pronounced spin, while Lock would wheel away to a packed off-side field, getting nobody out.

He was nothing if not determined, though, and a winter in an indoor cricket school made him a different bowler. After months of hard work, he discovered he could spin the ball on any surface – but it was at a price. Unfortunately, the net was too low for Lock to extend his arm fully, so he increased his delivery stride and bent his elbow to avoid catching his arm in the net. The following summer, Lock plundered a harvest of wickets and the Lock-Laker partnership began to terrorize batsmen, often on Oval pitches of inferior quality. Even Lock's own team-mates had their doubts about the legality of his quicker ball – the arm certainly seemed to be straightened just before delivery, and the result was a delivery of genuine speed. Once Doug Insole left the crease after Lock had flattened his middle stump with the wry comment: 'I agree I am out, but was I bowled or was I run out?'

Despite the mutterings, there were few umpires brave enough to 'no ball' a man who had become an England regular. So Lock continued pitching the ball around middle stump and hitting the off stump at medium pace. He was called for throwing in the West Indies but that was passed off as just a little local difficulty.

Ted Dexter vividly remembers the day when Tony Lock decided to change his action. It was in New Zealand in 1959 at the end of a tour where Lock's medium-pace style had proved ineffective. 'We sat down to watch a film of recent Tests and they showed Locky bowling. We could see the bend in his arm at the point of delivery and several gasped out loud. When the lights went up, there was Locky sitting white-faced and silent. The next day, he came into the nets and bowled very slowly, with no sign of the quicker ball.'

He decided to change his action again, to get a compromise between the gentle, flighty stuff of his youth and the medium-pace style of his pomp. Arthur McIntyre, his team-mate at the Oval, will never forget the work Lock put in at the nets over the next few months: 'I helped him as much as I could, but in the end he had to do it himself. He tried all sorts of styles until he hit on the right one. I don't think I've ever seen a greater trier than Locky – sometimes blood would be pouring from his fingers as he slogged away to get it right.'

Soon the transformation was complete and he took a hundred wickets in the rehabilitation summer of 1959. Ted Dexter took him to India with the England team in 1961–2 and he says, 'Locky bowled absolutely superbly for me on that tour. All the flight and variation you could wish for.' The success of the new bowling style galvanised the already legendary enthusiasm of Tony Lock. He went to play for Western Australia in 1962–3, bowled magnificently and decided to settle over there for good. He took a stack of wickets for Western Australia over the next few seasons and his joy was sealed when he led the State to the Sheffield Shield. Mike Smith captained the England side to Australia in 1965–6 and he remembers how fine a bowler Lock had become: 'He bowled much slower and the bounce on the wickets obviously helped him. He varied it so much more than in England – fiddling people out on good wickets. He was still a very big spinner of the ball and, by that stage, a slow left-armer of the highest class. It was a great feat by him.' John Hampshire agrees: 'I played a lot for Tasmania against Western Australia when Locky was captain and I thought he was the best slow left-armer I had ever seen. He had everything – control, flight, he used the breeze well and the responsibility of captaincy made him an even better bowler.'

Lock's inspirational qualities were not to be wholly lost to English cricket. Mike Turner, Leicestershire's far-sighted secretary, talked him

Tony Lock in 1962, three years after he had remodelled his action to become an orthodox slow left-armer in the classical manner into a three-year contract at Grace Road from 1965 to 1967. The effect of Lock's bowling and leadership was galvanic; within two years, he had taken them to second place in the Championship, the best position in Leicestershire's history. The captain had also taken a hundred wickets two seasons in a row – all this with wonky knees at the age of nearly forty. He even found the time to play a couple of Tests for England in the West Indies as a replacement for the injured Fred Titmus.

Lock's enthusiasm at Grace Road was infectious and became a legend. In his sojourn in Australia, he had picked up a number of extrovert habits that baffled the tough old pros at Leicester. Hugs and kisses became the norm under Lock's dynamic leadership and although the spectators warmed to his genuine enthusiasm, the players were sceptical. Stories abounded of the times when Lock remonstrated with a fielder who dropped a catch, only to be told: 'I couldn't stand another bloody kiss from you', but, for all his eccentricities, Lock was revered at Grace Road. When Ray Illingworth brought Leicestershire to a place in the sun a few years later, he generously nodded in the direction of Tony Lock – by then a reluctant former player. Not even Lock could ward off knee trouble and the relentless march of *anno domini* for ever.

It took guts to go through what Tony Lock suffered. The pro-Wardle faction are rightly aggrieved that their man never received his true rewards at Test level, but Lock showed his character by revamping his action at the age of thirty. He never knew when to give in. No captain could ever complain at Tony Lock's attitude or the crowd at his entertainment value.

---

If Tony Lock was the trier par excellence, then **Norman Gifford** is a worthy successor. A fine slow left-armer himself, Gifford is a master of strategic losses of temper. His team-mates and the regulars at Worcester look forward to the 'Norman Gifford funny half-hour', when Norman decides that the game needs a stimulus, even if only by a few choice words and gestures. It normally follows a period when the batsmen are playing and missing a lot or the wicket is not to Norman's liking. He will start kicking big lumps out of his follow-through, and stand with his hands on hips, doubting the parentage of the groundsman, batsman or fielder who happens to catch his eye. Once in 1979, the flat Worcester wicket was just too much for him; the match coincided with the influx of Vietnamese boat people into Britain and the papers were full of reports about the attempts to find work for the refugees. As Norman's temper boiled over, he bellowed: 'If those boat people want a job, they can come and bowl on this bloody wicket!'

Norman is renowned for trying to catch the batsman out before he has really settled for the delivery – a descendant of the 'Bomber' Wells school. Even as the batsman steps away, Normal will still deliver the ball, see it hit the stumps and then try his luck with the umpire. 'That's out, umpire, he's got to be out, what's going on?' while winking conspiratorially at his colleagues. He regularly pulls the leg of the intense 'Dickie' Bird by changing the line. 'Dickie' would be expecting Norman to come round the wicket, and when he sees the ball delivered from *over* the wicket, he will fly into a cry of 'dead ball, dead ball' while Norman is convulsed with mirth.

The players who have known Norman for years will vie with each other to get him going. Fred Titmus was a master at this: once at Lord's, Fred continually annoyed Norman by stepping away just as he was about to bowl. He complained about the spectators moving behind the bowler's arm, about paper bags going past his line of vision, anything to avoid getting many deliveries from Norman. Finally, a plane flew over the ground, part of the usual Heathrow traffic. Norman stopped halfway through his run-up and shouted: 'What about the plane, Fred? Shall I wait until the pilot sits down?'

On a hot afternoon at Worcester, that beautiful batting wicket was taking its toll of the Gifford feet and temper. Two Pakistani batsmen were enjoying themselves on such a good wicket that they were chattering away to each other in their native tongue. Norman, as usual, was doing most of the bowling and as the ball disappeared for yet another boundary, he shouted: 'For God's sake you two, this is an English game, so please speak in English. That way I'll at least know you're bloody enjoying yourselves!'

Dennis Amiss always looks forward to Norman's reaction to the Edgbaston wicket, a surface that favours the batsmen even more than Worcester. 'When Norman comes on, I'm waiting for the first explosion and it's never that long in coming. As soon as he knows the ball won't turn and that it'll keep low all day, he'll say, "That's my bloody day ahead, nothing but bloody toil", and he'll kick the wicket. When he gets really upset, he'll start frothing at the mouth and really have a moan. But at the end of the day he's always the first to have a drink and a laugh.'

43

Norman Gifford of Worcestershire, one of the most determined cricketers of the last two decades: a successful captain, a bowler with great powers of spin, with an enviable line in repartee

The vast majority of Norman's tantrums are simulated, his way of getting through the day. He needs to let off steam to prove he is still trying his utmost – 'if I played a week of cricket and nothing riled me, if I didn't get the red mists at all, then I'd think it was time to pack up. I wouldn't be sufficiently motivated in my eyes.' Norman actually looks forward to his verbal tussles with certain players – Derek Randall for example. 'Now Derek's a good lad, but he fidgets a lot at the crease. I often have to tell him to shut up chattering, so one game I got my own back. I was standing square of the wicket during an over and I started whistling as the bowler came in. Derek stopped, looked around and I stopped whistling. This went on for a couple of balls, till Derek shouted, "Umpire, Gifford's whistling, he's putting me off." It's harmless really.'

In the Worcestershire dressing-room, Gifford stories are as plentiful as his racing tips that never quite manage to make the finish. Glenn Turner remembers the time when Norman lost his run-up after eighteen years of county cricket. 'No one knew why it had suddenly happened but it was like watching an old hen as he tried to get to the wicket. He couldn't even remember if he took off with his left or right foot!'

Despite the colourful language and mock tantrums, there is no more genial, warm-hearted or affable man off the field in county cricket. There is no side to Norman, none of the prima donna about his response to the autograph hunters and the bar bores that are inevitably attracted to a cricketer of his status. He was a popular and successful captain with Worcestershire, and cogent proof that a bowler's form need not suffer just because he is captain. Apart from his idiosyncracies on the field, Norman will be remembered as a cricketer who gave everything he had. Warwickshire's David Brown has enjoyed many tussles with Norman and he says, 'I've lost count of the times he's pulled matches out of the fire by bowling over the wicket, pitching it into the rough or something like that. He imposes himself on the batsman and never really knows when he's beaten. A great bowler when people are blocking for a draw – he'll dangle the tempter at them, then the bouncer, then go over the wicket and try bowling round their legs. He never knows when to quit.'

Derek Underwood remembers Norman's untiring efforts on the tour to India and Pakistan in 1972–3. 'Norman was put in charge of nets and did a wonderful job. His enthusiasm was infectious and heart-warming in that he didn't expect to play in many Tests because

Pat Pocock and I had established ourselves early on in the tour. But that never affected Norman's attitude.' Finally, Norman got his chance at Hyderabad. The temperature was 110 degrees and Norman bowled more than fifty overs. Recalls Underwood, 'I can see him now, too tired to stand up in the shower. When he came off the field, covered in dust, he had a line of chewing gum around his mouth where he couldn't find enough saliva.'

It has been one of the great compliments to Gifford that he kept Underwood out of the England side for a time. Ray Illingworth felt that on good wickets, Norman's command of flight and spin was a better bet. In all types of cricket, Norman has been a great example and influence. Few captains are lucky enough to be a success in that job, remain a fine cricketer, and still be 'one of the lads' in the dressing-room. Many a disillusioned, introspective captain would like to know Norman's secret.

---

**Ray East** is one of the few players in the modern game who can make a crowd laugh. A true graduate of the Johnny Wardle College of Clowning, his routine of funny walks has graced county grounds from Folkestone to Blackpool. Like Wardle, he has the priceless gift of timing, all the more welcome in an age where the individualist seems actively to be discouraged on the cricket field.

One of East's more memorable comic strokes came at Ilford when Essex were playing Surrey. As East ran in to bowl to Mike Edwards, a car back-fired in the nearby High Street. East was in his delivery stride at that moment and he promptly collapsed on the ground in the best mock-heroic fashion. East enjoyed that one and he still relishes the time he confused John Arlott during a Sunday League match at Ebbw Vale. 'I was at mid-wicket and the ball was clattered past me. I clapped my hands together and threw up an invisible ball – I believe John Arlott told the TV viewers that I'd made a magnificent catch while the ball was sailing out of the ground.' I once saw him do the same thing at Edgbaston one Sunday – again at mid-wicket, but this time he essayed a full-length dive and threw the ball up as it was nestling against the boundary rope.

Once he was so bored with the endless diet of seam bowling and stodgy Essex batting that he dragooned a newspaper seller into lending him his cap and he went around the ground, selling papers and having a chat and a laugh with the crowd. John Lever remembers the time when East went one better: 'It was at Cambridge and it was bitterly cold. We were in the field and we saw Ray talking to a newsvendor at the end of an over. I thought no more of it until I looked round shortly afterwards. There was Ray, standing at square leg wearing a great big overcoat!'

Anyone who meets Ray East and expects to be clapped on the back and drowned in a sea of witty one-liners and back-slapping is in for a disappointment. He is soft-spoken and slightly intense, characteristics shared by many comedians. It would be wrong to paint a 'clown who wants to play Hamlet' picture, but Ray East is a thinking cricketer who has had to get used to his fair share of setbacks in the game. He is aware that many good judges feel that he should have played for England, that perhaps his fondness for the moment of slapstick held him back. As his former team-mate, Robin Hobbs, says, 'In the eyes of the selectors, you have to be a very good cricketer indeed to get away with antics like his, undoubtedly funny though they are.' Or Norman Gifford: 'A very good bowler indeed but perhaps the clowning has stopped him bowling six good balls an over, day after day, season after season. Sometimes little things can get to Ray – like a misfield – and he allows himself to get distracted from the task.'

Ray East's answer is endearingly direct and good news for the spectators: 'I won't change my ways, even if it has done me some harm in the eyes of the powers-that-be. There just isn't enough humour in the game today, too many fast bowlers are allowed to come charging in to aim at your head, rather than the stumps. I do take the game seriously and concentrate, but there are times when you can relax. It helps the rest of the side – especially when the ball is disappearing out of the ground.'

He admits that he goes too far on occasions and taxes the patience of even a calm man like his captain, Keith Fletcher. 'But Keith usually realizes that it's because I'm a nervous man. I'm a compulsive talker and watcher of cricket and all my joking around is a form of nerves.'

East is a great believer in cultivating the grass-roots of the game. He is the embodiment of village cricket to many of us, and it came as no surprise to learn that he was plucked straight from the village green into the Essex Second Eleven. Peter Smith, the Essex and England leg-spinner, was impressed with East when he took a side to his village ground. He arranged a trial and, within a year, East was bowling at M. J. K. Smith on a flat wicket at Edgbaston. He recalls, 'I had six on the off and three on the leg and the more I bowled at the off-side, the more MJK hit me over mid-wicket. My captain, Trevor Bailey, stood at mid-off and told me I wasn't bowling the right line. I said "It's alright leaving my end, Mr Bailey", but I still went for five an over. Things could only get better.'

They did. He was lucky enough to be able to learn his trade before limited-over cricket took over the English game. As a result, he uses flight more than most modern spinners and I could imagine East bowling particularly well on an overseas tour, where the bounce would suit him. 'I would have liked to have gone abroad with England,' he says wistfully, 'I think I would have been a good tourist on and off the field.'

His main philosophy is to get the crowd on his side. 'I'm sure many think I'm an idiot but it would drive me round the bend if I played cricket with a poker face.' Few bowlers have managed to pick up their best tally of wickets during their benefit season. It happened to Ray East. 'They all talk about the pressure but I loved it. I've always been a socializer and it was great going to all the pubs and local cricket clubs around Essex.'

East feels more and more disenchanted with the first-class scene in England. 'It bores me to tears watching seam bowling all day. There's no doubt in my mind that the game is less interesting to everyone, especially the crowd.'

One can only hope that Ray East will still be able to see something to laugh about for a few more summers.

---

'I'll miss the fun, but not the cricket' – a devastating indictment from **Robin Hobbs** as he contemplates the end of a first-class career that started in 1961 and ends with him being the only regular English leg-break bowler in the game. For Hobbs to state that he will not miss first-class cricket is tantamount to Mrs Gertrude Schilling spurning the charms of Royal Ascot. Robin Hobbs was one of the great enthusiasts of the post-war English scene – whether as a bowler, brilliant fielder or batsman with a taste for hitting the ball long distances.

At the end of a career that saw him play for Essex, Glamorgan and seven times for England, Hobbs considers that there is no chance of the leg-spinner having any real influence in top-class cricket. 'It grieves me to say it, but he would need to be able to score a lot of runs as well. You don't see them coming through from the schools, or through the league system. Yet when I started, every county side had at least one.'

Yet the leg-spinner gives so much interest to the game. I watched Hobbs wage a fascinating duel with the great Zaheer Abbas at Bristol in 1981. It was a slow wicket, one of those occasions when the seamers fancy grazing down at third man – so Hobbs had a long bowl. Zaheer played him well, but Hobbs always had a chance of getting him out – indeed he was dropped a couple of times. Finally, after tea, Hobbs had him caught at square leg for 140. It was challenging, attractive cricket with both bowler and batsman determined to triumph. Andy Brassington, the injured Gloucestershire wicket-keeper, said it was the best day's cricket he saw that season and the crowd savoured the sight of a class leg-spinner facing up to a world-class batsman.

There was an interesting sequel to that duel and it comes courtesy of the Gloucestershire captain, David Graveney. Apparently, Zaheer was so impressed by the bowling of Hobbs that he announced at tea to his colleagues that when he decided to get out, he would give the unlucky bowler his wicket. Says Graveney, 'From a man like Zaheer, that's the ultimate compliment.'

Hobbs always bowled with such relish, such communicable enjoyment that it is sad to hear him dilate on the game's ills. 'For me, it used to be wonderful to see a class leggie battling away against a great batter. But it's all so tight now, you have to bowl to contain. That's no good to a leg-spinner.' Yet Hobbs had to compromise over the years; he learned to bowl flat and he was as accurate a leg-spinner as anyone in the past two decades, even though he sacrificed his capacity to spin it. He became a 'roller' rather than a big spinner and consequently his value on overseas tours with England was diminished. He went on three major tours, a fact he justifies with characteristic humour: 'I got carried around because I never minded doing twelfth man. I loved fielding at any time.' In the opinion of David Brown, he was a great team man. 'I went to South Africa and the West Indies with Robin and I thought he was a tremendous tourist. He never moaned about doing twelfth man, and whenever he got the chance to bowl, he was in his element. No day seemed too long for him, he would bowl at anybody in the nets. He did such a good job for the game, because the crowd perked up whenever he came on to bowl. Robin was enjoying himself and he'd share that feeling with the spectators.'

The root of his enjoyment stemmed from the fact that he was lucky even to get into county cricket. 'I couldn't bowl anything other than leg-breaks, it was impossible for me to bowl an off-break. When Essex took me on, we had eight spinners on the staff and on the green wickets of that era, I shouldn't really have been in the side, bowling leggies. It was a seamer's paradise. After one season, I went for a trial with Kent, they got interested and Essex kept me on.' Fifteen happy years with Essex followed, during which the side established itself as the happiest in the championship, under the contrasting captaincy styles of first Brian Taylor, then Keith Fletcher. They were a talented team, with a capacity to enjoy life off the field. Says Hobbs, 'Essex was the biggest drinking side around then. I remember coming to Edgbaston after we hadn't bowled a ball at Swansea for three days. We were told there was no chance of any play next day at Edgbaston, so we went on a bender. It turned out fine and dry the next morning and we fielded all day. They got over three hundred and by tea-time, none of us could stand up!'

He still laughs at the way he got out some of the world's best batsmen – sometimes purely by accident. 'Rohan Kanhai went to hit a wide long-hop square and he dragged it onto his stumps from a long way out. He stomped off and I heard his bat go into the dressing-room a long time before him. Then there was a lot of shouting. At lunch, I was told he'd said that he'd been dismissed by the worst bowler he'd ever faced!'     .

The relaxed chuckle conveys the enjoyment Hobbs has had from the game, but it cannot completely hide his sadness at the demise of the leg-spinner. An enthusiastic student of cricket's history, he was full of the England tour to South Africa in 1909–10 when I talked to him. 'Jack Hobbs had to go and play all those great googly bowlers off the matting, because he couldn't read them from the hand. What a marvellous contest that must have been. I read about Grimmett and O'Reilly bowling together for hours against England, with the opening bowlers there just to take the shine off the ball. I'd love to have been around then. As a boy, I saw Doug Wright and Richie Benaud and then went home and tried to bowl my little leggies. Who can the kids copy today?'

Presumably a batsman or a seam bowler who runs in off 35 yards. But will they ultimately give as much pleasure to the public as Robin Hobbs?

# 3. The Artists

Certain slow bowlers have appealed to the public by their sheer personality, others by the quality of their bowling. Some of them were more than useful with the bat, but above all, they were worth the admission price just to see them bowl. They were not utility bowlers, filling in before the arrival of the new ball, or keeping things tight just for the sake of it. They were specialists – a regrettably dwindling breed of spinners. These then are what I call the artists:

If **Jim Laker** was not the greatest off-spinner the game has known, then a lot of cricketing experts have their lines crossed. A gloriously easy action, control, matchless variation in flight and the ability to spin the ball as sharply as anyone . . . Laker had everything. He prospered on the Oval pitches of the 1950s, it is true; but on a good wicket, he was still the master. He missed out on two England tours to Australia because he was labelled an Oval bowler, yet only a third of his tally of first-class victims were taken there, on the ground where he played more than a third of his cricket. When he finally made it to Australia, he showed what a great bowler he was, topping the England averages in both the Tests and all first-class games. Tom Graveney still talks with admiration of Laker's bowling on that tour. 'Apart from Neil Harvey, the batsmen could never quite get to him, because he was such a master of flight and line. In a match against South Australia, he tempted them all to self-destruction. I stood at long-on and took three catches off Jim's bowling, just like shelling peas.'

If Laker had never taken 19 for 90 at Old Trafford in 1956, his fame as a great off-spinner would still be secure. He was no stranger to freakish bowling analyses, after all. Had he not taken eight for two in a Test trial at Bradford? His reward for that astonishing performance in 1950 was a solitary Test that summer against the West Indies and no place on the tour to Australia a few months later. No wonder Laker appeared detached on the field and slightly sardonic when he was not playing: he had his share of setbacks and no one would ever accuse him of losing his Yorkshire commonsense.

Johnny Wardle always sympathized with Laker's treatment at the hands of the selectors. Wardle's recurring battle with Tony Lock for the left-armer's place soured his Test career, especially as Lock's action was doubtful during that period. Says Wardle: 'Jim was the greatest off-spinner I've seen, yet he had to watch men like Tattersall, Appleyard and McConnon get in over him. I couldn't understand that and we shared a common bond as we shuttled in and out of the England side for years.'

Ted Dexter believes Laker was in a class of his own. 'He used to do something that no modern spinner ever attempts; when a new batsman comes in, he's usually greeted by a quicker ball from the spin bowler. Jim did the opposite – he would put it up in the air, make the batsman move his head up and down. The ball would be really spinning and to do that and flight it at the same time is high class to me.'

Keith Andrew, the great Northants wicket-keeper, kept to Laker on several occasions and marvelled at his variations of pace and flight. 'He could land the ball on the same spot using different trajectories – releasing the ball a little early, a little later, a shade more round arm or even a bit higher. The batsman would be trying to pick up the arc without knowing it was going to the same spot.'

Alan Knott was lucky enough to experience Laker's greatness at first hand on a Cavaliers Tour to the West Indies at the end of Laker's career. 'Even then his control was immaculate and he really spun it. And his body action – he seemed to pause for an eternity on his front leg as if to say: "Now where shall I put it?" An education for me.'

Even when Laker joined Essex at the age of forty he still looked high class. Keith Fletcher recalls fielding to him at short leg: 'When he bowled, you could hear the ball buzzing on its way down. The pace with which the ball came off the bat showed how much he spun it. One morning we put down five catches close in off Jim, because we couldn't adjust to his power of spin.'

For Laker, the corollary to the ability to spin a ball is a sore finger: 'Unless you get finger trouble, you're not spinning it. The proper way to spin it is off the finger-tips, and then you have to work hard in the nets at your basic control. Hardly any of the modern spinners have sore fingers at the end of the season and that's because they don't really spin it.' He sees little hope of slow bowling making a dramatic come-

An unusual view from mid-on of the classical action of Jim Laker. The non-striking batsman is Roy Tattersall, Laker's rival for the England off-spinner's position for several years in the 1950s.

back in the modern game. 'That's a tragedy because it's a thinker's role. There are so many ruses, little tricks to get a top-class batsman out by slow bowling. I still get more satisfaction out of seeing a bail drop off than a fast bowler blasting them all out of the ground.'

---

**Doug Wright** was an inspirational leg-break bowler. He bowled at medium pace off a bounding run of about fourteen yards but although he looked bizarre on his way to the crease, the end product was thrilling. For a time after the War, he bowled more unplayable deliveries than any other bowler of any pace in England; no wonder his tally of seven hat-tricks remains a record. When all the parts were in smooth working order, Doug Wright could go through any side.

No bowler of such class could alternate between mediocrity and

Doug Wright, one of the greatest leg-spinners of all time. From a long, bounding run he would deliver leg-breaks that, on their day, would be too fast for anyone

inspiration within the space of a couple of overs. 'Roley' Jenkins dubbed him 'the Enigma Variations' and he was right. He was almost impossible to set a field for, because he attacked all the time. At the same time, he was a captain's dream because he could win a game in just a few minutes. As Colin Cowdrey puts it, 'If I'd gone up to Doug and said, "Come on, make them fight for a single", he'd laugh and say, "I'm sorry skipper, you'd better try someone else." He never bowled a defensive ball in his life. Can one say that about any slow bowler today? If he dropped it on the spot, he could bowl Bradman three balls running, because he was so unplayably fast. The modern game wouldn't know how to cope with Doug, he could bowl like a god for twenty minutes, beat the bat time and again and yet give away fifty runs by inside edges and nicks through the slips that went to the boundary because of his speed.'

Doug Wright decided to bowl quick leg-breaks early in his career with Kent. A. P. 'Tich' Freeman was still in the side and Doug was as slow through the air as the little master. 'I found that the quicker I bowled, the less I needed to be so accurate. If I bowled as slowly as "Tich" I had to be on the spot every ball. The quicker style also meant that any edges off me usually went to the boundary but I learned to live with that.' He thinks the googly was the main reason he picked up so many hat-tricks: 'I got used to seeing the leg-break go over the top or miss the edge, whereas the googly would come back in and bowl a tail-ender if it was pitched right.'

Doug Wright's modesty is genuine and even on balmy days during Canterbury Week, he has to be coaxed into talking about himself. He would rather pay tribute to 'Tich' Freeman than dwell on his own achievements: 'The longer I played, the more I came to realise what a great bowler "Tich" was. How did he manage to bowl leg-breaks so accurately and take so many wickets a season? It used to take me all my time to get the ball to pitch!'

Early in his career, he learned the importance of a philosophical temperament. No bowler surely beat the bat more often with so little reward, yet Doug maintains that was no great hardship: 'It was marvellous to pitch on leg stump and hit the off, but I used to enjoy beating a good player, all ends up, even when the ball missed everything. You know when you're bowling well.'

'Bomber' Wells tells a lovely story that epitomizes Doug's attitude to the game. Wells and Cook were engaged in their usual hilarious last-wicket partnership and 'Bomber' decided to enliven things further by asking Doug to bowl his quicker one at Sam. 'Now Doug's quick ball was really fast and when he came in to bowl it, I was ready for something spectacular. Unfortunately the ball slipped out of his hand and turned into a beamer. Sam yelped, just got his bat to the ball and it lobbed up to Doug for a simple caught and bowled. He ignored the ball completely, ran down the pitch, put his arms round Sam and apologized profusely. I wonder how many of today's players would do that?'

Let Colin Cowdrey have the last word on this diffident, gentle man: 'If I ever had to write an epitaph for Doug Wright's gravestone, it would be "he never wanted to bowl a dot ball". Doug gave us so much entertainment.'

---

**Roy Tattersall** flourished in an era of high-class off-spinners in England. If Jim Laker was the supreme artist, Tattersall was not far behind for a few years; indeed, he was picked for England ahead of Laker in the early 1950s. He was flown out to Australia as a reinforcement for the injury-hit England team on the 1950–1 tour.

Tattersall's early reputation was built on some wet wickets in the north. On a drying wicket he was almost unplayable, especially as he was backed up by great close fielders like Jack Ikin, Ken Grieves and Geoff Edrich in the Lancashire side. He was faster than the usual off-spinner but his variations of pace were subtle enough to trouble the best batsmen. Indeed Ray Illingworth considered Tattersall a better bowler than Laker on a good wicket: 'He had a bigger heart than Jim, he could take all the stick handed out.'

He started his Lancashire career as a medium-pace bowler, but soon the coach, Harry Makepeace, weaned him towards off-spin. 'I thought I'd have a longer life as a spinner, so I practised and practised. What Harry didn't know about cricket wasn't worth the bother of finding out.' The hard work paid off and, throughout Tattersall's career, he had the reputation of accuracy. 'I had to bowl correctly because lads were standing up close for me who had families at home. I was conscious of my responsibility to them.'

Although tall, Tattersall gave the air of being rather frail. He was never one to impose himself on the day's proceedings with a raucous appeal or an attempt to play to the gallery. He always seemed to be genuinely surprised at his success – the first Young Cricketer of the Year Award in 1950 and his late selection for the Australia tour embarrassed him.

He now lives in Kidderminster and delights in talking about the old days. A friendly, naturally modest man, he remains apologetic to Somerset's Bertie Buse for ruining his benefit match in 1953. The game was all over in a day, with the deadly Tattersall taking 13 for 69. 'I'm afraid the wicket wasn't a very good one at Bath. I opened the bowling with Brian Statham and if I hadn't got some wickets, I should have been sacked.'

He vividly remembers the Test at Lord's against the South Africans when he bowled 52 overs in the day – 'Jack Ikin took an astonishing catch at short square leg to get Eric Rowan. It came right off the meat of the bat.' His rivalry with Jim Laker was always friendly: 'Jim spun it a lot more than me, he had stronger fingers, I suppose. He was a great bowler.'

The fate of modern spin bowlers leaves Tattersall grateful that he played his cricket at a time when slow bowling had an important say in a captain's strategy. He still watches Worcestershire and local club cricket whenever possible and feels genuinely sorry for the slow bowler. 'He just doesn't get match practice. How can he be expected to bowl a side out when he goes several games without a proper spell?'

Roy Tattersall, of Lancashire and England; a splendid off-spinner in the 1950s, with the height and power to trouble batsmen on any wickets

It would be instructive to see how today's first-class cricketers would cope with a bowler of Tattersall's economy, resource and technique. After all, he was rarely collared by the Mays, Comptons and Graveneys of his day.

---

Some may query the inclusion of **Bob Appleyard** in a gallery of spin bowlers. It is true he was not a slow bowler, he was more of a cutter in the Underwood style, yet he employed finger spin and clever changes of pace to establish himself at the top for a tragically brief period.

After just three first team games for Yorkshire, Appleyard dominated the 1951 season with 200 wickets. From the boundary he did not look devastating but a combination of off-spin, in-swing and off-cutters, plus awkward bounce, was too much for most batsmen. Colin Cowdrey considers Appleyard the best spinner/cutter of his time in all conditions – 'he could bowl everything and his line was perfect' – Tom Graveney agrees: 'He was terribly difficult to get after because of his bounce and variation of pace. He used to jump at the moment of delivery and that would make the ball bounce like a tennis ball. You'd wait all day for a half volley.'

During his short career, Appleyard was always experimenting, forever trying to extend his already formidable repertoire of skills. In the spring of 1952, he was to be found in the Yorkshire nets, trying to master the leg-cutter: it was only the previous season that he had taken 200 wickets! Sadly, illness confined him to a single match in 1952 and he did not play at all in 1953. The effect on Appleyard's morale can be imagined; he was in his thirtieth year, but he had had no chance to add to his dramatic season of 1951. He recovered his health for the 1954 season, although it was significant that his off-break was nowhere near as fast as the 1951 vintage. Yet he managed to make a significant contribution to England's successful tour of Australia, heading the bowling averages in both Tests and for the tour. His accuracy impressed everyone on that tour: regularly he would bowl with just two men on the off-side, plus a slip, and nobody took him apart. As a back-up to Tyson and Statham he was invaluable and of his eleven wickets in the series, all were authentic batsmen.

By 1956, shoulder injuries and illness were robbing Appleyard of his cutting edge and he was never the same again. He retired in 1958. One wonders just what he might have achieved given decent health. It would be unfair to dub him a 'one-season bowler'; in just five full seasons he took 708 wickets at a cost of 15.48, a lower average than any other top-class bowler then playing. Ray Illingworth, after admitting that he resented Appleyard's harsh treatment of him when he first came into the Yorkshire side, is nevertheless fulsome in his praise of him: 'He was the best of all the spinners I've ever seen. A marvellous variation of pace, a devastating leg stump yorker and a loop ball that really bounced. He could spin it a lot as well. A master.'

There cannot be many bowlers with just 700 wickets who receive a tribute like that. All the major English batsmen of the 'fifties would heartily endorse it.

---

If Bob Appleyard's influence over a short period was impressive, that of **Bruce Dooland** was even more profound. In just five years with Nottinghamshire, he took 770 wickets with his leg-spin; he also did the 'double' twice, always fielded superbly and by his own example lifted the county from the foot of the table to a position of respectability.

Bruce Dooland was a superb leg-spinner and truly Australia's loss was England's gain. He played just three times for his country after the War and he came to England because chances for spinners were limited at that stage in Australia: for an experimental period, the new ball was available every forty overs and Dooland saw no future for his subtle skills. After a successful spell in League cricket in Lancashire he joined Nottinghamshire in 1953 and proceeded to outclass most batsmen. In addition to the traditional leg-spinner's gifts, Dooland had another deadly delivery under his command: the flipper. He spun that from out of the tips of his fingers and it zipped through from off to leg at speed. It was quicker than the googly and Dooland caught out countless batsmen with it: they would shape up for the pull, only to see it hustle through, bowl them off the inside edge or trap them LBW. 'Roley' Jenkins, no stranger to the arts and crafts of leg-spin says: 'How Bruce did that was beyond me. He bowled it at a different pace from the googly with no change in action and it would come off the pitch like an Alec Bedser delivery.' Doug Insole remembers: 'Bruce used to get me out for a pastime. To me, his flipper was indistinguishable from his googly. As far as I was concerned, he had seven or eight different types of delivery and I was on the edge of my seat all the time. He didn't bowl loose balls like Doug Wright, either. He was the best bowler I've ever faced, an artist.'

Johnny Wardle, an equally clever bowler, used to relish the battle of wits with Dooland. 'When I batted, Bruce would bowl me a googly, I'd spot it and give it a whirl. Next ball, I'd think, "googly again", but it wasn't, he'd done me with the flipper. Or sometimes I'd expect the flipper and he'd bowl me another googly and I'd play too soon. He could make you look very silly.'

Dooland was lucky enough to learn how to bowl on fast, bouncy Australian wickets. He had to spin the ball, rather than just put it on the spot; if he found the edge of the bat, he would be rewarded by the nick carrying to the close fielder. At just under six feet tall, he had natural bounce anyway and that served him well on English wickets where he adapted brilliantly to the slow wickets.

Reg Simpson captained Dooland at Trent Bridge. 'He was simply a captain's dream, a marvellous man to handle. To have an attacking bowler who could bowl all day was wonderful, especially on those flat Trent Bridge wickets. If he came back today, he'd get 200 wickets in his first season. It would take a couple of years for the modern batsmen to work out how to play him. He'd love to bowl at these chaps who push forward with bat and pad together, especially with fielders closer to the bat today, because they wear helmets.'

A calm, charming man, Dooland was admired and liked by everyone in county cricket. Simpson remembers just one occasion when his charm deserted him – and the cause was our old friend and master of the bizarre, 'Bomber' Wells. At Bristol, the ball was turning slowly on the usual sandheap and Dooland could not get many wickets. When 'Bomber' came in at number ten, Dooland had 3 for 105; he realized that in Wells and McHugh, Gloucestershire had the worst last two batsmen in the county championship, so – not unreasonably – he assumed his analysis would be improved. John Mortimore was the 'not out' batsman and 'Bomber' was told by his captain to instruct Mortimore to push the score along. Dooland bowled to Mortimore, he blocked the ball and started to run. 'Bomber', the worst judge of a run in the game, was left stranded halfway down the wicket, with Dooland shouting, 'for God's sake, don't throw the wicket down.' Wells run out. In came Frank McHugh – so bad a batsman that Sam Cook would be placed at number nine! Off the next ball, McHugh ran himself out after a brilliant stop by mid-off – Dooland shouted, 'No, no, no!' as the stumps were thrown down at his end. He had missed the chance of bowling respectability. 'Bomber' Wells still chuckles about that: 'Imagine it – a great bowler, two useless batsmen and there's a couple of run outs. I'd never seen Bruce so mad!'

No doubt, Bruce Dooland regaled a few cricket audiences with that story when he returned to Adelaide to settle with his family in 1957. He died young – in 1980 at the age of 56 – but he left behind warm memories of a great bowler and a charming person.

---

**Jack Walsh** and **George Tribe** completed the trio of brilliant Australian wrist-spinners who flourished with Midland counties at the same time. Like Dooland, they were indebted to the bouncy wickets of their homeland during their formative years: all three did 'the double' in England and made a tremendous contribution to the entertainment value of county cricket.

Walsh and Tribe were left-arm bowlers, wrist spinners who could turn the ball great distances. They were both masters of the googly and chinaman and their skills were admired by that other contemporary practitioner of the left-arm arts, Johnny Wardle. 'I really admired those two,' says Wardle. 'I was always quite happy with my chinaman but my googly was very ordinary compared to theirs. I could never turn it as much.'

Hardly any of the batsmen in English cricket could 'read' Tribe or Walsh. Doug Insole: 'If it pitched middle, you assumed it was a googly, and you played from the crease. That was my only hope. I once got three hundreds in a row against Tribe and I never picked him once.' Tom Graveney: 'It was always a case of bluff and double bluff. They'd show you a googly, repeat it, then bowl you a totally different googly that was either faster, slower or spun more. If the delivery arm was low, I would hope it was the chinaman, but apart from that it was all guesswork.'

Jack Walsh's prodigious spin and variety of delivery was regularly too much for his own Leicestershire wicket-keeper, Paddy Corrall. Walsh was often grateful to his fellow Australian, Vic Jackson, for nipping over from slip to leg-slip when he had bowled the chinaman: poor Corrall would be covering the off-stump, while Jackson was saving byes or taking catches down the legside!

'Roley' Jenkins recalls the time when Walsh showed his mastery by bowling two different googlies in the same over. At tea, the Worcestershire captain, Ronnie Bird, had told 'Roley' that Paddy Corrall had given him the secret to Walsh's googly: his little finger was wrapped

Two great Australian slow left-arm bowlers of the unorthodox variety from the 1950s – Jack Walsh, who played for Leicestershire, and George Tribe of Northants

round the top of the ball. 'Roley' went out to bat after tea with Bird and watched him being beaten completely by the first five balls of the over. The last ball – a googly – fizzed from leg to off, Bird chased it and was caught. 'In that over, he mixed up his googlies and the one that finally got Ronnie Bird turned more – but there was no little finger on the ball. Now that's high-class bowling.'

The ever-curious 'Roley' asked Jack Walsh which batsman played him best – 'Laurie Fishlock, he belts the life out of me', was the reply. When Worcestershire next played Surrey, 'Roley' could not wait to quiz Fishlock. He was staggered to be told, 'I haven't got a clue how to play him, I can't pick one from the other!'

Jack Walsh spun the ball more than George Tribe, while Tribe was also a little flatter. His wickets cost him less and Keith Andrew – who kept to Tribe during his career at Northamptonshire – considers him a better bowler than Walsh. 'Jack just enjoyed bowling for the sake of it. He could bowl out anybody in the world, but I think George was more astute, more professional, certainly more accurate.'

Andrew recalls the time when Tribe made batting rather embarrassing for Cyril Washbrook: 'He lasted three overs in both innings and George made the ball go all over the place. Cyril was playing at the ball and missing it by about two feet because he couldn't pick George. There was nothing wrong with the wicket and Cyril would've been better getting out first ball.'

Tribe would regularly bowl on green wickets, away from the dusty ones of Northampton, underlining the point that a great bowler can perform under any conditions. His field-placing was precise; he insisted on a good catcher at mid-wicket, because his short-pitched googly would often trap the batsman unawares and he would catch the ball high up on the bat, when going for the pull. He was superstitious about bowling to batsmen he thought could pick him – even his own colleagues in the nets. Keith Andrew says: 'If I went to bat in the nets, George would move out and bowl somewhere else, and it was the same against Jock Livingston. I think he was worried about losing his confidence if someone played him easily enough.' His approach to the bowling crease always impressed Keith Andrew. 'He didn't just bowl with his wrist or fingers, he spun it from deep inside of him. He bowled with everything.'

It must have been difficult to set fields for Walsh and Tribe because they spun the ball so much both ways. A split field was therefore necessary and there was always the chance that a loose couple of deliveries would let the batsman off the hook. Yet they had the priceless ability to bowl a man when he was well set and considering the margin of error involved, their career bowling averages are surprisingly low. Two-in-one bowlers . . . and double the pleasure for everyone but the batsmen.

---

'Give him another pair of legs and you've still got an England bowler' – not a bad tribute to **Fred Titmus** in his fiftieth year. It comes from John Murray, his old partner behind the stumps for Middlesex. The evidence for Murray's claim comes from the matches the two friends played together in the Old England side that delighted many spectators in Sunday friendlies during the 1981 season. Murray kept wicket to Titmus three times, and maintains that his greatness as an off-spinner remains undimmed. On reflection, it is not that startling an assessment, for Titmus returned to county cricket for several matches in 1980, and, apart from some creaking joints in the field, he still looked a formidable bowler. Why did Titmus put his reputation on the line and agree to return to the injury-hit Middlesex side when nearly forty-eight? 'Ego', is his honest answer. 'It was a challenge and I thought I could still do it without looking a fool. Anyway, why can't slow bowlers go on till they're my age?'

That reply shows the steel that always lurked beneath the slightly diffident, whimsical Titmus persona. He was one of the most determined of cricketers, a fact he proved when losing four toes in a boating accident in the West Indies in 1968. Within six weeks, he was playing at the start of the English season and it never affected his bowling. He was also mentally strong. His former England colleague, David Brown, says: 'Fred was as tough as a nut. Nothing would ever rile or upset him and he always wanted to bowl, whether it was Sobers or Kanhai walking to the wicket.' John Murray remarks: 'No matter how often they'd get after Fred, he'd still be in there fighting. Great off-spinners like Laker and Illingworth might pack it in at some stage – but Fred, never.'

Titmus showed that streak of determination early in his career. He joined Middlesex as a batsman who bowled seamers, but soon his natural ability was spotted and great pressure was put on him to become a slow bowler. He was sent to Alf Gover's Indoor School for a winter, yet he still ran up and bowled outswingers. Successive captains at Middlesex would nag him to bowl slower in matches, but Titmus insisted on learning his art his way. He saw no point in tossing the ball up for the sake of it and reasoned that if he could bowl a thousand tight overs in a season, he would take a hundred wickets. He was lucky to have the advice of England slow bowlers, Jim Sims and Jack Young, two men nearing the end of their careers. He bowled a lot of long spells in tandem with Young and gradually developed his own particular style. A conversation with Charlie Barnett at a Cheltenham match was a turning point; Titmus had failed to take a wicket on a pitch that should have asssisted him. He was distressed and he went to the former England batsman at the interval and said, 'Mr Barnett, the wicket's turning and I don't look like getting anybody out. Why?' Charlie Barnett replied, 'Look, son, all good players play the turning ball well. What you've got to do is get them to make a wrong movement *before* the ball turns. Don't let the ball go straight from your hand in a straight line – that way they can see where the ball is turning.' Titmus considers that the best advice he was ever given: 'I believe a slow bowler should beat the good batsman *before* he lets the ball go by getting him to move a little earlier. He can do that by lengthening the swing of the arm, or holding onto the ball a bit longer or holding back

Fred Titmus – master of the floater and the swinger, as well as orthodox off-breaks

the body action a shade. I've proved that time and again in the nets by running up to bowl and hanging onto the ball – usually the batsman has moved.'

So Titmus eventually realized he needed more than just accuracy and spin to become a great off-break bowler. He needed drift in the air, a little wobble *away* from the bat. Here his early career as a seamer proved invaluable. He developed two deliveries that brought him hundreds of wickets – the floater and the swinger. The floater would swing away and then spin back into the right-hander off the pitch, while the swinger never came back, it was an outswinger. The success of the floater depended on the conditions – if the wind was coming up from fine leg, that was ideal. Eventually, Titmus managed to judge the amount of float needed and he would under-cut the ball if he wanted it to zip back in at the stumps. He also determined to bowl wicket to wicket, middle stump to middle stump, so that if the batsman went for the sweep to either the floater or the swinger, an LBW was a strong possibility. He picked up an enormous amount of LBWs when the batsman went to sweep what he thought was an orthodox off-break, only to discover that the ball was not going to pitch on leg-stump, but middle-and-off. The swinger also brought many entries in the scorebook along the lines of 'c. Parfitt b. Titmus' (first slip) or 'c. Murray b. Titmus' (wicket keeper), when the batsman believed the ball was just a straight one. Titmus was a master at spinning, floating or swinging the ball *just enough*. 'I reckoned that if the bat was four-and-a-half inches wide and I could turn the ball two-and-a-half inches, I was therefore at the edge of the bat, so why turn it a foot and miss everything?'

He cannot understand why more slow bowlers have not examined the possibilities that come from learning how to vary slightly the grip. 'Jim Sims once told me to paint the seam white and see how and where it goes when you vary things. Any bowler can bowl four different balls, simply by altering the height of the delivery arm. Then you can change the position of your foot across the line of the bowling crease and now you've eight different balls for a start. And watch where the seam of the ball is travelling for all these deliveries – it never goes the same way.'

John Emburey greatly benefited from the commonsense of Titmus when he was making his way in the Middlesex side. 'In my first game, the wicket was turning square and I didn't get a wicket. I asked Fred why, and he told me to vary my pace, to get the batsmen guessing a little. In the second innings, I bowled much better.' Shades of a conversation at Cheltenham over a cup of tea twenty years earlier.

The styles of Emburey and Titmus mirror the changing attitudes to spin, as Emburey himself admits: 'When Fred made his comeback in 1980, I was amazed at how slow he bowled. Of course, I'd played several times with him before, but I hadn't seen him for a couple of years. I stood at mid-wicket and marvelled at his controlled slowness through the air. It was a throwback to a different age.' The point is not lost on Titmus. He sees little encouragement for spin bowling in the modern game and offers this bleak comment: 'If I came into the game now, I'd probably end up a number six batsman who bowled medium-pace dobbers. I'd be average at both and never get anywhere near the England team.' From a man who played first-class cricket in five decades, that is a telling indictment of the way slow bowling has been allowed to decline.

---

For a decade, the off-spin partnership of **John Mortimore** and **David Allen** adorned the game. They were worthy successors to the Gloucestershire tradition of great slow bowlers that stretches back as far as C. L. Townsend, and if less deadly than the Parker-Goddard and Goddard-Cook duo, the firm of Mortimore and Allen did good business for a time. Although both off-spinners, they were as different in styles as in temperament – Allen, a bigger spinner of the ball, was a better bowler on a perfect batting wicket, whereas Mortimore was the better all-round bowler. Mortimore flighted the ball subtly and his control meant he was a nastier proposition on drying wickets, and during his career, the pitches at Stroud, Lydney, Gloucester and Cheltenham provided plenty of encouragement. His career record is more impressive than Allen's, yet Allen played in thirty-nine Tests and Mortimore just nine. Lucky the county who could afford to play them at the same time.

They were a fascinating contrast in attitudes – Allen, with the genial air of a man out for a post-lunch stroll, Mortimore, the angular, efficient theorist. It came as no surprise to me to learn that Mortimore studied to be an accountant during his playing career; as he whittled away at a batsman, he seemed to have his own cricketing profit-and-loss book open at a relevant page. He would plan a dismissal in a series of overs, clinically manoeuvring the batsman into positions that would benefit only the bowler. In his field placings, the slide rule would come out, the product of long research into the strengths and defects of the batsmen he was facing. Tony Brown remembers the day when his colleague's mastery was not reflected in his appeals for LBW: 'Morty thought he should've had at least two LBWs that day. After play ended, he went into the groundsman's hut to get some string and pegs. He used them to create the line and angles he thought he was getting from both round and over the wicket. He wanted to make sure that his appeals had been justified. They were.'

Allen was more expansive. He may have looked unhurried and relaxed in the field, but when he bowled, the positive side to his nature took over. Arthur Milton recalls: 'He had Fred Trueman's attitude, he really expected a wicket every ball. He would impose himself on the game and try to dominate the batsman.'

John Murray, who kept wicket to Allen many times for England, agrees: 'He was very strong-minded. He knew exactly what he wanted to do and wouldn't be dictated to by the captain over field placings.'

Both Mortimore and Allen agree they were better bowlers because of their partnership. Allen: 'We came from a slow bowling tradition at Bristol, so we didn't have to look over our shoulders at the seamers. We were good for one another because we could both nurse each other along and compete for wickets. Mortimore: 'The advantage was that we would set out to achieve an objective together against certain players and therefore our side had double the chance of getting them out.'

Mortimore's analytical mind does not allow him to be over-sanguine about the prospects for slow bowling. 'The problem is that slow bowlers take a long time to develop. In the meantime, the county captains see that the seamers are doing a reasonable job for him, so he makes sure the wickets are left green. Then the spinner doesn't get a bowl because the wicket doesn't suit him. Modern captains forget that you need a selection of varied bowling.'

Allen prefers optimism, his natural psychological stance that was reinforced by a game he played for the Old England side in the summer of 1981: 'Fred Titmus, Morty and I bowled twenty-four overs between us and it was lovely to turn the clock back. and show our skills to each other. There was such a pleasurable feeling that we were doing our job well and I know the spectators felt that. Surely top-class cricket hasn't lost that for good?'

One hopes that David Allen's idealism prevails – but accountants do have a habit of getting things right.

**Ray Illingworth**'s career is cogent proof of the value a team gets from a good spinner. For more than a quarter of a century, Illingworth's guile and unflappability served the causes of Yorkshire, Leicestershire and England with great distinction. When he retired in 1978, at the age of forty-six, he was still high-class, even if his body was showing signs of wear and tear. Now he says: 'If someone had given me a new back and a fresh pair of legs, I would have been even better at the age of fifty. Slow bowling is a thinker's game and you never stop learning at it.'

He was brought up in a hard school and never let anyone forget it; in his early days at Yorkshire, he would be told to bowl, only to find a Wardle or an Appleyard at the crease with the encouraging message: 'Booger off, I'm still bowling here.' Says Illingworth: 'I was a quiet sort of a lad but I made up my mind to be as tough as them. It was a test of my character.' He quickly acquired the mental toughness to develop as a slow bowler and years later, when he captained England and Leicestershire with such distinction, he made it clear that team spirit was vital. Few players under Illingworth's command would say they were treated unfairly. No comparable English slow bowler has been such a successful captain.

The popular criticism of Illingworth is that, in his England days, he did not bowl enough. A Titmus or an Underwood would wheel away all day, yet Illingworth chose the times when he wanted to bowl. Roger Tolchard, Leicestershire's wicket-keeper during Illingworth's time, feels that sometimes the skipper himself needed to be captained: 'I occasionally had to bluff him when he wanted to come off after being hit. He'd say it wasn't his day and I tried to gee him up.' To be fair to Illingworth, he carried a painful back injury for several seasons and he *had* to ration his bowling. When he did bowl, few bowlers withstood pressure as well as Illingworth. Two Tests will suffice: at Leeds in 1971 and Sydney earlier that year. The Sydney Test was a tremendously tense affair, with Australia needing just 100 to win on the final day with five wickets left. John Snow was injured and could not bowl; Illingworth had hardly bowled recently because of back trouble. The captain nagged away, varying the angles subtly and psyched them out on a good wicket. He took 3 for 39 in twenty overs, effectively winning the Test and the Ashes. Alan Knott, England's wicket-keeper that day, says: 'That was a tremendous piece of pressure bowling from a man who hadn't bowled for weeks. Added to his captaincy, it was a wonderful effort.'

At Leeds, the strong Pakistani batting side needed just over 200 at the start of the last day with all their wickets in hand. Instead of opening with the seam bowlers, Illingworth defied convention and started with himself and Norman Gifford. He got Aftab Gul with the third ball of the day, then the prolific Zaheer for nought and England scraped home by twenty-five runs.

John Hampshire offers an interesting assessment of the character of his former team-mate: 'If Ray had been a fast bowler, he would have been very sharp and nasty. He liked to get his wickets cheaply and he didn't like batsmen. He wanted at least four men round the bat, but also a sensible back-up in the outfield. If he'd have been a quickie, there would've been a few bouncers flying around if the batsmen hit him for fours.'

Illingworth took very little out of himself in his action: a little chassis at the start, a smooth, poised approach and a classic sideways-on delivery in the Laker manner. He used to place his left foot in front of the middle stumps, so that the little away drifer he bowled off one finger would take the edge late – or if he simply bowled a straight one, an LBW was a strong possibility. Dennis Amiss enjoyed the tussles with Illingworth: 'You'd see the cocking of the wrist, the opening of the door and the ball being spun, but then the odd one might go straight on rather than turn, and you were never quite sure which was which.' Roger Tolchard says: 'It takes great talent to be able to bowl like that. He literally dealt in inches – I'd tell him I'd seen a spot and to come back two inches, and he'd be there next over.' David Gower remembers his awe at Illingworth's control when the young batsman had just come into the side and his captain was well into his 'forties. 'I noticed how late he could change his delivery,' says Gower. 'If he saw someone on their way down the wicket, he could change line, dart it down the legside for a possible stumping or switch to an orthodox off-break. I'd never seen a spinner so flexible.'

Flexible, shrewd, phlegmatic and resourceful – Ray Illingworth combined these qualities with an intense determination and pride. At the end of his career, he was still proving that a slow bowler with a canny head on his shoulders is more than a match for most batsmen.

---

Possibly there were greater slow bowlers since the War than **Bishen Bedi**, but none has been more admired for the purity and beauty of his bowling action. For five years, the Indian adorned county cricket and his performances in Tests established him throughout the world as a

Ray Illingworth's classic sideways-on action

classic slow left-armer. Here are just a few of the tributes from cricketers I interviewed:

Colin Cowdrey: 'A truly magnificent sight.'
Glenn Turner: 'He made it flow like music.'
M. J. K. Smith 'He enjoyed bowling for the sake of bowling.'
Norman Gifford 'An artist – one of the few players I'd always make a point of watching.'

And so on and so on. It all seemed so natural with Bedi – unhurried and beautifully co-ordinated, a marked contrast to his efforts with the bat and in the field. When Bishen Bedi had the ball in his hands, his limitations in other aspects were readily forgotten. He could bowl for hours without any apparent strain. Unruffled, balanced, and phenomenally accurate, the spider/fly analogy came easily to mind when Bedi bowled. Although he did not start to play cricket until he was thirteen, he was a natural bowler. He would drop into rhythm straight away and the coaxing, teasing and bluffing would begin.

In common with most contemporary batsmen, Glenn Turner considers him the best slow left-armer on good wickets he has faced. 'He could vary his pace without any change of action. Your subconscious would tell you where the arc of the ball was, but all of a sudden he'd bowl you one *above* that arc which you thought was driveable. Your eyes would light up, you'd be down the wicket to drive it, but he'd held it back and you were caught at mid-off or stumped. At his best, he had you on a piece of string and he'd tug you this way and that.'

Mike Brearley enjoyed the mental battles with him on the England tour to India in 1976–7 but concedes: 'When he let go of the ball, it was very difficult to know where it was going to land at your end. He never seemed to change his action, although the deliveries varied.'

Dennis Amiss toured India twice with England and his duels with Bedi are among the most satisfying memories of his long career. 'You'd be out there in front of 90,000 people in Calcutta and Bishen would take the ball in the third over of the innings. A mighty roar would go up and five men would gather round the bat. Bishen's first ball would explode, bounce and turn and the ground would erupt. His control was astonishing – middle-and-off most of the time to the right-hander, yet he'd toss one up higher and it would land on the same spot. Over after over, the ball would pitch on a spot the size of a handkerchief.'

Amiss also remembers a gesture from Bedi that explains why he

The art of spin was never in better hands than those of Bishen Bedi

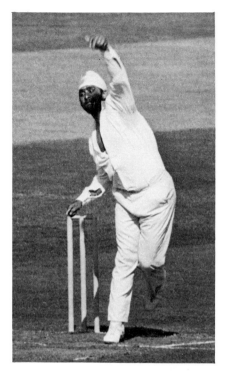

Bedi's flight, control and pace were
superb – perplexing to the batsman,
but a beautiful sight for the spectator

was one of the most popular cricketers of his time. Amiss had had a
terrible tour to India in 1972–3 and finally he was put out of his misery
and dropped for the last two Tests. He sat watching the Bombay Test,
marvelling at the way Keith Fletcher and Tony Greig played the
spinners; they used their pads and just ground them down. They both
got hundreds and Amiss mentioned to Bedi that he thought that was
the right way to bat against him. 'Of course, that's the only way,' he
said, and promptly offered to bowl to Amiss in the nets. Bedi brought
the off-spinner Venkat out with him and told him to bat for half an
hour to an imaginary field and then he would tell Amiss how many
times he was out. 'I just blocked it, using my pads. At the end of the
session, Bishen said I hadn't been out once. On those wickets, I
shouldn't have been bothered about smashing him out of sight.' On
the next tour, Amiss scored heavily and Bedi was less effective. Tony
Greig captained England on that 1976–7 tour and he devised a way to
break up Bedi's rhythm; he took a long time to look up when Bedi was
running in, so that he had to stop and start again. The effect was to
exasperate Bedi and throw him out of gear.

Bedi was never happy against batsmen who just set out to defend. He realized that a good player should not get out on a perfect wicket. His considerable gifts were testing enough, but he relied on self-destructive urges by the batsmen. Perhaps that is why he ostentatiously clapped when he was hit for six – he wanted the batsman to try the shot again. He thrived on challenging batting, rightly considering that eventually he would ensnare his man.

Geoff Cook tells a story about Bedi that sums up his attitude to bowling. Northants were playing Hampshire and the contest within the contest was clearly Bedi against Barry Richards. Bedi's first ball was straight-driven for six by Richards, who turned to Cook at short-leg and said: 'Now the real contest begins.' Cook takes up the story: 'For the next hour, we saw some fabulous cricket. Bishen tossed it up, using all his wiles and Barry played some magnificent shots. Finally, Bishen got him, when he was stumped for about sixty. It was the most exciting hour's cricket I've ever watched.'

Bedi's attitude that the wicket of Richards was worth 60 runs hardly endeared him to those who wanted cricket to be played on a more utilitarian level. Northants dropped him from limited-over cricket because of his ponderous fielding and mediocre batting. The writing was on the wall and Bedi became more and more disenchanted. A communications gap developed between him and the club's administration, and at the end of the 1977 season he was sacked. Many members were incensed, and Northants were threatened with an industrial tribunal hearing, but it was all to no avail. One of the artists of the game was lost to English cricket at the age of thirty-one.

In retrospect, it was wrong to drop a great bowler from limited-over cricket, yet Bedi's refusal to compromise his art was a factor. His gracious applause of Lancashire's David Hughes when he hit him for 24 in an over in the 1976 Gillette Cup Final was endearing – yet it was the last over of the innings and Hughes's onslaught made Northants' target more difficult to attain. One might ask why Bedi was selected to bowl the final over, when it was obvious that a hard hitter like Hughes would try for the slog and that Bedi would not alter his style, but that is another matter. As Norman Gifford, that most adaptable of left-arm spinners, says: 'Bishen just wouldn't alter his style, he still wanted to say, "Come on, see whether you can hit that one." He was a throwback to the old amateur days when the ball kept disappearing out of the park and there'd be three stumpings every innings.' Sad but true.

There was another criticism of Bedi – he did not like bowling on a wet wicket. While the Giffords and the Underwoods would lick their lips at a drying wicket and fire the ball in quickly, Bedi would amble in with his usual grace and bowl as if he was on a Bombay shirt-front. He would beat the bat, but rarely get a man caught in the bat/pad position by making the ball rear up off a length. The Northants wicket-keeper, George Sharp, remembers: 'We tried to get him to bowl like Gifford and Underwood on wet ones, but he said that wasn't his idea of cricket. He wanted to bowl his own way and this inability to adapt to the modern game was his fundamental weakness. At the time, our strength was in limited-over cricket and Bishen just wouldn't bowl negatively.'

So we lost Bishen Bedi. A specialist slow bowler of genius was sacrificed on the altar of expediency and professionalism. After 1977, Bedi's career swiftly declined and he retired four years later. Long after his records have been forgotten, he will be remembered for the beauty of his bowling, his Corinthian attitude to the game and for the days when spectators would rush to that prosaic ground at Northampton if the home side was in the field. Even that ground lost its functional air when Bedi was bowling: the football floodlights no longer assailed the eyes when the chunky figure with the bright turban ambled up to the umpire. When Bishen Bedi bowled, every day seemed bathed in sunshine.

---

**Don Wilson** was dissimilar to Bishen Bedi in all but two respects: his style of bowling and attitude to the game of cricket. Wilson bowled orthodox slow left-arm for Yorkshire and England in the best Peel-Rhodes-Verity tradition. He was a flight bowler first and foremost: the modern tradition of flat trajectory on leg-stump was never for him. Don Wilson also enjoyed his cricket and he saw no reason why that should be concealed.

His best days were those under the captaincy of Brian Close, an attacking captain. That suited Wilson; he liked men round the bat and in the deep and he and Ray Illingworth made a splendidly contrasting pair. John Hampshire considers Wilson was under-rated. 'Some critics reckoned that he only got his wickets because of Illingworth's accuracy at the other end, but he was a fine performer for us. He was a big spinner of the ball, not afraid of stick and he loved his cricket.'

At six foot three, Wilson was the ideal height for a bowler relying on flight. He was the kind of bowler who seemed to think the Fates were being unkind in denying him at least three wickets in the over. 'I honestly expected a wicket every ball. I was brought up in a side that expected to bowl other sides out. If the ball was going out of the ground, I still threw my hands up as if the batsman had been dead lucky.'

Perhaps Wilson's introduction to first-class cricket shaped his super-optimistic nature. In his first over he bowled George Tribe of Northants – 'he played for the turn but it went straight on, as usual. One colleague quipped: "I hope they close the gates, else this lad will run all the way home." The attitude of the side was that they expected a wicket every ball.'

One of the fortunate men to see silver linings in the densest of clouds, Wilson cites a game against Worcestershire as an example of the kind of cricket he relished. 'Tom Graveney and Basil D'Oliveira hit us all over the place. Ray Illingworth and I bowled thirty overs each and at no stage did we have a deep mid-wicket or a deep extra cover. Our lads were really enjoying it in the field, their attitude was "they're not getting the ball past us" and, on a good wicket, some magnificent shots were played. I thought it was wonderful cricket.' One doubts whether the more realistic members of that Yorkshire side – Illingworth for example – shared Wilson's genuine enthusiasm, but the day is fresh in his memory. So is the time when Peter May got off the mark in spectacular fashion at the Oval – 'He hit me over extra cover and it went out of the ground. That was after a low score in the first innings. Magnificent, challenging cricket.'

His refreshingly sporting attitude to the grim realities of first-class cricket was cemented by an incident early in his career that tells us much about the camaraderie of cricket in the 'fifties. The game was against Middlesex at Leeds and Wilson was brought on to bowl against Denis Compton. The rookie in his first season against the old master in his farewell year. The great man was on 82 when Wilson started bowling; paralysed with nerves, he bowled a clutch of full tosses in two overs before lunch and Compton made no attempt to score off them. He went to lunch, still on 82 with Wilson wondering how he had managed to bowl two maidens in a row against him. Just after lunch, Compton was caught at leg slip and on his way back to the pavilion he made a point of coming over to the gauche young spinner. 'Young man,' he said, this is the start of your cricket career and the end of mine. You will have a tremendous time if you get as much fun out of the game as I have done.' That day, Denis Compton became Don Wilson's hero and he continually tried to play by his precept, even in the tensest of situations.

Today, he presides benignly over the youngsters at Lord's. He is chief coach there and his enthusiasm rubs off on all who come within twenty yards of him. He honestly feels he is bowling better than at any time of his career – at the age of 44. 'It's because I bowl so many overs. I get through about a thousand in the summer in the nets, and I bowl for about five hours daily in the winter. I concentrate like hell when I'm bowling to anyone, because I'm head coach and therefore expected to get the chap out. I treat every day like a Test Match and I really think I could play in a county side if I wanted to, because I get so much more bowling than the slow bowlers in first-class cricket.'

Heaven knows how Don Wilson will cope with life when he finally puts his flannels in mothballs. At this rate, he must be good for another forty years.

---

The *joie de vivre* of Wilson is in marked contrast to the intense absorption of **Derek Underwood**. A relaxed, friendly man off the field, he seems to find the game of cricket very hard work; during a bowling spell, he is wrapped in a cocoon of concentration, the embodiment of the maxim that genius is nine-tenths perspiration. For Derek Underwood is a genius, a unique bowler of his time. If one dubbed him a left-handed Bob Appleyard, it would probably be an over-simplification, but that is the nearest comparison. Underwood is difficult to classify as a bowler: he is more of a slow-medium cutter than a spinner, yet he can, and does, impart spin and flight when the conditions suit his tastes. For the past fifteen years, he has been two bowlers in one – a stock bowler of staggering accuracy and a match-winner when the pitch is favourable, 'Deadly' the wet-wicket sorcerer.

Alan Knott feels it is wrong to label Underwood as a wet wicket bowler. 'He has a great record in Tests abroad on good batting tracks. Ask the Chappell brothers, he always had the sign on them. His accuracy is invaluable on flat wickets – I remember a game in Pakistan, where not one delivery from Derek came through to me in a two-and-a-half-hour session. He can sow seeds of doubt in the batsmen's minds with a single delivery; it happened at Brisbane in 1970 when he bowled one to Paul Sheahan that just took off. I caught it and the later batsmen looked at the pitch very suspiciously. But the wicket was a beauty, they didn't realize that it was Derek's pace which made that ball fizz.'

For Underwood, the important thing is to judge the pace of the wicket and then bowl accordingly. He likes to start off with a maiden, gently easing himself into the combat and finding out the speed of the wicket. 'I might bang the ball in, see it come off slowly, so I'll try a very slow one. Usually the right speed for me is between the two extremes. I suppose I'm still learning how to bowl slow, because I know there are times when you have to hold it back a little on a wicket with some speed in it.'

He admits that in his early days, he bowled too flat, a style that served him well on drying wickets. He points out that he was still in his mid-twenties when the criticism was at its height and that maturity in his style was still at least ten years away. With some justification, Underwood defends his speed of delivery by maintaining that the wickets in England have got slower and lower – 'Without bounce, you have to push it through or the batsmen has too much time to hit you.'

Despite his towering achievements, Underwood has always been a little insecure as a cricketer. He felt the pressure of being saddled with the 'Deadly' image and the times when he was kept out of the Test side by Norman Gifford affected him. Ray Illingworth had been disappointed with Underwood's bowling on good Test pitches. In 1971 and 1972, England played India and Australia at the Oval and on both occasions, Illingworth felt he had erred in picking Underwood. 'At that time, there was little to choose between Derek and Norman,' says Illingworth, 'but Norman spun it more and I think he would've won us those games. Derek wasn't spinning it off the straight and we were carrying him around for wet wickets that never materialized. In the India Test, I encouraged Derek to bowl slower. He got two wickets, but after lunch, he told me he'd lost it and went back to firing it in, which was no good on a dry, wearing wicket. Yet it worked for him before lunch.'

So Underwood was unsure of his England place for several years, although Illingworth thinks that insecurity made him a better bowler. Underwood agrees; he feels he returned an even more determined bowler with greater variety.

He is unashamedly a specialist cricketer in an age of mediocre 'bits and pieces' players. He considers it unfair that the specialist slow

Derek Underwood's familiar delivery stride – body bent, concentration
intense

bowler should be in danger of extinction when a mundane all-rounder is plainly not good enough at either batting or bowling. 'It's very easy for a chap to get thirty with the bat, but is he then in the right frame of mind to do a stint of slow bowling? You can fall between two stools; if an all-rounder has held the tail together and batted well, what frame of mind is he in when he has to bowl? If he's as tense with the ball in his hand as he was when he batted, well that's fine, because I think you *should* be tense at the start of a bowling stint. How many times does that happen though? I believe cricket should be doing more for the specialists.'

An uncomplicated bowler, Derek Underwood; therein lies his true greatness, according to Fred Titmus: 'He's a natural sort of bowler, he just runs up and bowls, puts in a slower one now and again, but that's all. He relies on line and length with the odd bit of controlled variation thrown in, and that's usually enough.' Mike Smith feels the greatest compliment to him is that he has always been reliable. 'I don't think I could ever say that he bowled badly. He may not have bowled as well as he might have done by his own high standards, but it's incredible that he never lost it. He's always been there or thereabouts. A tremendous bowler under any conditions.' To Tom Graveney, the fascination of Underwood is that he was so good so soon: 'As soon as he came onto the scene, he was a very good bowler. It seemed he didn't have to learn his trade, he was at us right away at the age of eighteen.' John Hampshire speaks for thousands of frustrated batsmen around the world when he pays this tribute to Underwood: 'It's always "grit your teeth" time when you face him. You have very little chance of getting after him, all you can do is try to work him away for singles. Even on good wickets, I've never seen him slogged around the park. For the last fifteen years, he's been the first name in the England team for me. A great craftsman.'

One wonders if the modest Underwood realizes just how good he is. Probably not – for he has little to be modest about.

---

Any off-spinner who takes more than 1000 first-class wickets under the present structure of the game can be said to have enjoyed a successful career – but in the case of **Pat Pocock**, there is a sense of comparative failure. This feeling is in its own way a tribute to the skills of the likeable Surrey bowler, yet there is still a hint of untapped potential. For more than a decade, he has been England's best

Pat Pocock's lovely high action gives him a fine command of the off-break

off-spinner in terms of sheer ability – and yet he has played in just seventeen Tests.

Pocock has all the physical assets needed to be a great off-spinner – a lovely, high action, an enviable range of variety and power of spin. He follows Jim Laker's dictum by having chronic finger trouble, yet, as Laker says, 'at least that means he spins it'. He is a skilled bowler in limited-over cricket and a joy to watch on good batting wickets, as he rings the changes on his varied and fascinating art. Yet that same variety that makes him such an attractive bowler seems to be his undoing; he does not nag away at the batsman on turning wickets, leaving the ball to do the work in conjunction with favourable conditions. A Titmus or an Illingworth would find a good enough stock delivery for the occasion and if it was dangerous enough, they would broadly stick with it. Not Pocock. His laudable desire to extemporize and keep the batsman guessing by variety means he bowls more bad balls than other high-class spinners. Alan Jones, the Glamorgan batsman, has relished his tussles with Pocock over the years, yet considers that Pocock has spun the ball too much for his own good. 'On occasions, he's turned the ball about eighteen inches and I've been able to watch it go past my off-stump. Now Titmus would always be at me in similar conditions and he would probably get me out. Pat seems to have a leg-spinner's temperament while bowling off-spin.'

Dennis Amiss agrees: 'He wants a wicket with every ball whereas the greats would say, "if I can't get you, I'll bowl a dot ball". Pat doesn't think as a batsman, we don't like being pressurized and wondering where we can fiddle a run.' Norman Gifford has a great admiration for Pocock's ability but considers he has never been a pressure bowler: 'You can't bowl a different ball every over and expect to create pressure, because some of them will be loose. If they're scoring off you, they aren't under any pressure.'

Pocock accepts the criticism but feels he is now a more consistent bowler: 'I've taken my game apart on several occasions and now I'm 200 per cent better than the time when I played my first Test back in 1968. I remember Jim Laker telling me that I should not even consider myself a good spinner till I was thirty. I was in the England team at the time and that age seemed an eternity away to me, but he was right.' He agrees that too many runs were being scored off him; now that he counts his analysis during a session, he thinks he has tightened up his approach. He pays generous tribute to the coaching ability of Fred Titmus during his short stint at the Oval. 'He got me to bowl closer to the stumps. My arm comes straight over the top now and if the ball doesn't turn, I can pitch off-stump to hit off-stump. Now I don't get cut so much because the batsmen know they're doing that off the stumps and I'm getting more LBWs because I'm bowling wicket to wicket. If I saw the way I bowled ten years ago, I would be very critical. You can't sit back and be blind to your own technical defects.'

One can only hope that the perennial Pocock optimism is well-founded. At thirty-five, time is still on his side and there is no reason why he cannot get better. He has an openness of mind and a refreshing attitude to criticism, vital assets when things are going wrong. What a prospect he was at twenty-one! He toured West Indies with the England team in 1967–8 and Tom Graveney remembers: 'He bowled absolutely beautifully, he looked so mature for his age. He kept Sobers quiet in the game against Barbados with some superb bowling.'

Pocock justifiably points out that he received little encouragement from the selectors. He was dropped following the First Test against Australia in 1968 after taking 6 for 79 and subsequently Ray Illing-worth's ascent to the captaincy meant he had little chance to be the number one off-spinner. Of his seventeen Tests, fourteen have been abroad and eight against the strong West Indies batting sides – 'no wonder my wickets have cost me 41 in Tests! But I'd love to bowl against those blokes now that I'm a better bowler.'

His most satisfying bowling performance is not the time in 1972 when he took seven wickets in eleven balls against Sussex ('they were just chasing runs') but a return of 0 for 152. It was at Kingston in the second Test against the West Indies in 1974. 'I bowled 57 overs from round the wicket to a 7/2 field with a 55-yard straight boundary against men like Lloyd, Kanhai, Kallicharran and Sobers. Derryck Murray was at number nine. And I went for less than three an over.'

Cheerful, philosophical and talented, he must wonder in his darker moments just where he went wrong. One hopes there is enough mileage left in the Pocock engine to revise the opinion of one of his greatest admirers, David Brown: 'It's one of the biggest mysteries of cricket that Pat Pocock didn't become one of the great off-spinners of all time.'

---

Pat Pocock will feel a little strange bowling for Surrey in 1982 without the company of a rotund, smiling man at the other end. For **Intikhab Alam** has been lost to English cricket. At the age of forty, he has

One of the last international leg-spinners, Intikhab Alam, of Pakistan and Surrey, retired at the end of the 1981 season

returned for good to the family textile business in Lahore. With his departure, the art of leg-spin in England is no more. His first Test, back in 1959, was watched by President Eisenhower of the United States and now, a little over twenty years on, leg-spin is about as relevant to our game as Dwight D. Eisenhower himself.

'Inty' is sad at the demise of his art in England; he blames wickets with no bounce and is quick to praise the efforts of the Oval groundsman, Harry Brind, to rectify that in recent years. He feels that captains have a defensive attitude to leg-spin: 'If you are a good bowler, you can bowl on anything, whether it's a green wicket or a slow turner. Although leggies are still being produced in India and Pakistan, there is no incentive for them in England. Everything is geared up to winning.'

Anyone who has enjoyed Intikhab's career knows that the avuncular, charming personality concealed a hard, professional attitude to the game. Not only fast bowlers want to win. In his pomp, 'Inty' was a splendid leg-spinner – accurate and brisk enough to prevent the batsman having fanciful ideas about going down the wicket to him. He was also a powerful, uncomplicated hitter with the bat and his all-round qualities have been invaluable in both Tests for Pakistan and in English county cricket.

He worked hard at his art: as a boy, he was made to bowl for no less than four hours a day in the nets, despite his protestations that he wanted to have a bat. He came over to spend a year as a professional in Scotland to learn how to bowl on slow, dampish wickets. 'Length and line were the important things to learn, then how to spin the ball. I never really needed to turn the ball a lot, I usually bowled from different angles to keep the batsman guessing.'

In his last season, it was a delight to see him picking up a respectable tally of wickets. Young players who had hardly seen a class leg-spinner were regularly undone by his 'flipper' and the oldest practising exponent of the art ensured that his valedictory message was that leg-spin can still thrive. Even the great Viv Richards fell to his wiles: a planned dismissal, bowled sweeping round his legs. Says 'Inty': 'Very few modern players, including Viv, play the sweep shot correctly.'

Colleagues and opponents are fulsome in their praise of 'Inty' as a man and cricketer. David Brown: 'One of the true gentlemen of the game, he sums up the philosophy of the leg-spinner to me.' John Hampshire: 'A fabulous bowler and man. He did an awful lot for Surrey on and off the field.' Pat Pocock: 'If you conducted a poll around the world to find the three most popular men in cricket, Inty would be one of them. I have fantastic respect for his ability as a cricketer. Some of the Pakistani Test players have told me that when Inty was captain, they would bend over backwards to make things happen for him, even if he made a daft tactical decision. They just didn't want to let him down.'

'Inty' has no qualms about choosing leg-spin for a career: 'If I came back again, I wouldn't change a thing. I know how much the public have wanted me to do well and I'm truly proud and grateful for their support.' Ever since he took a wicket with his first ball in Test cricket (Australia's Colin McDonald, bowled trying to cut), 'Inty' has given more to the game than he has taken. In a uniform era of cricket, he has brought us light and shade.

---

Another Pakistani leg-spinner gave great pleasure to the English public at the same time as Intikhab. **Mushtaq Mohammad** was primarily a batsman, but a good enough bowler to take more than 500 wickets for Northamptonshire. He was less accurate than Intikhab, but he had a better googly, spun the ball more and could be unplayable on his day. George Sharp, the Northants wicket-keeper, remembers how effective he was against the tail: 'You'd get these blokes playing down the line against the seamers, then 'Mushy' would come on and bamboozle them. He'd bowl flippers and googlies, and roll them over – they'd play back and be trapped in front by the flipper, or they'd try to off-drive and get bowled through the gate by his googly.'

Mushtaq feels his lack of height (just five feet seven inches) hampered his attempts at accuracy, so he compensated with extra turn: 'I bowled more with my wrist to give it air, whereas "Inty" was always very physically strong and bowled with his shoulder. That meant he could drop the ball on the spot.'

He started bowling leg-spin because he was bored with just fielding. He admired Richie Benaud and tried to model himself on him, copying Benaud's bustling run-up, and the Australian passed on several tips when the two men actually met. Such encouragement is lacking today for the young leg-spinners, Mushtaq feels: 'The captains are too stereotyped. They say leg-spin is a luxury, but they won't give it a consistent try. Then a leg-spinner is brought on at the wrong moment, gets some stick and the captain says "I told you so!" You need a big heart to be a leg-spinner. I feel he could do particularly well in England where the English players don't use their feet. I used to love seeing a batsman stay in his crease and push and prod at me, that meant I could attack him without worrying about getting hit.'

His sad prognosis is that any spinner has to be able to bat to get into an English county side. 'In Pakistan and India, you can still see the specialist slow bowlers, but the one-day game in England means a need for all-rounders who bowl medium pace.'

His message for English leg-spinners is: 'If you win a match for your captain, you can turn to him and say that the art hasn't died, it's you who has forgotten it!' Unfortunately, it has to be said that you cannot win a match for your captain unless he gives you a bowl.

---

In the seventies, Leicestershire were one of the more interesting sides to watch in the field. They usually played two slow left-armers and two class off-spinners. One of them was Ray Illingworth and the other an underrated, classical slow bowler – **Jack Birkenshaw**. In his time,

Birkenshaw was one of the best flight bowlers in the game. A slow bowler in the best traditions, he never really came to terms with limited-over cricket. He was at his best tossing the ball up to the batsmen, beating them in the air, rather than by containment. Roger Tolchard kept wicket to him for Leicestershire – 'when he bowled it quicker, he was never right. But when he lobbed it up, it was a treat to see a batsman running down the pitch and never quite getting there. Shades of Bedi.'

At the age of fifteen, Birkenshaw played for Yorkshire Second XI. Len Hutton told him he would never make a great off-spinner because he was too small; yet the young Birkenshaw was lucky enough to be coached by Johnny Lawrence, himself a fine leg-spinner and later mentor to Geoff Boycott. Lawrence lived next door to Birkenshaw in Leeds and, from the age of twelve, young Jack was taught the basics. 'He made me bowl and bowl in the nets. It was organized net practice, though – he made sure I wasn't tired out just for the sake of it.' At the age of eighteen, Birkenshaw played for Yorkshire and he would watch wide-eyed the spinning talents of men like Dooland, Walsh and Tribe.

Opportunities were limited at Yorkshire, so he joined Leicester-shire in 1961. His batting developed and soon he was an invaluable member of that emerging side. Birkenshaw believes he was at his best in the mid-sixties under Tony Lock's captaincy. 'Everyone tried to get after me, because Locky was so dominant at the other end. I was encouraged to keep on flighting the ball and I spun it quite a bit too.' Ironically, England calls never came for another few years and then only because his county captain, Ray Illingworth, did not want to tour India and Pakistan.

Jack Birkenshaw was one of those talented cricketers who missed the boat of eminence by a hair's breadth and had to make do with an honourable seat in the main supporting tug. The presence of Illing-worth in the same county side meant that this quiet, dapper man was overshadowed by a great off-spinner. His flighty method of bowling never really prospered on wickets that became slower over the years; and limited-over cricket disrupted the smooth, easy rhythm of his bowling. He tried dropping his arm and firing the ball in on the leg stump. 'I ended up bowling almost round arm from around the wicket into the batsman's feet. I sacrificed my flight – my best quality – for the sake of stopping them scoring. It messed me up and I wish I'd stuck to my own method.' Ray Illingworth agrees: 'Jack was always an impressionable lad, a great theorist, and all the changes in action did him no good at all. But that beautiful flight of his meant that, on his day, he was the best off-spinner in the country for a time.'

At the end of his career, he looks forward to his new post as a first-class umpire and to continue coaching in the winters. The words of Johnny Lawrence are still fresh in his mind from the days when he would bowl all afternoon in the nets – 'Remember lad, whether it's batting, bowling or fielding, cricket should be beautiful to watch.' Jack Birkenshaw did not fail on that score.

---

**John Emburey** has recently held the number one off-spinner's spot in the England team that Jack Birkenshaw could never make his own. Emburey's hold was tenuous – not because of his defects, more to do with the strategy of modern Test attacks. Despite his undoubted class, he has had to steel himself to the prospect of carrying out the drinks and missing tours; a year after an impressive tour to Australia, he was not selected for the 1979–80 trip, and only joined the party because Geoff Miller was injured. He only really looked at home in the England side when Mike Brearley returned to the captaincy midway through the 1981 Ashes series – and Emburey's bowling at Edgbaston proved what an asset he is when his insecurity is pushed aside.

At six foot two, he has the height of a Laker and the easy, unhurried rhythm of the master. At his best, the arm is high and the bounce surprisingly profitable from the most sluggish of wickets; he undercuts the ball skilfully, to give him drift away from the right-hander. He is working at the kind of away floater that made Titmus great, but time is on his side. At Emburey's current age, Titmus had only played two Tests, he was still in limbo, cultivating his matchless skills. The demands of one-day cricket do not help Emburey; sometimes his line is too flat and on occasions, he is annoyingly loose. At Edgbaston on that tense Sunday in the 1981 Australia Test, Emburey bowled beautifully for most of the time, removing Border and Yallop. Australia, needing just 151 to win, were 105 for 5 when the dangerous Rod Marsh entered. Every run was vital and Emburey's off-spin would surely test the patience of the impulsive Marsh – yet the first ball was pitched short outside off stump, and Marsh leaned back to crack it square to the boundary. In the end it did not matter, Ian Botham saw to that – but a mature Titmus or an Illingworth would not have given a first-ball present to a new batsman at such a tight stage.

Norman Gifford, a man who worked out his method of bowling in a less pressurized age, rates Emburey highly, but feels he is still searching for consistency: 'He's the sort of lad who does think about his bowling and I reckon he can't be happy about being hit in certain areas. I've seen our right-handers hit him square on the off-side and that's no place for an off-spinner to go. He does tend to drag the ball down sometimes and a good player steps back and hammers those.'

Fred Titmus, a man who moulded Emburey's early career at Lord's, feels he will develop into a high-class bowler: 'But he has to keep his arm up, there are periods when he bowls it a little too quickly and he loses his flight. But he's a natural bowler, with good variation in pace. Once he finds a stock ball, sticks to it, then works out his pattern of variety around it, then he'll go even further.'

Emburey insists that the one-day game does not bother him – 'I grew up with it, so I'm used to its demands' – but he agrees that finding a rhythm is essential. That can only come with regular bowling. 'It's a little difficult in Tests nowadays, where a spinner is looked on as a bit of a luxury. That puts pressure on me and I have to work at making myself indispensable to the team. I agree that it's important to get your hooks into a batsman and never let him go, but it takes a lot of experience to be able to keep him quiet while still varying the flight to try to get him out. I'm still learning about things like that.'

Success sits easily on his unflappable shoulders; he has known many disappointments in the game and sees no reason to get over-worried about temporary lapses in form. You learn to be stoical after being sacked by Surrey in the early stages of your career, then playing a dozen first-class matches for Middlesex over a period of six seasons, as Titmus continued to demonstrate his greatness. He watched, waited and learned a great deal from the master in the same way that Jack Young and Jim Sims helped young Fred. By the time Titmus left to coach at the Oval, a mature, confident bowler was ready to take his place.

John Emburey has achieved much since the day in 1970 when Surrey told him he would not make the grade in county cricket. He now approaches his thirtieth year – the time of life when a fine off-spinner starts becoming a great one, in Jim Laker's opinion. We can only hope Emburey can cross that great divide.

A high action, nagging accuracy, and bounce, combine to make John Emburey England's chief Test spinner.

If John Emburey is still waiting to fulfil his potential, the verdict of 'not proven' can be readily hung round the broad shoulders of his Middlesex spinning partner, **Phil Edmonds**. Here is a slow left-arm bowler with all the gifts – tall and strong with a gloriously high action, bewitching loop, pronounced spin and a crisp follow-through. At times he has looked a great bowler, notably with England on the tour to Pakistan in 1977–8, but he remains frustratingly reminiscent of a left-hand Pat Pocock. Sometimes great natural talent can be almost a millstone.

There are, of course, valid reasons why Edmonds has not consolidated his place in the English team, a place that he first occupied so excitingly at the age of twenty-four, when he took 5 Australian wickets for 28 in the Leeds Test of 1975. He has faced competition from Derek Underwood and has become a casualty of modern Test cricket's antipathy towards slow bowlers. His undoubted potential with the bat has perhaps distracted him from his greatest gift of a slow bowling style redolent of the masters of yesteryear. The staccato structure of English domestic cricket means he is always trying to come to terms with the demands of different competitions – one day giving the ball some air, the next trying just to keep the score down. Fred Titmus noticed several technical flaws in the Edmonds style when he returned for a few games for Middlesex in 1980: 'He was bowling too wide of the crease and wasn't well-balanced when letting the ball go. I'd always been impressed by the way he stood up when delivering the ball. Technically he should be one of the great slow left-armers.'

Edmonds thinks such problems would be eradicated if he could bowl more overs: 'There really is no substitute for doing it out in the middle. I have some sympathy with the critics of the tracksuit brigade, who see us running around at the start of the season. Although I agree that it's important to get fit for cricket, I would love to bowl myself into fitness by sending down about 1500 overs a season.'

We spoke at the end of the 1981 summer, a season that was ending on a high note for Edmonds as he gathered a haul of wickets in the last few weeks. His frustration was twofold – he wanted the season to go on, because he was bowling so well after teething problems earlier in the summer, and he was disappointed his good form had not arrived earlier to get him on the England tour to India. John Emburey agrees with Edmonds' assertion that he is as good a bowler as he was in 1978, when he seemed to have made the England slow bowler's position his personal property. He enjoyed the Pakistan tour and his 7 for 66 on a lifeless Karachi pitch was the best bowling return by anyone in a Test in that country. He acknowledges his debt to Geoff Boycott for some intensive work in the nets. 'He made me treat nets seriously by instilling an intense rivalry in the proceedings. We simulated match conditions – he didn't want to get out to me and I didn't like him hitting me for four.'

Edmonds needs such a stimulus. A cultivated man, he acknowledges that his concentration lets him down sometimes: 'I could never be a hundred per cent professional like John Emburey, although I do try hard and would not want to let my team-mates down. But my mind does occasionally wander, especially if I'm fielding down on the boundary in an early season match, when the seamers are on for hours.'

He views his sensational debut for England with characteristic whimsy: 'I was embarrassed that I got so many out with bad balls. I suppose I must have bowled some good deliveries to get 5 for 28 in twenty overs, but I can't remember them.' A return of 0 for 118 on a dead Oval wicket in the next Test soon put Leeds in perspective and Edmonds departed the England scene until Underwood signed for World Series Cricket.

Only a cerebral man like Edmonds could attribute his emergence as a slow bowler to political reorganisation of Central Africa in the mid-sixties: he was born in Lusaka and by the time he was twelve, many white people were reacting to the changing pattern of politics by returning to England. Top-class cricket was dying in Zambia and the young Edmonds was given the chance to join his brothers in senior cricket at a flatteringly early age. He soon had to drop his fast bowling against men who would hit it straight back over his head, so he turned to spin. After a Blue at Cambridge, he looked the most talented young bowler of his generation. A decade later, he is still searching for a consistent backbone to supplement the strains of brilliance.

He sometimes gives the impression of aloofness and detachment on the field of play. That would be unfair to a man who possesses a keen desire to win but sees no reason why he should take refuge in the clenched fist and tight-lipped image which many cricketers love to affect. Certainly some England cricketers have failed to understand him – his two England tours coincided with Mrs Thatcher's period as Leader of the Opposition and the disputatious side to Edmonds' nature led to the nickname 'Maggie'. There is no reason why an enquiring mind and facility with words should disturb England cricketers, but Edmonds experienced a depressing tour of Australia after he

Phil Edmonds bowls in determined fashion for England

was dropped for the Second Test. Thereafter he played hardly any cricket, and found little in common with the rest of the tour party. Yet his keen sense of humour still glittered on occasions: during that series, he was asked his opinion on yet another England batting collapse. He replied, 'I really don't know, Test cricket has changed so much since I last played it.'

It remains to be seen how long the game can hold the attention of Phil Edmonds. One can imagine him flourishing in the Edwardian Era – tossing the ball up to invite the slog, launching into his booming straight drives with optimistic vigour and dazzling self-indulgently in the field. He would probably have captained England. Instead he battles to come to terms with a more fustian age of cricket – 'my ideal is to get a lot of wickets bowling well, a due reward for performance,' he says. 'I don't know if that will ever happen. That's why I'll probably play longer than I might.' If Phil Edmonds does manage to take wickets consistently, the game of cricket will be the richer.

---

**David Acfield** has the same Cambridge educational background and lively mind as Phil Edmonds, but they are poles apart in bowling attitudes. Acfield sees no point in quixotic gestures towards flight: he is a modern off-spinner who will not toss the ball up for good batsmen to hit. 'I think that one of the great arts of slow bowling is to stop the batsmen from scoring runs. People at a game might say 'Oh, jolly good show, he's tossing the ball up and it's going for six,' while someone later picks up the paper and says, 'I see Acfield went for five an over, he's not very good.' In those circumstances, we can't win.'

In Ray East and David Acfield, Essex have had one of the best and most consistent pair of spinners in recent years. Keith Fletcher calls Acfield 'a Scrooge bowler – I never have to tell him where to bowl,' and certainly Acfield's line and length are a tribute to his powers of concentration. He says: 'It's nice to be able to tie good batsmen down by ability rather than petrifying them. 'I've never had the big spin of a David Allen or the subtle away drift of a Fred Titmus, so I've had to set my stall out and work at my own major asset – in my case, it's accuracy.'

Although a product of his age in his attitude to bowling, David Acfield has much of the behavioural traits of another era. A gentle, droll man, he is quick to see the funny side of modern cricket: 'I think cricket's new hard image left me behind some years ago. When you're an off-spinner, there's not a lot of point in glaring at a batsman. If I glared at Viv Richards, he'd just hit me even further. Cricket is not World War Three and never has been and that's an unnecessary way to play the game. I'm a fairly philosophical kind of chap, although I admit that can be difficult when the ball is disappearing a lot off your own bowling!'

Over the years Acfield has needed his sense of humour. An admittedly mediocre fielder and a natural number eleven bat (career average just under nine), he has only his intelligent bowling as credentials for inclusion in an Essex side packed with all-rounders. Too often for comfort, he has been twelfth man for the big games; he understands the reasoning behind the decision, but that makes it no easier for a man who has given away less than four an over in one-day matches throughout his career. Acfield says: 'In a few years' time, specialist slow bowlers like me will be extinct. How many young boys will want to be spinners pure and simple when they see ones like me missing out on the glamour games? Most youngsters want to be involved in the big matches and the only ones who'll bowl spin in those will be useful batsmen.'

Acfield teaches at a comprehensive school in Chelmsford and coaches at Essex's indoor nets in the winter and regrettably he sees few slow bowling prospects: 'They tend to tear in and bowl short. They copy what they see on television, I'm afraid.' He was luckier; he had to learn how to bowl with discipline on the perfect wickets at Fenner's and when he first came into county cricket, there were no overs limitations and he would bowl for long spells. At that time, Essex had the luxury of three good spinners – Ray East, Robin Hobbs and Acfield, and Acfield only really established himself with Hobbs's departure in 1975. A long apprenticeship, but at least it helped him to work out just what he was doing in county cricket: 'I reckon that if I help to win at least two county matches a year, then I've played my part in the side.'

Some would say the genial Acfield under-estimates himself. Yet his many friends would reply that, despite Keith Fletcher's sympathetic support, the evidence of team selections supports David Acfield's realistic assessment of his worth.

---

In the last thirty or so years, Gloucestershire's production line of spinners has been impressively varied. Since the retirement of Mortimore and Allen a decade ago, the county has been bereft of a top-class spin bowler. Now they have one – **John Childs** – and an interesting cricketer he is.

He came late to county cricket – at the age of twenty-four, having completed a five-year apprenticeship in sign-writing in Devon. He is that rarity in the current game, a genuine slow bowler, left-arm, with a fluent run-up and delivery. A natural bowler, he is also a specialist – top score only twenty and a slow mover in the field – so his progress will be a useful litmus paper test of a slow bowler's prospects. As a bowler, he is more than good enough to play eventually at the highest level, but will he be allowed to play enough regular cricket?

Until the 1981 season, John Childs had been wheeled out by Gloucestershire for certain games. He would always be certain of a place for the Cheltenham Festival, where the spinners traditionally fare well. The turning August wickets in Kent have appealed to him also. Yet he hardly featured in Gloucestershire's plans for one-day cricket, a reflection on his batting and fielding as much as his bowling. Not unnaturally, Childs wondered about his future at Bristol; several counties were casting envious eyes at his position and after all, he was getting no younger.

The 1981 season was a bad one for Gloucestershire but a good one for John Childs. Covered wickets helped him, as did the abolition of the hundred overs limitation on first innings of a championship match. He managed to get a couple of thirty-five over stints under his belt early in the season and with Mike Procter and Brian Brain injured, he soon looked comfortably the best bowler in the team. He even made the side for some limited-over matches and on August Bank Holiday, he took 9 for 56 against Somerset, the best figures by anyone in the season. Fleet Street suddenly woke up to the fact that a class slow bowler was alive and well in Bristol and he was even tipped as a dark horse for the England winter tour.

John Childs had arrived – but for how long? This friendly, modest man is not sure, but he is happier with his lot. 'Before, I used to be looking over my shoulder, but now I'm getting used to the responsibility. There's so much to learn about my craft – I have to think about each batsman before I go out to bowl. If I don't bowl well, I can at least console myself with the fact that there's always tomorrow. That was never the case before. When I first started, I would just pick up the ball and send it down. Now at the age of thirty, I'm just coming to terms with it all.'

He is working hard at eliminating the one bad ball an over that still dogs him – 'the good pro will put that away for four' – and he is trying to improve his batting. His colleagues stare in disbelief when he tells them he used to open the batting for his village side near Torquay. Fielding is another area that occupies his attention – 'I'm a slow starter, a little flat-footed. I think my catching is satisfactory, although I shall never forget dropping Clive Rice three times in a John Player game – it was on television, too.'

As a bowler, he is highly rated by that illustrious trio of Gloucestershire and England spinners – Cook, Allen and Mortimore. They consider him good enough to have flourished in any era. We can only hope that John Childs does not become an anachronism, or that he compromises his feathery skills. It would be satisfying to contemplate a decade in which Childs does not need his sign-writing trade to make a living.

# 4. The Psychology of Spin

Like most sports, success in cricket can usually be gauged by the amount of thought the player puts into his own game. In the case of slow bowling this is vital; it would be wrong to approach the mental aspects of spin bowling in a Freudian manner, but it *is* a taxing, demanding art. As Arthur Milton told me, 'It's all a matter of inches – those between your ears.'

A successful slow bowler – whether a 'character' or an 'artist' – needs talent, of course, but he also needs the brains and the luck to maximize that talent. Some high-quality slow bowlers, however, have failed to last the pace in first-class cricket for the simple reason that, in the final analysis, they were not mentally tough. Basil Bridge is one of the cruellest examples – at the age of twenty-two, he took 123 wickets for Warwickshire in the 1961 season. A talented orthodox off-spinner, there seemed no reason why he would not make the England side in the near future – yet in the next five seasons, he took just thirty-three more wickets before disappearing from the game. Quite simply, Basil Bridge lost the ability to bowl, a phenomenon that still causes him anguish today. A minor stomach muscle operation perturbed him unduly, but there was nothing physically wrong with Bridge during the rest of his sad career. It was all in the mind: 'It got to the stage where I'd dread bowling. If they threw the ball to me, I'd go stiff and unco-ordinated. I couldn't guarantee hitting a car from twenty-two yards, let alone stumps.' Jim Laker and David Allen tried to help, and in the end, Warwickshire sent him to a psychiatrist for a spell. Even hypnotism was tried on the hapless Bridge – 'just one word was enough to put me under, but my confidence kept falling apart when I had a cricket ball in my hand'.

In the end, Bridge was played for his batting in the Second Eleven, and he would spend most of his time in the field avoiding the captain's eye in case he wanted him to bowl. David Brown, who played in the same side as Bridge, calls his case one of the biggest personal tragedies he has known in cricket: 'He was high class and he completely lost it. It

A wicket for leg-spinner Warwick Tidy in 1972 – Majid Khan, for Glamorgan, is easily stumped by Warwickshire 'keeper, Derryck Murray

was shattering for us to see one of our team-mates fall apart at the seams and for Warwickshire it was a tragedy, because Basil was our Norman Gifford, a man to bowl spin for us for the next twenty years.'

Brown had the chagrin to see the career of another talented slow bowler disintegrate at Edgbaston. Warwick Tidy was just seventeen when he first played for Warwickshire in 1970; a leg-spinner who bowled it quicker than many of his breed, Tidy impressed most shrewd judges from the start. Experienced batsmen would try to get after him from down the pitch, but he was a little too fast through the air for that – in his first season he even succeeded in keeping Clive Lloyd quiet in an astonishingly mature and confident spell. His accurate, waspish style of bowling was reminiscent of the great leg-spinner, Eric Hollies, and it was reassuring to learn that Warwickshire's leading wicket-taker had sorted out the youngster's run-up and approved the finished product. All seemed bright for Tidy; within a year, however, he had lost almost everything. David Brown still cannot believe it: 'It was just like Basil Bridge all over again – the boy would bowl alright in the nets, yet when he was out in the middle, the ball would shoot off to square leg. It was so embarrassing for him. I reckon someone at our club got at him to try to spin it more – he spent a winter in the nets, trying to learn that, rather than concentrating on his strengths, and next season he could hardly pitch the ball. No one has ever admitted ruining Warwick Tidy and he wouldn't say anything.' At the age of twenty-one, he left first-class cricket. He now sells insurance in the West Country.

Roger Harman was just twenty-three when he took 136 wickets in 1964. A slow left-hander, with good flight, high action and the gift of spin, he was just what Surrey needed to fill the gap left by the departure of Laker and Lock. Nearly twenty years later, Tom Graveney remembers Harman taking ten wickets in the match against Worcestershire during that 1964 season; Norman Gifford took seven wickets in one innings and the young Harman lost nothing in comparison. In those pre-Underwood days, the slow left-armer's spot in the England team was there for the taking – Gifford had made his England debut that year – and there seemed no reason why Roger Harman would not soon be challenging for contention. Five years later, he was not re-engaged. He never took more than 63 wickets in a season after 1964. Arthur McIntyre, the Surrey coach at that time, believes Harman lacked that crucial spark of sensible aggression: 'He'd rather bowl in the nets where people wouldn't criticise him. We knew that experienced players would sort him out a little after 1964, but we assumed that Roger would keep on learning. But he got dispirited at being in and out of the side and soon the full tosses and long hops became a regular thing. In the end it was a question of nerves and Roger didn't come through. It was such a shame – a nice man, a good bowler but a low level of aspiration.'

Alan Jones can understand McIntyre's frustration. In his first season as Glamorgan's captain, Jones thought he had unearthed a slow left-arm bowler to serve the county with distinction for many years. In the summer of 1976, Tony Allin came up from Devon and immediately looked the genuine article – a return of 8 for 63 against Sussex only confirmed his potential. He took 44 wickets in just thirteen matches at under 23 runs apiece. Alan Jones nurtured him, keeping him away from the big hitters when a declaration was imminent. He was delighted with his twenty-two-year-old protegé. Then in the winter of 1976, Allin decided he did not want to play county cricket again. He said the pressures were too much for him. Alan Jones tried reasoning with him but he was adamant. Says Jones: 'He seemed to enjoy it, and I was amazed when he packed up after just one season. He said he just couldn't live with all the pressure – this after doing so well. How would he cope with 0 for 100?' Allin now farms in his beloved Devon, and turns out for the Minor Counties occasionally – a long way from bonus points, interminable hours on the motorway between fixtures and a mauling at the hands of Viv Richards.

If Tony Allin did not fancy the traumas of county cricket, another Glamorgan spinner would have willingly embraced them. The problem was that eventually he could not bowl the off-breaks that had once looked so impressive. In 1968, Brian Lewis took 56 wickets at under 22 runs each; he was just twenty-three and ideally the natural replacement for that fine, underrated bowler, Don Shepherd, when he retired. Yet Lewis never played another game for Glamorgan. The winter nets that ruined Warwick Tidy at Edgbaston affected Lewis in the same way. When he said he had lost his off-spin, he was persuaded to try seamers just to get his arm going. A failure – the ball wouldn't pitch. Alan Jones recalls: 'It was pathetic to see. The lad was such a trier, such a great listener that we were shattered. He just tensed up every time he had to bowl in the indoor nets.' Brian Lewis still plays club cricket in Wales – he bats. He cannot even bowl seamers now.

These are just five examples from recent years. They were all comparatively inexperienced bowlers, but their gifts were indisputable. Yet even England slow bowlers go through the horrors that plagued Harman, Bridge and the others. Johnny Wardle had a nightmare year after being advised to alter his action by Bill Bowes, the former Yorkshire and England fast bowler. Bowes told Wardle his pivot was wrong and he remodelled the action that had served Yorkshire and his county for several seasons. The results were disastrous: Wardle was dropped from the first team for a dozen games and he remembers the time with embarrassment: 'They were quite right to drop me and the worst moment came when I played in the Huddersfield League as a stand-in pro. I took 0 for 70, bowled like a drain and I overheard one player say, "It's no bloody wonder Yorkshire dropped him." Yet Bill Bowes told me it could mean an extra hundred wickets a season.' In the nick of time, Wardle reverted to his former action, worked very hard in the nets, and soon regained his first-team place.

Phil Edmonds sometimes experiences those baffling periods when, in the dressing-room vernacular, 'he can't bowl a hoop down a hill'. Instead of his classical slow left-armer's flight and loop, he sends down full toss after full toss, and the harder he tries, the more embarrassing it all becomes. It happened to Edmonds at the start of the 1981 season, when a grisly half-hour's stint from him on the final day of one of the early matches did the cause of the slow bowler no good at all. One full toss would have hit first slip smack on the forehead if the wicket-keeper had not taken it; he bowled ten overs and got worse as the spell continued. 'I should have come off,' he says, 'but Mike Brearley thought it best to carry on bowling in the hope that it would come good. I think the main reason was that I had had little bowling. I'm the type who needs a lot of hard work and in the last couple of winters, I haven't played any cricket. So I was still very rusty when I bowled against Essex.'

Edmonds has a specific response to these occasional lapses when he loses all control of the ball: he refuses to bowl any differently. 'I've always been an attacking bowler and I don't see what good it does you to fire it in on the leg stump when you're having a bad time. I like to make things happen and I think my natural inclination is to be a fast bowler, not a waiter and a watcher like Bishen Bedi.'

Derek Underwood gets very annoyed with himself when he feels he is not doing himself justice. 'So many people tell me that I'm always frowning when they see me playing on television, but they don't realize that I feel responsibility weighing very heavily on me. I thrive on success and enjoy it, but I am expected to do well – the 'Deadly' thing.

The fact that so much is expected of me brings its own pressures, never mind the actual ones involved in bowling at great players.' Insecurity seems an occupational hazard for a slow bowler – hardly surprising when one considers the amount of obstacles that are placed in the way of the modern spinner. Even a balanced, rational and humorous man like David Acfield feels it: 'More than a decade after being capped by Essex, I still feel on trial when I go out to play. The game is weighted against the spinner today and we have to battle all the way. You never really get used to being left out of the side after proving that you're a productive part of it – yet that happens to me regularly for the one-day games. I find myself thinking that no matter how well I am bowling, I can't get into the side because another batsman is needed – and that's hard.'

It is also hard for Acfield when he is expected to switch on his skills in a championship game once the wicket is turning. He and Ray East faced that problem in 1979 when Essex just had to beat Nottinghamshire to stay in the title race. In the previous eighteen days, East had bowled only seven championship overs, Acfield none at all – hardly the greatest preparation for the responsibility they faced on the last day of the Nottinghamshire match. Notts needed 170 to win and they had reached 87 for 1 when the spinners found their touch. They were all out for 123, with East and Acfield taking five wickets each. East says: 'Even though I've been playing a long time, that kind of pressure worries me. David and I were rusty, yet we're supposed to run in and drop it on the spot with men all round the bat and no runs to play with.'

That kind of pressure eventually broke Don Wilson. He would dread Yorkshire's match at Swansea because he knew the ball would turn and that his captain expected him to reap a harvest of wickets. 'I could hardly sleep for a couple of nights before going to Swansea,' he says, 'It's ridiculous for a slow bowler to admit this, but I was no good on a slow turner. I preferred bowling on good wickets where I wasn't expected to get 7 for 20.' Ultimately, Wilson's bowling fell apart; he would drop the ball on a handkerchief in the nets, then hit the wicket-keeper on the chest with a full toss in the match. He became a nervous wreck and retired earlier than his ability and fitness warranted. 'It's even worse today for slow bowlers than when I packed up ten years ago. All this limited-over cricket would've finished me early, because I just wouldn't get enough bowling. And my confidence was always on a knife-edge, it didn't take much to shatter me.'

Nottinghamshire's Championship success in 1981 owed much to the
renewed confidence of their off-spinner, Eddie Hemmings

Not every spin bowler is lucky enough to possess the mental strength of a Norman Gifford. Like a dog with a juicy bone, he simply will not give up the battle. Gifford knows what it is like to be out of favour and disillusioned – he was dropped by his county just one month after playing for England. 'When I was in my early 'twenties, I wouldn't tell my captain I was going to try something different, because he would've told me to stick at my usual line. That was wrong, I should've been more positive. It takes a long time for a spinner to develop confidence in himself, but when he's got it, he must never let it go – if you're worth your salt, you must say to yourself, "right, this is my day" when the wicket helps you. Never dread going out there to bowl under any circumstances and wait for the chance to get your own back for all the hammerings you've had on flat wickets.'

That kind of positive attitude has at last imbued Eddie Hemmings. After a long apprenticeship with Warwickshire he moved to Trent Bridge and his 90 wickets in the 1981 season were decisive factors in bringing the championship to Nottinghamshire. For Hemmings, life is sweet after some dreadful times at Edgbaston; the crowd never really took to him, their favourites were the glamorous Test players. When he came on to bowl, he says he could sense the hostility of the crowd and when he was hit around the field, the cries of 'take him off' were cruelly delivered. Hemmings suffers from asthma and eczema and those experiences did nothing for his health and peace of mind: 'I'm a very uptight sort of person and after a bad day, I'd just sit there and have an attack. I had no confidence in myself as a cricketer or as a person.'

By the end of the 1978 season, Hemmings was ready to finish with county cricket. He was certainly through with Warwickshire. A call came from Trent Bridge at just the right time and for the last three seasons, the transformation has been heartening. He pays tribute to his captain, Clive Rice ('he just lets me get on with the job'), and the support he gets from the faithful at Trent Bridge. 'Above all, I've now got a sense of responsibility and I'm being continually encouraged. I'll never be a star but my county think I'm their best spinner and that's very important to me.' For Hemmings, the pressures have been lifted from his shoulders and transferred to the batsmen – 'As far as I'm concerned, they have all the pressures. I've got six mistakes an over to hope for and if he makes just one, then I've got a wicket.'

Hemmings is lucky that he now enjoys continuity of cricket; he plays in the one-day games and appreciates the varying challenges.

Dilip Doshi envies him. The 1981 season was a great disappointment for him after taking a hundred first-class wickets in the previous season. Stricter regulations on overseas players and a proliferation of one-day cricket meant Doshi was no longer an automatic choice for the Warwickshire team and as the season progressed, the Indian became more and more depressed. When he *did* play, his punctilious insistence on placing his field exactly in the right spot occasionally irritated colleagues who faced fines for their slow over-rate. He did not seem to be on the same tactical wavelength and he has a theory for this: 'Warwickshire hadn't had a proper spin bowler since Lance Gibbs and they couldn't come to terms with precise field-placing. They didn't realize that the batsmen are winning the struggle when the slow bowler can't get his message across to the fielders.'

Doshi did not like tossing the ball up to assist a declaration; he wanted to bowl properly with his fielders in the right places. He had enjoyed that feeling of responsibility which so attracts Eddie Hemmings, but felt disappointed that, in his eyes, he seemed less important to the club in 1981 than in the previous year. 'I need to be part of a team and when I don't play, I feel a sense of deprivation. It is not good for an established player to be told at 10.30 on the morning of a match that he is out. You feel a sense of humiliation.' Warwickshire point out that Doshi was not the bowler of 1980. David Brown, the manager, thought he was tired after an arduous tour of Australia with the Indian side; his wickets cost a lot more and his arm had dropped, making him bowl down the legside. He bowled a lot of no-balls, something a world-class spinner should avoid. Brown says, 'He was a better bowler than most of our staff and if he'd bowled well, he'd have bowled a lot more.' So Doshi left Warwickshire. With the quota of overseas cricketers being reduced, it is difficult to see where he can return to first-class cricket in England.

While Dilip Doshi relished the 1980 season, for Derek Underwood it proved to be the most schizophrenic of his career. In first-class cricket, he bowled just 585 overs to take 61 wickets – and two-thirds of that total came in the last six games. Bad weather and overs limitations meant that Underwood had very few of the long spells he likes and by the time he was selected for the First Test against the West Indies, he was not in the best frame of mind. He was made twelfth man for the Test and in the next fortnight, he bowled just fourteen first-class overs. Then, in the Second Test, Ian Botham threw him the ball and told him to bowl at Viv Richards, who was 42 not out at the time!

A fascinating sequence of pictures of Dilip Doshi, the Indian left-arm spinner, showing a full follow-through

Richards hit him for four boundaries in an over, he finished with 1 for 108 at the most un-Underwood rate of three runs an over and he was banished from the Test scene for another eighteen months. 'I desperately wanted to play for England but I suppose I should've said no, because I hadn't bowled at all in the previous few weeks. It was a ridiculous state of affairs and shows what pressures the spinners face. The seamers never need to worry about a lack of bowling.'

Kim Barnett would simply love a bowl at any time. Barnett is a Derbyshire batsman. More importantly, he is the only English leg-spinner left who plays regular cricket. Correction; he plays county cricket regularly but does not bowl. In his three seasons with Derbyshire, he has bowled just 270 overs and most of them came to aid a declaration target. Some will say Barnett does not get to bowl because he is a mediocre leg-spinner – if so, then Mike Brearley and Keith Andrew have suddenly become bad judges of a player. Andrew went with the England Under-19 team to Australia in 1978–9 and was impressed by Barnett's capacity to bowl the 'flipper' and by his

108

attitude to hard work in the nets. On that tour, he bowled at Brearley at Adelaide as the senior England team prepared for a Test Match. The net wickets were fast and bouncy and Barnett troubled both Brearley and Gooch. Brearley feels that some counties are just not used to handling slow bowlers and in the case of Kim Barnett, that seems to be the case. He worked very hard before the start of the 1981 season, yet hardly bowled in a game; by mid-season he was so depressed that he started to bowl medium-pace in the nets. He sees little prospect of a change in attitude and is now resigned to developing his batting: 'The county like to talk about having a young leggie on the books, yet I never get a bowl. Perhaps the game itself is at fault.'

Perhaps those who run cricket occasionally forget that it takes a long time to master the art of slow bowling. David Brown has had to learn patience in his two years as manager of Warwickshire: 'It's so easy to say a youngster won't make it, but then you have to pinch yourself to remember that he's only 18 or so. That's no consolation to him as the ball keeps flying out of the ground, but it's something those of us who determine their destinies must never forget.' Johnny Wardle believes there should be more slow bowlers on coaching staffs: 'A bowler *must* know more about cricket than a batsman. He has to study all the batters, what shots they play and he must know about field placing. A batsman gets his runs, sits down afterwards and that's it for him. A good slow bowler always watches the game and tries to learn from it.' Ray Illingworth has cause to be grateful to a slow bowler/coach for giving him precious encouragement in his formative years. Arthur Booth, a fine left-armer in his time, used to make other youngsters come and watch Illingworth in the nets. 'That's the way to bowl,' Booth would tell them. 'It did wonders for my confidence,' says Illingworth, 'I just wish every budding spinner had the same guidance.'

The encouragement of a Booth, the sheer grit of a Gifford, the good fortune of a Hemmings to bowl long spells – a spin bowler needs all three to survive in modern first-class cricket. Otherwise he may as well start learning how to bowl the bouncer.

# 5. Captaining Slow Bowlers

'In the last fifteen years, seam bowling has proved to be more versatile than spin bowling.' The speaker is Mike Smith, a man who led Warwickshire and England with distinction. Smith had a reputation for being seam-orientated in his captaincy, but he insists his opinion is not coloured by anything other than a realistic assessment of the facts. 'In the old days, you'd open with a slow bowler on a wet wicket, but seamers have been proved to be more productive in recent years in such conditions.' That is partly because the footholds are now covered, so the seamers can stand up to bowl on a wet wicket. Smith disagrees with his image as a captain antipathetic towards spin bowling; he stresses that Warwickshire never had a consistently good spinner in his time, and that when he led England, he always played two spinners. David Allen, who played under Smith for England, supports him: 'I never felt I was bowling against Mike as well as the batsmen. He relied on the expertise of the bowlers in his side and never imposed his views on field placing.'

Mike Smith does not blame modern captains for relying predominantly on seam; he regrets the passing of the specialist slow bowler and hopes his day will return, but for the moment, he understands why the fast bowler holds sway. Conditions are generally against the slow bowler in England and much of the nostalgic rhetoric of the old players skirts round that fact. Sir Donald Bradman is aware of that. From his home in Adelaide, he told me: 'You cannot blame modern captains; they are given teams virtually without spin, and the selectors don't pick spin, because, in their judgment, spin – given the physical conditions and rules – will be relatively unsuccessful. No captain in his right mind would continue to use bowlers under conditions unsuited to requirements. It is largely cause and effect. The pushing of spin into the background is of course preventing the development of top-class spinners. But until the legislators are willing to take the bull by the horns and adopt rules and conditions that will break the domination of fast bowling, the present state of affairs will continue.'

Sir Donald's period as captain against England confirms how he adapted to the conditions; in 1936–7, his slow bowlers took 55 wickets against England, while the seamers picked up just 29. In 1938, in England, the ratio was 37:13. It was a different story in 1948, when he led an unbeaten Australian side to England – the new ball was available every 55 overs, and he had a great fast bowling spearhead in Lindwall, Miller and Johnston, backed up by the nagging medium left-armers of Toshack. Bradman would have been a fool to ignore such advantages – 'I did not use this class of bowling because I preferred fast bowling to spin, but because the quality of these men was so perfectly tailored to take advantage of the laws and conditions of the day.'

Bob Willis agrees: 'It's all about self-interest. We county captains all sit round the table at meetings at Lord's and the discussions are often enlightening – but in the long run, the captains will vote for a playing structure that benefits their own sides.' Willis, Warwickshire's captain, finds that sad but painfully logical. 'It's simply a better game when the spinners are around. Most of the memorable matches I recall have been when the slow bowlers have got men round the bat and the batsman has had to play shots to survive. But it's all about winning now and that means seam bowling under existing conditions and regulations.'

Yet 'winning cricket' can also feature slow bowling. The last three sides to win the county championship have enjoyed the valuable assistance of some fine slow bowlers – in 1979 Essex had Acfield and East, a year later Middlesex had Edmonds, Emburey and Titmus, and in 1981 Eddie Hemmings took 90 wickets for Nottinghamshire, more than any other spinner in the country. These teams won because they had balanced attacks, able to function properly under any conditions.

Clive Rice, Nottinghamshire's dynamic captain, believes he would have had the title sealed up a month earlier if he had had a top-class slow left-armer in his side. 'Balance is essential. You have to know when to use a spinner, but he's a godsend when the fast bowlers are bushed. A lot of county captains are inexperienced and they panic when their spinner goes for four – it looks bad when the close fielders have to duck in fear of their lives as the ball is pulled away. But if you look at the scorebook, you'll see how many fours are squirted away off the seamers. There's just no point in moaning at a slow bowler if he gets hit. He needs confidence, rhythm and a lot of bowling.'

Keith Fletcher's Essex side is perfectly balanced, but he realizes the

The positive attitude of Nottinghamshire's captain, Clive Rice (first slip) had much to do with their success in 1981 – here, five close fielders exert pressure on Younis Ahmed as Nottinghamshire strive for victory

importance of match practice for his spin bowlers, East and Acfield. 'You can't expect them to run through a side on a turner, when they haven't bowled for a fortnight. The beauty of having good spinners is that you can keep the pressure up. There's no easing of tension when the fast men are taken off. We keep men round the bat even when the wicket's doing nothing. The secret is to create the illusion that the ball is turning.' David Acfield feels this is one of Fletcher's strongest points as a tactician: 'He's tremendous at pressure. Sometimes the ball might only be turning at one end, but his attacking captaincy makes the batsmen think it's doing it at both ends.'

Mike Brearley thinks it is essential to give a slow bowler close fielders to make him feel confident. 'When John Emburey first played in the Middlesex side, he was loath to have a silly mid-off for the bat/pad catches. He was worried about the odd bad ball; we worked at him and instilled an attacking attitude in him.' Brearley gave an object lesson in this to his opposite number, Graham Yallop, in the series in Australia in 1978–9. He always had men round the bat for his two off-spinners, Miller and Emburey, and the Australians' defective footwork and traditional weakness against off-spin played into Brearley's hands. Yallop, on the other hand, never quite knew when to attack with his main spinner, Jim Higgs, the leg-break bowler. In the Sydney Test, Yallop's tactical naïvety played into England's hands; Boycott went to Hogg for nought at the start of the second innings, when England were still nearly 150 behind. The situation cried out for attack, for Higgs to pressurize Brearley and Randall yet, as Brearley recalls, 'He bowled at us with one slip and no one else close up. This was on a turning wicket with the batsmen thinking defensively against a good, accurate leg-spinner.' Brearley and Randall added a vital 100 runs, and England won by 93 runs, with their spinners taking seven wickets in the last innings.

Brearley feels that some county sides do not have a tradition of slow bowling and therefore do not know how to use a spinner. 'Teams like Essex and Middlesex have developed a positive attitude to slow bowlers on their staff, but others just don't know how to use a spinner when he arrives on the scene. You need to know how to use a slow bowler, when to bowl him and when to keep him out of the firing line.'

It is no coincidence that slow bowlers from other counties admire the way that Fletcher and Brearley treat their own spinners. Dilip Doshi, the Indian slow left-armer, had a frustrating season in 1981 with Warwickshire, partly because of a communication problem between his captains (Bob Willis and Dennis Amiss) and the manager David Brown. Doshi says 'Some captains say "let's see what happens" when a slow bowler suggests a field alteration. But a good captain of spin can anticipate things. Fletcher and Brearley understand the con-

A good player against spin, Mike Brearley is a captain with the experience and confidence to encourage the slow bowlers in his own side

cept of spin, because they are both very good players of slow bowling and they have two good spinners in their sides. They see the need to have patience and sympathy, they understand that a slow bowler mustn't have a hazy mind when he's running up to bowl.'

No one could ever accuse Ray Illingworth of having a hazy mind and his positive attitude to slow bowling was rewarded when Leicestershire won the championship in 1975. When he came to Grace Road in 1969, he insisted that conditions should be made more conducive to the spinners; the boundaries were extended, the outfield was shaved so the ball did not retain its shine for too long, and the wickets were made harder with little grass left on them. The result was a season of attractive, positive cricket in 1975 with the county's four spinners playing a decisive role in the title victory. Their seamers bowled nearly 1,300 overs in championship matches, while the spinners sent down just over 2,000 overs. It was a dry summer, which clearly helped the slow bowlers, but they proved their effectiveness. Says Illingworth: 'There was nothing wrong with the Grace Road wicket, either – more centuries were hit on our ground that year than any other county ground. We also bowled more overs than any other county side, keeping our over rate up while winning the title. As far as I'm concerned, successful cricket means bowling a lot of deliveries.' Certainly Illingworth was lucky in that all four of his spinners (Steele, Balderstone, Birkenshaw and himself) were more than adequate batsmen, but the over rate was over twenty an hour, so the entertainment value was enhanced. The medium-pacers who relied on a shiny ball were smashed all over the large Grace Road ground and slow bowling proved gloriously effective.

Now Illingworth has returned to Yorkshire to help the county rediscover its palmy days of the 'sixties. He is convinced that two good spin bowlers are a vital adjunct to a seam attack, a view endorsed by the captain, Chris Old. During the 1981 season, Old received hundreds of letters bemoaning Yorkshire's lack of success; many of them reminded him that the county lacked slow bowlers of high quality. 'They didn't need to tell me that,' he says, 'I'm conscious of our great reputation for producing England slow bowlers. I just wish I could find a Verity or a Wardle. They'd be in the side like a shot.' Old is aware that the limited-over nature of league cricket in Yorkshire inhibits the production of slow-bowling. His solution is a drastic one – 'We should increase our playing staff, get sixteen-year-old spinners to the nets at Headingley every day and make them bowl over after over. If we could find a couple of good young spinners, we'd be up there at the top again because young batsmen just don't know how to play them. Ray Illingworth bowls at our young first-team batsmen in the nets and they really struggle. They end up slogging.'

Chris Old's sentiments are admirable, but in common with other county captains, he has to be convinced that a spinner can prosper on all wickets. Too many think that a slow bowler can only be used when the wicket is dry and the ball has lost its shine. Peter May's opinion that a good bowler performs well under any conditions is backed up by the fact that Jim Laker often bowled sides out on green wickets that ostensibly suited the seamers. Tom Dollery, Warwickshire's sagacious captain of thirty years ago, will never forget the day when his great leg-spinner, Eric Hollies, bowled out Yorkshire with the new ball. 'They didn't need all that many to win and Eric wanted to get at them straight away. He told me, "I can spin the new ball as well, Tom." and he was right.' Yorkshire all out 49, Hollies 5 for 12 in twenty overs.

In the great Yorkshire side captained by Brian Close, the spinning partnership of Ray Illingworth and Don Wilson was regularly seen in action on green wickets. Says Wilson, 'We thought that good bowlers could bowl on anything and our skipper agreed. Today's captains need educating – often they don't bring the spinner on till the last day.' Under Norman Gifford's successful captaincy, Worcestershire won the county championship and the John Player League and he trusted spin to do a good job for him in all conditions. 'You never know how a wicket will play until you've actually played on it. I always assumed that the wicket would be misleading, so I wanted a balanced bowling attack. There are times when you go out to play on a green wicket without a spinner and it costs you a game. I just wish all county captains thought the same way.'

Kim Hughes fell into the stereotyped trap of relying on seam during Ian Botham's wonderful innings in the Leeds Test of 1981. No praise can be too high for the way Botham flogged the Australian attack – but it was a tiring attack, made up of three willing seamers. Graham Dilley and Botham enjoyed their good fortune and played them so well that the case for the introduction of Ray Bright was overwhelming. Dilley, an inexperienced player of slow bowling, must surely have struggled if Bright had bowled over the wicket into the rough outside the left-hander's off-stump. Botham, a naturally attacking player, would surely not have altered the uninhibited way he was tackling the seamers – and any reputable slow bowler likes to see the

Ray Bright noticeably altered his action during the 1981 Australian tour, going from almost round-arm round the wicket to delivering the ball at full height over the wicket

ball in the air. Bright would have brought variety into the attack, making Botham wait a little longer before the ball came to him – and if he collared Bright, the spinner would merely have suffered the same fate as the overworked seamers. Eventually Bright was given a token couple of overs near the end of the day, when Botham was well past his century; predictably, Botham could not resist temptation, he swung wildly in Bright's first over and the ball just missed the stumps. In the innings, Bright bowled just four overs.

Of course, the Leeds pitch was a seamer's wicket with the ball taking off on a length, a situation brilliantly exploited on the final day by Bob Willis. Yet within the context of an innings, just *one* wicket can be the crucial one, not five cheap ones. Kim Hughes played it in the conventional manner and missed the chance of tempting Botham with slow bowling. He seemed to have learnt his lesson in the next Test at Edgbaston when Bright enjoyed a long and profitable spell in the England second innings – but it was too late to save a Leeds Test that Australia lost by just eighteen runs. And who took the vital wicket at

Batting against spin is never easy when a ball suddenly pops up off a length. Here Mike Gatting takes the crucial catch to dismiss Alan Border of the bowling of John Emburey in the Fourth Test, 1981

Edgbaston, as Australia crawled to the comparatively easy task of getting 151 to win? Not Ian Botham, despite his magnificent burst of 5 for 1 at the end – it was John Emburey, who, at a crucial moment trapped Alan Border with a ball that popped off a length. Border had played more comfortably than anyone else in the match but, once committed to the front foot, he could not keep down Emburey's delivery and short-leg took a simple chance. That made Australia 105 for 5 and the door that had opened was brutally kicked aside by the inspirational Botham. In similar circumstances, would Kim Hughes have shown the same faith in his spinner as Brearley?

Faith, coolness, flexibility – a captain needs all those qualities to get the best out of his spinner. As Phil Edmonds rightly says, 'It's up to the captain to look after a slow bowler. If he has picked him, then he must nurse him along on occasions, and bowl him at the right time. You don't become a good spinner by standing at third man watching the seamers all day.'

The dominant influence on post-war Test cricket has been the fast bowler. Immediately after the War it was Lindwall and Miller, then Tyson and Statham, Heine and Adcock, Trueman and Statham, Hall and Griffith, Procter and Pollock, through to the awesome West Indians of today. Of the 175 post-war Tests played in England, only 26 were won by the spinners (the qualifications being ten or more wickets in the match taken by the victorious slow bowlers). The last time a spinner had a decisive effect on a Test in England was at Manchester in 1977 when Derek Underwood took 6 for 66 in the Australian second innings. Not since Chandrasekhar bowled so marvellously at the Oval in 1971 has a Test series in England been won by slow bowling.

The trend has now become a pattern; if a spinner manages to make the squad, he invariably ends up carrying the drinks or is used as a last resort when the battery of seamers has failed. With the declining over-rate seemingly destined for a permanent place in the ICC pending tray, there seems little hope of Test captains re-assessing their unsympathetic attitude to slow bowling.

With modern Test cricket so much in the hands of the seamers, it is instructive to recall four matches when spin bowling played a decisive part. In three of them, the game was won by a spinner while in the other, a great slow bowler was broken on the rack of an historic partnership.

At 5.20 on a sunlit afternoon in July 1956, the Australian wicket-keeper Len Maddocks misjudged the flight of an off-break. Instead of playing forward, he went back and the ball hustled on to strike him on the pads. The appeal was a formality and Maddocks walked up the pitch to shake the hand of the tall, lean man who had made cricket history – Jim Laker. His bowling figures in that Fourth Test were sensational – 10 for 53 from 51.2 overs, to add to his 9 for 37 from 16.4 overs in the first innings. Australia had lost to England by an innings and 171 in what will always be known as 'Laker's Match'. A quarter of a century later, the figures are still astonishing – 19 for 90, two wickets more than anyone in a first-class match. All this in an England team including bowlers of the calibre of Statham, Bailey and Lock.

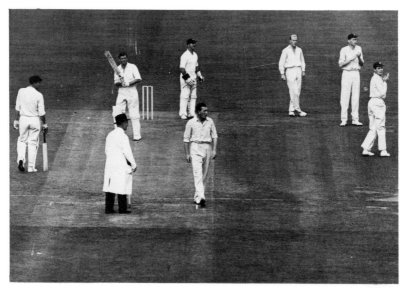

Jim Laker displays the sangfroid that served him so well during the historic Old Trafford Test of 1956, when he took 19 wickets for 90. Richie Benaud has been caught by Brian Statham (out of picture) and while Laker saunters back to his mark, the England fielders (left to right), Evans, Lock, Oakman and Sheppard show more satisfaction than the great Surrey off-spinner.

Laker's first innings was astounding enough on its own – in the space of 22 balls he took seven wickets, one every three deliveries. On that second day, Australia had replied to England's 459 with an abject 84 all out. The pitch, of course, was dubious – yet at tea, Australia were 62 for 2. Just 35 minutes after the interval, they were all out. Yet the only ball that really did something was the one that bowled Neil Harvey – it pitched on leg stump and took the off. Harvey stared at the pitch in disbelief before he walked back to the pavilion; could it be that the reaction of Australia's best batsman to an unplayable ball coloured the judgment of his team-mates? That might explain why Ken Mackay looked as if he had never batted against spin in his life before prodding lamely to gully, why Richie Benaud hit a catch to long-on and why Ron Archer charged down the wicket to give Godfrey Evans a routine stumping.

120

On that Friday, the light was good and the pitch dry with some turn. Earlier in the day, the Australian spinners Benaud and Johnson had extracted little turn and the feeling that the wicket was not exactly a terror was hardened in the remaining sixty-five minutes of play on that second day when Australia followed on. In that time Australia made 51 for one with some ease and the only wicket to fall was a fluke – Neil Harvey hitting a full toss straight to mid-wicket to give him the first 'pair' of his career.

On the following day, just three-quarters of an hour's play was possible. The only wicket to fall was that of Jim Burke, caught in Laker's leg-trap for a sensible 33. Rain again interfered with Monday's play, restricting the action to a matter of fifty minutes. Ian Craig and Colin McDonald added another twenty-seven runs, and Australia finished on 84 for 2. Although Laker had taken both wickets, the wicket was too damp for him; with one day to go, there was no inkling that we would be witnessing a phenomenon.

It rained until dawn on that final morning. The Australians, mindful of the eighteen wickets taken by Lock and Laker in the previous Test at Leeds, were doubtless praying for more rain during the day. Unfortunately for them, a strong wind appeared later in the morning and lingered to play a decisive part in the match. Yet until lunch, the Australians seemed in little trouble; the pitch was still sluggish and the England captain, Peter May, switched the bowlers around. England prayed for the sun to come out while the Australians looked for the rain clouds to dampen the optimism in the English camp.

During lunchtime, the clouds disappeared and the sun started to shine brightly. At 2.25, Laker beat Craig in the air and off the pitch and trapped him LBW. He had batted four hours for just 33, an impressive technical performance from a 21-year-old. At the other end, McDonald was playing a memorable innings which had begun on the Friday night; his impeccable back-foot play allowed him to commit himself late and his cool adjustments were driving Tony Lock to distraction. The more Lock tried, the better McDonald played him and in the end Lock bowled too fast.

At the other end, Laker pulled the string tighter round the neck of the Australian batting; six fielders clustered around in a space of five yards and Mackay, Miller and Archer perished in supine fashion, all for nought. Archer steered an off-break into the leg-trap with almost exaggerated care, Miller uncharacteristically elected to use his pads rather than his bat and was yorked leg-stump, while Mackay's misery ended with a catch to slip. Benaud joined McDonald and played sensibly, mostly off the back foot, but leaving himself scope to play forward if necessary. On a wicket which was beginning to form a crust under the hot sun and drying wind, this was a risky tactic, but Benaud survived to use up a precious eighty minutes with his accomplished partner, who was punishing the wayward Lock severely on the legside.

By tea, Bailey and Oakman had been introduced into the England attack and it looked as if the series would remain at one-all with just the Oval Test to come. Australia had two hours left, with four wickets in hand. Surely they were safe? The second ball after tea answered that question – McDonald could not keep down a ball that turned sharply and Oakman held the catch in the leg-trap. McDonald out for 89 after a display of 337 minutes that, years later, Colin Cowdrey still describes as one of the best he has seen on a bad wicket.

Perhaps McDonald's departure deceived the eye but now the pitch seemed to be taking spin quickly. Benaud played back to Laker for the umpteenth time and the ball hurried on to bowl him. Laker had now taken seventeen wickets in the match to equal the world record. A win was obviously more important to the England players – not least of all to Lock, who was still desperately seeking some compensatory wickets – but perhaps the crowd valued the record more. Even better if England won and Laker beat the record. At a quarter past five, Lindwall was caught at leg slip by Tony Lock – Laker's Surrey colleague had guided him to posterity. Five minutes later, after yet another committed over from Lock, Laker bowled the second ball of his 52nd over. Maddocks was beaten for pace and Laker had all ten. Handshakes all round for Laker, a pat or two on the back and the laconic off-spinner walked from the field with the air of a man expecting his dog to catch up with him after a diverting stroll in the park.

From a distance of 25 years, Laker still views the match with his customary detachment. 'If that game was played again a million times over, you'd never get the same situation. Locky didn't exactly have all the luck in the world, you know. I wasn't particulary excited inside – nobody kissed me, that's for sure. I was doing my job and I tried to detach myself from everything. I gave a thought to every ball I bowled. I never ran up to bowl without some plan in my mind throughout my career.'

In fact, Laker considers his performance earlier that season against the Australians was just as meritorious. Unbelievably, he also took all ten – and McDonald also made 89! Laker recalls, 'That Oval wicket was a very good one and I'd been up all night with two sick young children. I hoped we would win the toss, but they batted first. Thanks to the cajolery of my captain Stuart Surridge, I bowled 46 overs and cleaned up. But unlike at Old Trafford, there was nobody at short leg and there was little turn for me. Most of my wickets came from catches at slip or by the wicket-keeper'.

Colin Cowdrey stood at slip for most of the Old Trafford match and the unhurried air of Laker's performance stands out in his mind: 'Jim was a calm destroyer. The batsmen played and missed so often, yet you couldn't tell from his expression. He was in perfect rhythm.' Cowdrey maintains that if McDonald had gone earlier in the day, the wickets would have been shared round, but Lock became increasingly frustrated as McDonald elected to deal with the left-hander rather than Laker. 'Jim made the batsmen play at every ball, with a little drift in the air and just enough turn.'

Godfrey Evans still maintains that Laker was the only bowler who ever looked like getting anyone out. 'Locky kept pulling the ball down and I was taking it chest-high. When it turned for him, it just went too far. Jim had the right idea – pitch the ball up and let it turn a little off the pitch.'

Peter May disagrees that Lock tried too hard. 'There was never a greater trier and he thrived on that commitment. I think the crucial thing was that his deliveries were going away from the bat and the Australians could leave a few. On that kind of wicket, you wanted them to play at every ball and Jim's off-spin meant the ball was turning *in* to the right-hander. Jim just dripped away at their nerves, realizing that they had got a little obsessional about him and the wickets that year. To be honest, the wicket was not that difficult.'

Richie Benaud disagrees about the quality of the pitch but generously praises Laker's mastery, particularly the way he would force the batsman onto the back foot if he looked comfortable playing forward. And he acknowledges his own defects as a bowler in that match. 'Ian Johnson and I should've done better. I wish I could have had a go a few years later, when I'd developed a few more wiles.' Benaud's most vivid memory of that match is the delaying tactics of his captain, Ian Johnson, on that last afternoon. 'He even appealed against the sawdust blowing across the ground, which I don't think was terribly subtle. Mind you, he couldn't appeal against the light, could he?.'

Johnson also appears to have been less than diplomatic to the Old Trafford groundsman, Bert Flack. Now living in retirement in Devon, Flack told me: 'When we went out for an inspection on that last morning, he wanted me to protect the bowlers' run-ups which seemed odd, considering that his boys weren't doing the bowling. He was just trying to hold things up – and I shan't tell you the reply he gave me when I asked him what roller he wanted for the follow-on!'

'Gubby' Allen, then chairman of the England selectors, was not at all surprised by Laker's performance. He had looked at the wicket on the day before the start and prophesied it would break up. 'I thought it would have turned even earlier because I rubbed it with my thumb on the side and took the top off. This after Cyril Washbrook, a fellow selector, had told us that it would be the greatest batting wicket of all time. At our selection meeting the previous weekend, we had considered picking an extra seamer in the light of Washy's prophecy. After a couple of hours discussion we agreed to keep Lock and Laker in the twelve until we saw the Old Trafford wicket. When we did, the side picked itself.'

If Cyril Washbrook had been proved correct; if Tom Graveney had not dropped out with a hand injury – that meant a place for Alan Oakman, a specialist fielder in the leg-trap, who proceeded to take five catches; if Graveney – a safe slip fielder – had played instead of Oakman, would Laker have taken so many wickets? Oakman recalls that the Rev David Sheppard had started the Australian first innings in the leg trap but after a few overs he asked Peter May to take him out of it, because he felt a long absence from top-class cricket had affected his timing in such a specialist position. 'I was at mid-on and Peter May asked me to go in close, a position I was used to occupying for Sussex with Robin Marlar bowling off-breaks. Twenty years later, I sat next to Jim at a dinner and when I was billed as the man who took five great catches in Laker's match, Jim leaned over and whispered, 'Christ, you're not still living on that are you?'

Oakman remembers the mesmeric effect Laker had on that Australian team *off* as well as *on* the field. During the periods when rain held up play in the Old Trafford Test, Laker would spend his time tending to his sore spinning finger. 'Jim would take out the cork and wedge the little bottle between his fingers. He'd do this while strolling into their dressing-room for a chat. Each time, the Aussies would stop playing cards and just look at him, and then his fingers, as if he was a witch doctor!'

Oakman gives a graphic account of the uniquely combative nature of Tony Lock, a man who genuinely admired Laker. 'To start with, Locky was pleased that Jim was getting a few wickets. But he got more and more annoyed and in the end, if he caught one, he'd curse and throw the ball away. When we came off the field, Jim poured himself a drink and went out to the balcony for a quick wave to the crowd. In that short space of time, Locky had changed and left!'

One other incident from that astonishing day tickled the wry nature of Jim Laker. On the way back to London that night it suddenly dawned on him that he was hungry. He stopped at a pub in Lichfield. 'It was packed out. I stood at the bar, with a sandwich and a pint, saw about eight of my wickets on the television news and listened to the bar chatter about this bloke Laker. I took my time swallowing my pint and walked out. Nobody had recognised me!'

Five years later (to the very day), Richie Benaud had his revenge in a match that encompassed all the best features of Test cricket. After four days of contrasting fortunes, Australia faced defeat twice on the last day – just after midday, when they led by just 159 with their last pair together, and again at ten to four, when England needed only 106 in 110 minutes with nine wickets in hand. Australia's eventual triumph by 54 runs stemmed from several fine individual performances, but the match-winner as captain/bowler was Richie Benaud.

It had been an unhappy tour for the Australian captain. A serious shoulder injury had restricted his appearances and at no stage had he looked like the man who had matured into a top-class leg-spinner since the last tour to England. By the end of July, the fibrositis that had troubled him since early May was at last clearing up; just before the Old Trafford Test he had taken nine wickets in the Middlesex match. His side needed him; the rubber stood at 1-1 with just the Oval Test to come.

To the relief of the Australians who played in Laker's Match, Old Trafford 1961 was a completely different wicket. Groundsman Bert Flack had prepared a hard, true pitch with even shafts of grass; the bounce would be true and there would be some turn as the game progressed. So it proved. Over the first four days, England held sway – Australia all out 190, England 367, a lead of 177. It looked as if Peter May would be taking a 2-1 lead to the Oval, some compensation for the 4-0 thrashing in Australia in 1958–9.

At the start of the final day, Australia stood at 331 for 6, a lead of 154. Bill Lawry had compiled his second hundred of the series to stiffen the backbone of the innings and Alan Davidson and Ken Mackay – men of proven Test Match temperament and capability – were the not out batsman. In the next half-hour the off-spin of David Allen claimed Mackay, Benaud and Grout at a cost of one run. At 334 for 9, the first crisis of the day loomed for Australia. Yet Davidson was still there, a composed, dangerous left-hander with the nerve and ability to gather quick runs, and the technique to defend when necessary. His partner was Graham McKenzie, a man destined to become a great fast bowler, but playing only his third Test at the age of twenty.

Davidson decided to take Allen while McKenzie struggled to come to terms with the seam bowling of Brian Statham and Ted Dexter. May replaced seam with the off-spin of Brian Close, the sort of ploy that often breaks up a stubborn partnership. In two overs, however, Close bowled five full-tosses, three of which were struck to the boundary by McKenzie. The stand was consolidated and Davidson decided to quicken the tempo. Since taking Grout's wicket, Allen had bowled six overs – all but four deliveries had been taken by Davidson. In Allen's seventh over of the day, he was hit by Davidson for twenty – all superb shots in the arc between cover-point and the straight drive.

The tactical pendulum had swung to Australia; Allen was immediately taken off, May took the new ball and Statham and Trueman were treated with calm insouciance by McKenzie and rugged dominance by Davidson. The last-wicket pair began to bat like openers. Time was now as important as runs. At one o'clock, McKenzie was bowled by Jack Flavell, the sixth bowler to be tried that morning. The stand had been worth 98 precious runs and the grandeur of Davidson's unbeaten 76 had not eclipsed the serene assurance of young McKenzie.

England needed a total of 256 in three hours and fifty minutes – a rate of 66 an hour. The openers – Geoff Pullar and Ramon Subba Row – did all that was needed in the awkward twenty minutes before lunch, scoring a run a minute. That lunchtime must have felt like an eternity to the crowd; the runs/wickets/time equation looked as if it might yield a positive result after several years of fairly mundane safety-first Test cricket. Surely England would go for the runs? If they did, Australia would need to take all ten wickets within four hours. A draw seemed the least likely outcome.

After lunch, the England opening pair prospered at a good rate until Pullar mistimed a hook shot off Davidson. At 40 for 1, Ted Dexter came in to play one of the great *short* innings in Test cricket. An imperious off-drive for four off Davidson announced his intentions; battle was joined and from three overs by Davidson and Mackay, 27 runs came. At the other end, Benaud – who had come on as early as the seventh over – was being treated with respect, but he seemed to hold no terrors. He was bowling over the wicket to Dexter, but round the stumps to the left-handed Subba Row – aiming for a few footmarks outside his off-stump, courtesy of Fred Trueman's follow-through. As Dexter punished Davidson off back and front foot, we entered the crucial phase of the match. How long could Benaud bowl Davidson? He was no doubt tired after his magnificent efforts with the bat and the second new ball was due at 200, a total that would be reached uncomfortably quickly if Dexter continued in this dismissive vein.

Benaud rested Davidson and then saw eleven runs come off McKenzie's first over. The crowd was ecstatic – a dour Lancashire gathering, people who knew their cricket, they did not expect anything fancy so that they would never be too disappointed. Yet here was Dexter batting in a Test Match like a stunning amalgam of Hammond, Trumper and Bradman. At last a modern English batsman had transcended the pressures and demonstrated that a half-volley in a Test goes to the boundary as easily as in a Festival game.

By ten to four, Dexter had made 76 in 82 minutes, and England were now 106 adrift with 110 minutes left. Benaud had continued to attack, using the leg-spin of Bobby Simpson at one end while he wheeled away at the other. Benaud finally went round the wicket to the right-hander. The first five balls of the over yielded no run, the last was a top-spinner that Dexter tried to hammer through the covers off the back foot. Wally Grout, the wicket-keeper, took the outside edge. Dexter was cheered in like the cricketing prince he was – it was a disappointment that he had missed his century, yet he had won the game for England. After all, the man walking to the crease was Peter May, the greatest English batsman of his generation. . .

Subba Row played a maiden and May took his first ball from Benaud. From round the wicket, he bowled on May's leg stump and he played it back to the bowler. The next one landed further outside leg stump in the rough of Trueman's footmarks. May, possibly surprised by a wide ball outside his legs, played a shot not usually in his extensive and impressive range – the sweep. He failed to put his pad in line, the ball broke back to the off and hit leg-stump. It was the only ball Benaud dropped outside the

Peter May is bowled round his legs for nought by his rival captain, Richie Benaud, at Manchester in 1961 . . . a Test the Australians snatched out of the fire by dint of slow bowling.

leg-stump to a right-hander that day. Never the most diffident of cricketers, he looked like a small boy who had been given a chocolate factory.

If May's dismissal was a jolt to the English nervous system, the performance of the next man in was enough to make spectators reach for tranquillizers. Brian Close, always an idiosyncratic cricketer of great natural talents, had clearly worked out the way to play Benaud. He would sweep him. The first ball was skewered in the air from a cross-batted swing that seemed to owe everything to the village green. The ball dropped behind the square leg umpire, where Benaud immediately placed a fieldsman. For the last three balls of that over, Close tried the same shot. Each time he missed. After Subba Row played a maiden, Close seemed to have changed his tactics. He hit Benaud straight for six – a marvellous stroke, full of timing, strength and mastery. The lesson had surely been learned? Not a bit – the next ball, the

129

sweep shot again, failed to make contact. Three balls later, he top-edged a sweep to the waiting hands of Norman O'Neill, standing precisely in the spot demanded by Benaud in his previous over.

Five runs later, the unthinkable happened. Subba Row had played throughout the afternoon with his customary good sense. All he had to do was play for tea and receive new instructions from his chastened captain. It was not to be; he played back to Benaud, rather than forward, and was bowled off his pads for 49. It was the last ball before tea.

In twenty minutes, England had slumped from the prospect of a resounding victory to the abyss of defeat. At 163 for 5, Benaud had taken the last four wickets for nine runs. John Murray remembers walking out to bat with Ken Barrington after the tea interval, with England needing 93 to win in 85 minutes. 'We were still going to have a go. Kenny and I reckoned that Richie would keep himself on, and possibly bring back Bobby Simpson at the other end, so we would get enough overs bowled at us. All we needed was to get among them in the first half-hour after tea.' Soon England's strategy was in tatters. Murray and Allen were both picked up at slip by Simpson off Benaud's leg-breaks, Barrington was LBW to Mackay, Trueman was tempted once too often by Simpson. At the start of the extra half-hour, Flavell and Statham were together. For a few minutes, they handled the spinners with some aplomb. Then, at twenty minutes to six, Benaud called up Davidson with a view to taking the new ball. It was never needed – Davidson's fourth delivery bowled Statham. The game – and the Ashes – were Australia's. A glorious victory, proof incarnate that cricket can yield the most bizarre and unexpected twists.

John Arlott called the events of 1 August, 1961 'a dramatic day's cricket which will be recounted, mulled over and disputed as long as anyone who saw it is alive to talk cricket.' Although a record total attendance of 131,000 was established for an Old Trafford Test, just 12,000 witnessed one of the greatest final days in Test history. The scene was in strong contrast to Laker's Match five years before, when the delighted Lancastrians were still gathered round the wicket two hours after Len Maddocks had been dismissed. This time the ground had emptied twenty minutes after the end, and the partisans were wistfully shaking their heads about the inadequacies of the English batting as they streamed up the Stretford Road.

Since the start of that over to Dexter, Benaud had taken 6 for 30 to win the game almost single-handed. For the engaging Australian captain, that over was indeed the moment of truth. He had bowled 17 overs unchanged from the Stretford End. His analysis stood at 0 for 40. In the first innings it had been 0 for 80. In the previous Tests, he had taken just five wickets for 190 runs. His batting had fallen away – a 'pair' at Leeds and only three runs at Old Trafford in two innings. With Davidson tired, McKenzie, Mackay and Simpson hammered by Dexter, only one man could be relied on to remain economical. That same man also had to bowl out England. Benaud had pulled it off by sheer force of character and the tactical nous to unveil a strategy before it was too late.

Benaud maintains to this day that the dismissal of Dexter was the vital one – 'another twenty minutes of Ted and we were finished' is his verdict. A conversation with the great Ray Lindwall the previous evening was perhaps equally important. Earlier in the match, Benaud had noticed Trueman's foot marks; they were perilously close to the leg-stump and therefore the left-hander would struggle just outside his off-stump if the ball was pitched in the right place. England had five left-handers in their team – Pullar, Subba Row, Close, Flavell and Statham. At close of play of the fourth day, Benaud went out to look at the effect of Trueman's follow-through. There were four marks, no longer superficial scratches as they had been earlier in the match. They were deep holes and the surrounding area was dusty. Benaud reasoned that it would be a difficult area for the left-hander and that if he bowled *round* the wicket for the right-hander and aimed for the footmarks, at least the batsmen might be tied down.

That night, Benaud discussed his idea with Lindwall. His advice was cogent – give it a try but if he strayed off line Dexter and co would smash him out of sight. Benaud considers that if Lindwall had not encouraged him, he might have left his plan till it was too late.

131

Once Dexter was established, it suddenly dawned on Benaud that a draw was impossible; even if Dexter got out, there was always May to come. He told Neil Harvey, his vice-captain, what he planned to do. 'Our only chance was for me to go round the wicket to Dexter, get him quickly and press for a win.' After Dexter's dismissal, Close was the batsman who worried Benaud most. 'I thought he was right to sweep with the spin, wait for the shorter one to pull, and get as many as possible at the other end. If he had succeeded for about twenty minutes, England would still have won.'

For Peter May, the memory of that nought still makes him wince. 'That wasn't a shot I normally played, and I can't ever remember being dismissed that way before or since,' he told me. After paying due tribute to Benaud's bowling, May believes that the England close catching was the crucial aspect of the match. 'We dropped some fairly easy catches, you know. They took some fine ones, particularly Bobby Simpson.' A relevant point indeed – in the Australian second innings, Harvey and Lawry were both badly missed at gully and slip. They went on to score another 110 runs, more than twice the victory margin.

David Allen still feels slightly aggrieved that he got little chance to test McKenzie at the start of his historic partnership with Davidson. 'The seamers wouldn't give Graham a single, so that I could have an over at him. All I got was four balls. When you've rolled over three useful batters early on, you have to fancy your chances against a youngster. Then Peter May told me to toss it up at Davidson, I did so, went for twenty in the over and I'm off!'

John Murray agrees that Allen was unlucky. From his position behind the stumps, it seemed to Murray that Allen would soon ensnare McKenzie. 'If he'd had just a few balls in a row at Graham, he would have gone. David was also unlucky that Closey was brought on at the other end; most of his stuff didn't land and the game started running away from us. So David had to suffer, even though he'd bowled superbly.'

Ted Dexter modestly plays down his great innings – 'it was simply a case of good old Dexter giving it a go, if he comes off we might win the game. I thought Richie's tactics were absolutely right; bowling outside leg to the right hander is good business when there's rough around, and his control was very good. I also think Brian Close was unfairly castigated – if you're trying to attack the ball when it's pitching and turning in the rough, you can't go for the big drive in case it does you through the gate. The only chance is to go for the sweep. The funny thing about that match is that we lost the game *because* we got into a winning position, but then that's cricket isn't it?'

Yet if only the ball that dismissed Dexter had bounced another quarter of an inch to miss the bat; if only Fred Trueman's laudable desire to get close to the stumps for his outswinger had not created rough for Benaud to exploit; if only Peter May had eschewed the sweep shot; if only Colin Cowdrey had not been ill with pleurisy, he might have taken some of those slip catches; if only Benaud had been the kind of captain to play his tactics strictly by the book. But if all those possibilities *had* come to pass, we would have missed the rare sight of a magnificent Test that was won by a slow bowler.

The time was 5.55 on a grey August afternoon at the Oval in 1968. A slim, bespectacled man was about to take strike against a fair-haired bowler whose fierce concentration furrowed his brow in a manner that belied his tender years. If the batsman fancied a pleasant word or two with a fielder he did not need to strain his voice – ten of them were within a space of a few yards around the bat. The young left-arm bowler wheeled in on his precise, smooth run; the delivery was well up on the middle-and-off stumps, the batsman began to play a shot, then changed his mind and stuck out a pad as an afterthought. The ball had come in with the arm rather than moved away from the off-stump and the LBW appeal was a formality. John Inverarity did not bother to look at the umpire as the bowler was congratulated by his exultant team-mates. Australia all out 125, a defeat by 227 runs and England's Derek Underwood had sealed a performance that established his legend as the best wet-wicket bowler in the world.

The deceptively unathletic Underwood had made his first-class debut five years earlier – now, as he sheepishly acknowledged the acclaim of the crowd, he could reflect that a return of 7 for 50 was due reward for 31 overs of nagging accuracy. The years of introspection and frustration lay ahead for him, but from that afternoon onwards, England captains would trail Underwood around the world in the hope of encountering conditions similar to those on that amazing final day at the Oval.

That Fifth Test was notable for other milestones – Basil D'Oliveira scored 158, arguably the most historically significant innings in Test cricket. It led to his selection for the winter tour of South Africa, the subsequent refusal of Prime Minister Vorster to allow him to tour and the eventual isolation of South Africa from Test Cricket. D'Oliveira's century and another from Edrich gave England a commanding total of 494. Australia replied with 324, their captain Bill Lawry compiling a typically watchful 135. On the fourth day, a brisk three hours' batting by England led to a declaration asking Australia to score 352 at 54 an hour, a tall order in a Test against bowlers like Brown, Snow, Illingworth and, above all, Underwood. Perhaps Colin Cowdrey should have declared earlier, but such considerations were shelved in the final half-hour of the day when the crucial wicket of Lawry fell to Brown, then Redpath padded up to Underwood's quicker ball, to be given out LBW. Australia were 13 for 2 and England had six hours on the morrow to take eight wickets.

There was precious little for the Australian peace of mind in Underwood's first over of that final day. Ian Chappell snicked a ball that spun away sharply and the edge fell just short of slip. Soon Chappell played back to Underwood and fell LBW. Doug Walters lasted half an hour for a single before getting a ball so unplayable that he did well even to touch it – the ball pitched on leg stump, zipped to the off and Knott took the edge high up. Australia were 29 for 4 and three of the wickets to Underwood.

Inverarity now began to wrap a cloak of respectability around the innings; never the most stylish of batsmen, this modest pragmatist knew his priorities. He realized that a 'killer' ball from Underwood would arrive at some stage and he made sure he would not perish the same way as Walters. He simply shielded his stumps and kept his bat away from the ball that threatened the edge of the bat by late adjustments; the cordon of eight close fielders did not seem to ruffle his calm temperament, nor the cacophony of appeals for bat/pad catches that clearly came off the pad alone.

The elegant Sheahan kept him reassuring company for a time until Sheahan pulled Illingworth to mid-wicket, the only man anywhere near that part of the field. Such things happen when defeat threatens. Jarman, the wicket-keeper, battled through the anxious minutes to lunch at 86 for 5. By then, the remaining five wickets had become less of a problem than the weather. The sultry heat haze of the morning gave way to a thunderstorm of Caribbean proportions. Within half an hour, the ground was almost completely waterlogged – spectators cursed the rain that had ruined the fourth successive Test, journalists filed their 'hard luck England' stories and the players of both sides started to change from their flannels in varying degrees of resignation and glee.

One man remained optimistic – Colin Cowdrey, the England captain. As the sky cleared, and the sun came out, he watched the covers drawn back and examined a wicket that was damp but not yet out of action for the rest of the day. The outfield was the problem, the more so on a huge ground like the Oval. How could a groundstaff of four cope with mopping up seven and a half acres of sodden ground? Cowdrey than played a public relations masterstroke; realizing he could tap the crowd's reserves of frustration and goodwill, he appealed for volunteers. Within minutes, pin-striped executives, truant schoolboys and amused students were wielding pitchforks and blankets. As the water seeped deeper into the ground, the umpires conferred and decreed that play would resume at 4.45 if there was no further rain. Surely this blighted summer would grant just a couple of hours' pleasure?

There *was* no further rain and Inverarity and Jarman started to bat for a draw. The odds favoured them – England needed five wickets in just seventy-five minutes and even more crucially, the ball was not turning for Underwood. The pitch was too damp, it had been anaesthetized by the rain and moreover the sun had disappeared. It looked as if England would have to make do without the classic combination of sun and wind on a drying wicket that had served Laker so well in 1956. As Underwood

Derek Underwood traps John Inverarity lbw to end the Australian
second innings at the Oval in the 1968. The entire England team was
gathered round the bat . . . from left to right, Illingworth, Graveney,
Edrich, Dexter, Cowdrey, Underwood, Knott, Snow, Brown, Milburn
and D'Oliveira.

nagged and probed, three bowlers were used in five overs at the
other end. The batsmen were unmoved. At 5.25 – with the extra
half-hour looming, but probably not worth the bother of claim-
ing – Underwood was rested. After forty minutes, no wicket had
fallen. Who could make the breakthrough? Basil D'Oliveira, a
cunning, underrated bowler, was brought on – a man who occasionally managed to succeed where more talented bowlers failed.
D'Oliveira bowled to Jarman; one of his modest little floaters
bemused Jarman into playing a half-cock shot. The ball hit the
roll of the pad and kissed the off stump.

With his job done, D'Oliveira was replaced by Underwood,
who ripped through Mallett and McKenzie in five balls, both to
agile catches by Brown at short-leg. With twenty-five minutes

left, Gleeson walked in – a cricketer with a relaxed attitude to the pressures of Test Matches and a man sporting enough to spurn delaying tactics. For the next quarter of an hour, Gleeson sold his wicket dearly, with the pad an effective buttress. Inverarity reached a splendid fifty that was worth ten times more than a hundred in many other Tests. It was ten minutes to six and Underwood was beginning to fret; he started to go round the wicket but Cowdrey waved him to continue his line from over the wicket. He could not afford to lose any time in re-adjusting the line of Underwood's attack. With Underwood's next ball, Gleeson was beaten for pace and he lost his off-stump. One wicket left, ten minutes to go and three – possibly four – overs in which to accomplish the improbable.

Connolly blocked the last ball of Underwood's over, Inverarity took a single from Illingworth's fourth ball and Connolly negotiated the last deliveries with some ease.

Inverarity against Underwood: the immovable against the inspired. Inverarity had battled throughout the innings for more than four hours to shame his more accomplished colleagues with his resilience; his sensible technique enabled him to alter his stroke selection very late. Just five minutes more and Inverarity's would be a new name on the élite list of great match-saving innings.

It was not to be. At the wrong moment, he chose to rely on his pad rather than his bat that had seemed so broad all day. As Underwood received a hero's welcome, one had a genuine sympathy for the teacher from Western Australia who had been undone by his only mistake in a very long day.

For Derek Underwood, the Oval 1968 proved a bittersweet experience. After two years of being an occasional selection for the England side, he was established, an acknowledged match-winner in favourable conditions. No wonder he came to be known as 'Deadly'. Yet Underwood began to feel the pressure of great expectations on his slim and rather diffident shoulders. He told me, 'Whenever there was rain about, the lads used to say. 'Oh, we'll be okay, we've got Deadly' – but that was pressure on me, even though meant as a compliment!' Over the next few years, he was indeed a destroyer on certain occasions, but his bowling became rather flat and mechanical and it took some time for him to come to terms with the variety needed to threaten good batsmen on wickets that nullified the bowler.

Underwood pays generous tribute to Colin Cowdrey – 'to me, he was always a giant of a man and he carried me along on his shoulders that day. He was sympathetic, yet he made me realize that every ball had to count; I was tense but I kept thinking that the batsmen must be equally on edge. By no stretch of the imagination could you say it was a spiteful pitch; there was a little bit of bounce eventually and the ball occasionally skidded through. But as Inverarity proved, a man with a good technique could survive'.

Alan Knott considers that the Australians were more concerned with Underwood's growing reputation as a dangerous bowler than the pitch. 'It really wasn't a typical "Deadly" wicket. The ground was so dry when the cloudburst came that the water just seeped all the way through and never altered the character of the pitch that much. It was simply pressure cricket that won it for us. The atmosphere was fantastic – that crowd got so involved and they really lifted us. In those days, players didn't show much emotion and I vividly remember David Brown running down the pitch towards Derek with the ball held high in his hand, after taking two bat/pad catches in an over!'

Brown remembers that as well – with great embarrassment. 'I saw it on television a few months later and I thought I looked a complete idiot. I was elated at hatching a plan that actually worked – when Graham McKenzie came in, I told Colin Milburn to stay where he was when Underwood bowled, just in case it lobbed up to him. I was a couple of yards away from him, so I decided to dive forward as soon as the ball left Derek's hand. It dropped straight down from the bat and there I was, the leaping salmon!'

Clearly the Australians lost the game through circumstances, rather than conditions. Panic set in when the England players had almost given up all hope. For all the batting inadequacies, it was a tremendous finish, an old-fashioned piece of melodrama with every fielder round the bat, the opposition bulwark collapsing just in time and the young hero carrying off the prize. One thought nags away, though – how would the England team have reacted if they had been in an overseas Test and told to play through an agonizing last hour or so in conditions similar to the Oval in 1968?

At 6.30 on the evening of June 1, 1957, England faced another ignominious home defeat at the hands of the West Indies. Or more pertinently, the fingers of Sonny Ramadhin. In this, the First Test of the 1957 series, the spin and flight of Ramadhin had triumphed over a slow, flat Edgbaston wicket and re-awakened memories of the way he and Alf Valentine had mesmerised the England batting in 1950. Seven years previously, Ramadhin and Valentine had harvested 59 wickets in the series. Ramadhin with slow right-arm spin and Valentine with orthodox slow left-arm. Now in this Edgbaston Test, Valentine was missing through ill-health, but for Ramadhin it was clearly a case of 'business as usual'. On the first day, England were all out for 186, Ramadhin 7 for 49. The wicket was blameless but the batsmen's footwork was not; Ramadhin undid them with flight and deceptive changes of pace, rather than sharp turn. They were still playing him as a leg-spinner, despite the accumulating evidence that the majority of Ramadhin's deliveries were off-breaks to the right-handed batsman.

Over the next two days, West Indies built a massive lead of 288. Then in the last hour of play on Saturday evening, the little man struck again as England started the long haul to respectability. In successive overs, Ramadhin had Peter Richardson caught and then bowled Doug Insole for nought. Peter May – then at the peak of his career – joined Brian Close and they lasted till close of play. England 102 for 2, still 186 behind, with two days stretching ahead and the weather set fair. Certainly Ramadhin would be looking forward to Monday; with the England tail starting at seven with Tony Lock, there seemed no hope. Yet as Peter May (not out 21) unbuckled his pads on that Saturday evening, he had some interesting words for 'Gubby' Allen, the chairman of the England selectors – 'I've rumbled him, chairman, I'm going to play him as an off-spinner'. Allen recalls, 'Peter had certainly played him very well that evening, but I remember wondering if they were famous last words. Fortunately I was wrong.'

Within twenty minutes of the start of play on Monday, the pressure on May had become even greater. Close was out – caught off Gilchrist – and England were 113 for 3 as Colin Cowdrey walked out to join May. With only Trevor Bailey left of the recognised batsmen, this was the decisive phase of the innings, the match, the series, and indeed Ramadhin's glittering career.

The two batsmen exchanged confidences. Later May admitted he told Cowdrey that he could not pick Ramadhin's leg-break; his advice was to play forward all the time. Ramadhin's deadly quicker ball had bowled four batsmen in the first innings. Slowly the partnership developed roots while Ramadhin toiled away, using every nuance of his art – a high leg-break, a floating off-break, a quicker ball, even one that went straight on, hoping the batsmen would play for non-existent turn. At the other end, Denis Atkinson bowled over after over of off-cutters and occasional off-spin. How their captain John Goddard must have wished for a Valentine of 1950, rather than the disconsolate figure who could not even make the team!

Throughout the afternoon, Cowdrey used his pads almost as much as his bat. Ramadhin, sensing the tactics behind such passive resistance appealed and appealed for LBW, to no avail. May was considerably more fluent and the arrival of his century warmed the crowd. At least they were getting their money's worth for this fourth day – the game would be all over early on Tuesday, but it was nice to see a brave hundred from the captain as the ship went down with colours still defiant.

At this stage, Cowdrey exerted himself – not with the bat but his cricketing intelligence. He noticed that May's concentration had snapped after reaching three figures. He was playing some loose shots and his concentration was clearly wavering. Between overs, Cowdrey cajoled him to leave the bowling to him for a few overs, to calm down, take fresh guard and play for Tuesday. As May recalls, 'there comes a time when you have this uncontrollable desire to attack the bowling, even though you know it's not wise. Colin was very good at those moments'.

The crisis passed and at close of play, the captain was 193 not out and Cowdrey on 78. They had added 265, to give England a lead of 90. May's dominance of the day was striking – of 276 runs scored, his share had been 172.

It was a little easier for England on Tuesday morning. The optimism, will and ability visibly drained from Ramadhin as May and Cowdrey made it quite clear there would be no easy pickings for him. The LBW appeals continued to rain on deaf ears as the batsmen set about demoralizing one of the most dangerous of post-war bowlers. The spell had not only to be broken, but obliterated. Cowdrey pointed out later that this grinding-down process was also for the benefit of the later batsmen: to some, he was still something of a sorcerer. Still there was no respite for Ramadhin as Cowdrey reached his century after nearly eight hours. When the batsmen finally decided to increase the tempo for a declaration, he was still bowling. At 2.50, Cowdrey was caught at long-on for 154 – not off Ramadhin. This momentous partnership had yielded 411 in 511 minutes, a record for the fourth wicket in all Tests. Considering the period of crises the batsmen encountered in their historic stand, the scoring rate was commendably brisk – or perhaps that was because the West Indies bowled their overs faster than a quarter of a century later?

After a frisky little partnership between May and the ebullient Godfrey Evans, the declaration came. May was 285 not out. He asked the West Indies to get 296 in 160 minutes and immediately the depth of their demoralization was clear when they went in to bat. They were quickly 27 for 4, then 61 for 6, and 68 for 7. The pitch was turning more than at any other stage of the match and when the match was left drawn at 72 for 7, Peter May was criticised in some quarters for delaying the declaration. He admitted to me that it was only a token declaration and that he had no idea England would get so close, with Lock and Laker snapping away at the tail. 'I saw that Test as one in a series of five and my object was to save the game and sort out Ramadhin. Now in my mind's eye, I can see an LBW appeal by Tony Lock against John Goddard that was so close. If he'd been out then, they would have been eight down with a few minutes left.'

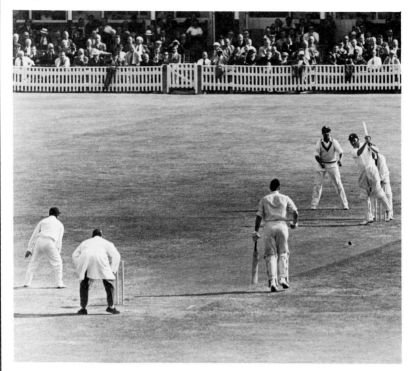

Colin Cowdrey plays Sonny Ramadhin to mid-on during his historic stand of 411 with Peter May against the West Indies in 1957 at Edgbaston – a partnership that finished Ramadhin as a world-class slow bowler.

May said that the England policy in the first innings was to attack Ramadhin. Australia had had some success with that strategy two years earlier, yet for England the plan misfired at the first attempt. 'He was a really fine bowler with all the subtleties. When I walked out to bat on the Saturday evening, I told myself I could only do my best. Early on, I managed to hit him for a four and that calmed me down a little. I couldn't read him from the hand at all, so I decided to play him from the pitch off the front foot.' Did he feel any great pressure during that wonderful innings? 'I think pressure is very much a modern word in sport. It's all a matter of what you make of the situation. I was honoured to play for, and captain my country and although I was very tired at the end, it was an unforgettable experience.

Godfrey Evans can vouch for the fatigue May suffered near the end of his innings. When Cowdrey was out, Evans came in, full of his usual bounce and energy, determined to run as many quick singles as he could. 'I pushed one through the covers and said "come two, skipper", to which he replied, "don't forget, I've been here bloody hours".'

Colin Cowdrey felt the England second innings gave the batsmen breathing space against Ramadhin. 'He was such a wonderful bowler, you know. The ability to bowl off and leg-spin at various speeds with no discernible change of action meant that he could bowl a Test batsman off-stump with a leggie as he was aiming to hit him through mid-wicket. He regularly made good players look stupid, so it was vital to sort him out. In the next Test, I played much more freely to get 152 and Ramadhin took some more punishment, so the hours I spent taking him in at Edgbaston paid off.'

Ramadhin's analysis in that Edgbaston second innings was awesome – 98 overs, 35 maidens, 2 for 179. Even though he was ground into the dust, he only gave away two an over. No other man has ever bowled more balls in a Test (774) or overs in a single innings. It was a shattering experience. Ramadhin still shudders at the memory as he talks in his pub in Lancashire. He admits it broke his spell for good, even though he was still too clever for lesser batsmen – indeed he was still taking a hundred wickets in a season in league cricket at the age of fifty, before heart trouble restricted his activities to the golf course. Ramadhin still cannot believe that his LBW appeals against Cowdrey in particular were unsuccessful – and he is supported by the England twelfth man for the match, Johnny Wardle. 'I could have cried for Sonny', says Wardle. 'I watched all that partnership and if he appealed forty times, I reckon a good proportion of them were absolutely plumb. He was the kind of bowler who could pitch six out of six on the same spot, there was no bounce, so the ball never got about bail-high, and I reckon the ball was hitting the stumps time after time until the pad got in the way'.

Reg Simpson, the former Nottinghamshire and England batsman, joined in the chorus of disapproval of the pad play in the May/Cowdrey stand. He estimates that Ramadhin bowled at least fifty balls that pitched on or just outside the off-stump which would have hit the wicket, but were padded away by the batsman, without attempting a stroke. Simpson feels that partnership ruined English batsmanship for years, ushering in an era of pad-play that became ugly to watch but effective, because it nullified the spinners. It was to be another fifteen years before the LBW law was revised to penalize the batsman who had no intention of playing a stroke, but in the intervening period there is no doubt that the quality of batting suffered in England. Batting became a contest between pad, bat and ball, rather than just bat and ball.

Colin Cowdrey counters: 'I didn't just thrust out my pad. I knew where my stumps were and the place to intercept the ball was just outside the off-stump. Under the existing law, I couldn't be out, so why should I have made it easier for Ramadhin? He appealed himself hoarse, but the umpires were in the best position.'

Jim Laker bowled 78 overs in that famous Test and sympathizes with the brave little man who never knew when to take a rest. 'John Goddard should have given Sonny a breather or two. There was always the danger that they would overbowl him, because they relied on him so much, especially with Valentine in decline. They wound him up, pushed him out onto the pitch and expected him to bowl on a beautiful wicket for two whole days. They wanted him to be a stock bowler as well as a strike bowler.'

Sonny Ramadhin was never the same bowler after that, despite a couple of productive seasons with Lancashire, some enjoyable times with Lincolnshire in the Minor Counties and a regular haul of wickets in the league around Lancashire. His eclipse was as dramatic as his rise (he conquered England in 1950 after playing in just two first-class matches before the tour began). After the Edgbaston nightmare, he took 1 for 83, 0 for 95, 0 for 34 and 4 for 107 on an Oval wicket turning square. At the age of 27, Sonny Ramadhin's great Test career was on the way out; he played just ten Tests after that 1957 tour, taking 31 wickets, but he was never a real threat again. Doug Insole – who was bowled twice by Ramadhin at Edgbaston – put his finger on the reason for Ramadhin's drift into obscurity; 'Word quickly gets round when a class cricketer is rumbled, whatever type he is. When May and Cowdrey showed how to play him on a good wicket, everyone else took note and the whole approach changed to batting against Ramadhin.'

It was a personal tragedy for Ramadhin and for those who value variety in cricket. After all, Lance Gibbs – his successor as the number one spinner in the West Indies team – was only four years younger, and still playing for his country at the age of 42, in 1976, a matter of sixteen years after Ramadhin played his last Test. Sonny Ramadhin would have been around for a long time *if* Peter May had not played the archetypal captain's innings at Edgbaston, *if* Colin Cowdrey had not known exactly where his stumps were, *if* John Goddard had been able to recognise the sight of a great slow bowler at the end of his tether. . .

# 6. Batting Against Spin

Today's top batsmen in English cricket prefer batting against spin – on the face of it, a complete vindication of the current trend towards fast bowling. The object of the exercise is to make life hard for a batsman and the following comments hardly advance the cause of the slow bowler:

Glenn Turner: 'A spinner gets you out nicely, rather than blasts you out with your gloves in front of your face.'

Dennis Amiss: 'To play a spinner is a pleasure, because in the last ten years the game's been about getting away from the ball to avoid being hit. When the spinners are on, it's a quieter game, no one's trying to knock off your head.'

Allan Lamb: 'When a spinner comes on, your eyes go round like dollar signs on a fruit machine. Everyone wants to hit him, because they can't smash the fast bowler.'

The slow bowlers who have played for more than a decade agree that the class batsmen hit them harder than a few years ago:

Derek Underwood: 'The high standard of fast bowling means they think, "We'd better get after the spinner now that the quicks are resting".'

Pat Pocock: 'Players are stronger today, they train harder, use heavier bats and they're much better at whacking you.'

Norman Gifford: 'You can't afford to leave the ball hanging too long in the air these days.'

That sounds fairly gloomy until one realizes the amount of world-class batsmen in county cricket at this time. It may be that the overall standard of batting among English players has sadly deteriorated but almost every county side now has a batsman of the highest class. In the

1940s and 1950s, England had several world-class players in county sides – men like Compton, Hutton, May, Cowdrey, Graveney – but strict curtailment of overseas players meant the quota of great batsmen was much smaller than in 1981. So any slow bowler who succeeds in the modern game – especially on so many wickets that do not favour him – is automatically a fine performer.

The methods of playing spin bowling have changed in the last twenty years or so. The great English batsmen of the post-War years played classically straight 'through the V' (the arc between mid-off and mid-on). A slow bowler's task was comparatively easier, because he could try to bowl a certain line against a particular type of batsman. If it was Peter May, the off-spinner would try to keep him away from his favourite on-drive; in the case of Tom Graveney, to force him onto the back foot and avoid the off-stump area. Great players they undoubtedly were, but a scoring chart of a long innings would be fairly predictable. Today, the growth of limited-overs cricket means the top-class batsman is more adept and flexible about where he gathers his runs. Norman Gifford: 'It's much harder bowling at the top players today than when I first started. I might bowl a couple of balls outside the off-stump which are played to my packed offside field, then all of a sudden, you can see the batsman has decided to change his line of attack. I'll bowl the same delivery, he'll play across the line and work me through to the on-side, where there aren't so many fielders.'

The facts back up Gifford's assertion. Modern batsmen are scoring faster than at any other period since the First World War:

| Year | Runs per 100 balls |
|------|-------------------|
| 1914 | 47.70 |
| 1925–8 | 42.26 |
| 1935–8 | 45.54 |
| 1946–9 | 43.33 |
| 1955–8 | 41.00 |
| 1965–8 | 39.37 |
| 1975–8 | 45.79 |
| 1980 | 47.38 |
| 1981 | 47.68 |

(See Appendix B)

So the great days of Hammond, Hobbs, Compton, Edrich, May and Dexter cannot match today's scoring rate per hundred balls. The tragedy is that, although current batsmen are scoring quickly, the bowlers do not deliver enough balls per hour.

Pat Pocock finds that it is not so easy to keep men round the bat to today's top-class batsmen. 'A man at bat/pad to Ian Botham is at considerable physical risk, despite the protection from helmets. He and his type hit the ball so hard. I've seen many of them top-edge the ball for sixes in recent years.'

Alan Knott has noticed how the attitude to loose deliveries has changed in his time: 'Very few balls come to me behind the stumps now without the batsman trying to play a shot. They're all looking to run it down to third man, or go for the big drive. When I first started, the batsmen would leave the ball alone outside the off-stump for the first two hours of his innings.'

The professional approach to batting by today's tail-enders does not advance the cause of spin bowling at all. The slow bowlers of the 'fifties would expect the later batsmen to enjoy themsleves, to have a big wind-up and put the ball in the air. Today's breed are better players: they go in the nets, don the helmets and play studiously down the line. Normally they have to be frightened out by fast bowling. The philosophy of dear old 'Bomber' Wells now seems positively antedeluvian: 'I would try to get four in one ball every time. Today, number eleven takes about half an hour to scrape four together.'

The style of batting against modern spinners, the lush outfields that keep the ball shiny all day, the slow wickets, occasional short boundaries – all these factors have combined to make spin bowlers more negative. Glamorgan's Alan Jones has played first-class cricket for twenty-five years. He says: 'Until recently, spinners always used to try to bowl you out – now they wait for you to make a mistake. I used to look forward to fixtures like the Northants game because I knew that Bedi and Mushtaq would attack me. Now you're either getting your head knocked off, or the slow bowler lacks the confidence to throw it up at you.'

It would be interesting to see how today's top batsmen would fare against a great leg-spinner like Bruce Dooland. By the mid-1950s it was clear that the leg-spinner's influence was on the wane. Just after the War, they were the best bowlers in England (men like Wright, Jenkins, Hollies, Peter Smith and Jim Sims), because there were few fast bowlers around and off-spin was not yet the vogue. A decade later, an analytical form of defence had started to limit the wrist-spinner's deadliness. Doug Insole was one of the men who worked out a method to play them: 'I'd play wicket to wicket at what I suspected was the googly, shoulder arms to the ball that was missing the off-stump, and just wait for the inevitable bad ball and whack it. During my time, batsmen stopped going down the wicket to the leg-spinners. The old cavalier attitude from the pre-War amateur had gone for good.'

The off-spinner then took over the main responsibility for slow bowling. With the ends of the wicket uncovered, he could stand up to bowl on a wet wicket – unlike the seamer – so he had regular opportunities to play a decisive role. In the 'fifties, many batsmen were bowled 'through the gate' by the off-spinner as they tried to drive; there were more close fielders behind the bat (often two leg-slips), because there was sufficient bounce in the wicket to make the ball carry. Today, the bat/pad position has replaced leg slip on slow wickets and there are generally more fielders in front of the wicket than twenty years ago. Batsmen also play forward a good deal more today, a fact that distresses Arthur Milton, one of the best bad-wicket players of spin since the War: 'Fifty per cent of back play has gone. The front foot gets stuck up the wicket automatically.' David Allen agrees: 'The average player today stands on the front foot and just slows the game down when the spinner comes on. You can see them get on the front foot before the ball is delivered. I just wish the wickets were quicker to catch them out.'

The slow bowler has been frustrated by pad play for the last twenty-five years or so. Colin Cowdrey popularized the passive method in his historic partnership with Peter May at Edgbaston in 1957; during their stand of 411 against the West Indies, Cowdrey played forward interminably against the predominant off-breaks of Sonny Ramadhin and nullified his effectiveness. Ramadhin appealed himself hoarse for LBW but the pad/bat strategy worked and he was broken. Cowdrey, like all great players, knew where his stumps were and he realized he would not be given out under the existing LBW rule – but this technique was soon imitated by lesser players. Soon we had the unedifying sight of average batsmen kicking away the spin with their pads, while making little or no attempt to play the ball with the bat. Tom Graveney watched this change in defensive techniques with horror: 'It was very unfair to the spinner. The bat's for hitting the ball, not for hiding behind the pad. I first noticed Colin using this method against the Australians in 1956, when he padded away the off-spin of Ian Johnson. I'll never forget Johnson appealing – 'How's that, ump? Pad first!', all to no avail. It worked for Colin, but too many copied him.'

150

Today the average English batsman clings to the same pad/bat technique. Fine players like Dennis Amiss use the pad as a second line of defence if the ball is turning, but in most cases the front foot goes down the wicket automatically. Glenn Turner has noticed how many English players hide behind their front pad; 'They get too tied up with their pads, tending to double-check as if each delivery has something vicious up its sleeve. The young players in particular don't seem to have the confidence to play the ball.'

Could this be because the young English players see little enough of spin on their way up to the first-class game? When they come up against Pocock or Underwood on a rare turning wicket, they just rely on pushing forward. Norman Gifford has spent hours in the nets with Worcestershire's two promising young batsmen, Phil Neale and Dipak Patel, trying to hone up their defensive technique against spin. 'They play at the ball very early, probably because they're so used to pace. I will bowl at them in the nets and occasionally hang onto the ball – they'd be lunging forward and I hadn't released the ball. They play the *reputation* of the spin bowler, rather than the delivery. Too many young lads lunge forward, rather than wait to see the ball in the air before committing themselves.'

Gloucestershire's young batsmen looked vulnerable against experienced spinners in the 1981 season and the secretary, Tony Brown, asked John Mortimore to come into the dressing-room and advise them how to play an off-spinner. After Mortimore had recovered from the amazement of being told by a regular first-team batsman that he always played a spinner *off* the pitch and never watched the ball from the hand, he proceeded to give a masterly exposition of commonsense. He told them to work out where they were going to score their runs *before* they went to the crease, that there was no point in expecting to pick up easy runs against experienced slow bowlers without a plan. It was noticeable how much young players like Phil Bainbridge and Chris Broad improved against spin for the remainder of the season.

By common consent, Keith Fletcher is the best English player of spin bowling still in the game. He considers it 'batting suicide' to lunge forward to the spinners: 'Everyone seems to be coached to play forward these days. This may sound obvious but batting is simply a matter of playing forward and back to the right balls. I play back a lot to the off-spinner, so I can watch the ball a little bit longer and I'll also use my feet to go forward if necessary. I stay at home for the slow

151

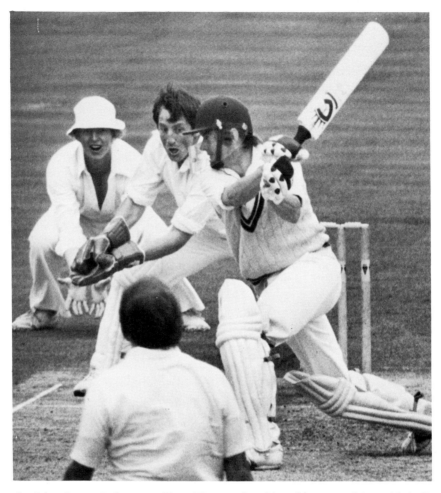

A wicket-keeper's dream – Glenn Turner gives himself room to hit a wide ball outside off-stump and is left stranded as Geoff Humpage whips off the bails

left-armer, in case he beats me on the outside edge and I may get stumped. It never bothers me about playing and missing, I've done it too often. I'm very lucky in one respect – we have two good spinners in Ray East and David Acfield on our books and I get a lot of practice in the nets against them.'

Ted Dexter's batting method against slow bowling was equally simple and sensible: 'The art is picking the length. You have to be able to play back and still attack the ball. I always wanted to hit the spinners over the top, because I could never see the point in hanging

around for half an hour to get a little nick onto the pad and be caught at short leg for eight. It's such a grisly death, isn't it? Make the captain change his field – get rid of those close fielders with your bat, not by boring them to sleep.'

Glenn Turner has evolved his own way of playing the spinners during his decade in English cricket. Turner's defence was always sound in his early days, but he had to come to terms with the need to keep the score ticking along. He is expert at rolling his wrists to turn a ball off the face of the bat through the close fielders; he chips the ball

153

skilfully over the inner ring, so that the fielder has to turn and chase while Turner picks up two runs; and his flat-bat slash square on the off-side to the slow left-armer has brought him many runs. 'That's a percentage shot to a ball that's wide. If you hit it powerfully, it'll go through the field for four and if you nick it, there's a reasonable chance that slip will drop it because it's going so fast.'

On a turning wicket to an off-spinner, he disciplines himself to playing through the on-side, unless he gets a full toss or half volley. 'I try to get down the wicket to play it away for a single, and if the bowler's seen that, he may drag the ball down and I can cut it away through the off-side. The secret is to know where your off-stump is, and when to play the good length ball defensively. I tend to play that one half-forward, stand up and watch it; that gives me a fraction of a second longer to adjust. If your body weight is coming forward later than normal, you're not able to absorb the impact of the ball on your bat and kill it.'

In recent years the sweep shot seems to have expired peacefully.

One method of playing the sweep shot, by Derek Randall; conception and execution from an original idea by Rohan Kanhai

David Gower falls prey to the catch at bat/pad position off the bowling of Ray Bright, Edgbaston 1981

Hardly one English batsman plays the sweep shot correctly, with the bat coming *over and down* rather than being swung across the line. The front leg bends if the bat is swung across, that takes away the pad as a second line of defence which invariably means the batsman is bowled round his legs – a fate that befell Peter Willey and Mike Gatting against the slow left-arm of Ray Bright in the Edgbaston Test of 1981. Alan Knott plays the sweep shot well, playing to the *length* rather than the line, and avoiding getting a glove to the ball if it pops. Few others master the sweep in the manner of a Compton, admittedly a genius, although Don Wilson points out how sound Compton's technique was: 'If you bowled on or outside leg stump, Denis would sweep you, but if it pitched outside off-stump, it would be the cover drive, not a sweep across the line.'

Most modern batsmen take the view that the sweep is not worth the risk. Glenn Turner: 'It usually only means a single and I can get one elsewhere with less risk, using the full face of the bat.' Quite a contrast to the style of Mike Smith, a terror of off-spin in his prime. Smith swept a lot because he felt it was important to disrupt a bowler's line. 'I'd often make a slow left-armer bowl with four men on the leg-side

155

Emburey bowls to Martin Kent at the Old Trafford Test, 1981, with the rare sight of seven fielders round the bat

rather than three, so then I could pick gaps on the off. I was stronger on the on-side anyway, and although it looked unorthodox to sweep from outside the off-stump, the method broadly worked. In simple terms the objective is to hit the ball away from a fielder and it doesn't really matter where you hit it as long as you get away with it consistently.' One other factor was in Smith's favour – the limitation of fielders to five on the leg-side. Before, an off-spinner would often have seven fielders on the leg when the ball was turning into the right-hander. By the end of the 1950s, he had lost one of his short legs, possibly deep mid-wicket and a man out for the slog. Fine players like Mike Smith licked their lips and picked the spots, while off-spinners such as 'Bomber' Wells moaned about the injustice of it all: 'It was the biggest single factor to destroy the off-spinner's influence. It enabled the lesser players to have a slog, so captains simply brought on the military-medium seamer, who'd bowl short of a length to five men on the leg side. And to think the rule was brought in to nullify the medium-pacers doing just that.'

Most current Test batsmen see the spinner as a dangerously relaxing bowler. Graham Gooch admits: 'I get out to them a lot because I play my shots too soon. You can't help relaxing a little when it's just a case of batting rather than getting hit by bouncers.' David Gower: 'It's such a different kind of contest and it's so easy to lose concentration; for example Viv Richards bowled me in the Barbados Test when I was well set.'

Tom Graveney was always fascinated by the moment when you had to take risks to break up the spinner's rhythm in a Test Match. 'Richie Benaud was a wonderfully accurate leg-spinner and now and then you just had to take a chance, like hitting him on the up through the covers or sweeping him.' He remembers his innings of 151 against the Indians at Lord's in 1967. 'Bishen Bedi tied me down with some beautiful bowling. I just couldn't get him through the covers. I made up my mind that I was going to hit him over square leg if he bowled wide enough outside off-stump. I managed to hit him for six, it messed up his line a little and things were easier after that.'

Peter May reckons a spinner often dismissed him when well set:

A fine photograph of the unlucky batsman's feet behind the crease but off the ground. Dick Spooner, the Warwickshire wicket-keeper here, had 73 victims in the 1951 season

'I'd get used to the fast stuff and then there was a change in the diet. After facing a few quick bowlers, I had to re-think my batting and play differently. Because of the change in pace, I would sometimes get myself out. Modern captains should remember that when they go into a match with bowlers of similar speed.'

Alan Jones, the veteran Glamorgan opener, is one of the few non-overseas batsmen who use their feet consistently to the spinners, a method that has served him well over the years. 'I know that if I stay in the crease on a turner, they'll do me with the bat/pad catch, so I try to stop them bowling on a length. I've been stumped a lot but rarely caught at bat/pad! When the spinners come on, I really have to steel myself to concentrate. They can do you so easily on the change of pace – John Emburey once bowled me with his first ball after I'd been bounced a lot by Wayne Daniel. I felt a sense of relief when Daniel came off and I was bowled on the back foot. But that's the fascination of batting against spin bowling.'

A fascination that is a rarer experience than the days of 1955 when Alan Jones joined the Glamorgan staff and cut his teeth on bowlers like Tom Goddard in the second team. Colin Cowdrey found a musical analogy to describe the dwindling appeal of batting today: 'If you play against seamers all day long, it's like asking Yehudi Menuhin to play the same set of routines on his violin. Eventually he would throw his violin into the fire.'

# 7. Keeping Against Spin

'It's just a better game for the 'keeper when the spinners are on. There's more action, more concentration needed and more brains involved. I just feel like a first slip with pads on when I'm standing back.' The speaker is one of the few surviving embodiments of the all-round wicket-keeper left in the modern English game – Bob Taylor of Derbyshire and England. His assessment of the attributes needed to stand back from the stumps are characteristically modest – nobody would deny the demands of athleticism, nerve and swiftness of reaction needed to keep to quick bowlers – but can anyone who respects the art of wicket-keeping disagree with Taylor? It is significant that the best two wicket-keepers left in English first-class cricket are men who learned their trade in a different era – Taylor and Alan Knott. An era when the slow bowler would be on before lunch in a county championship game, when a legside stumping was a commonplace and the demands of limited-over cricket were yet to transform most of our spinners into defensive bowlers with sights set firmly on the leg stump. The one-day game has spawned a breed of athletic 'stoppers' with the agility and fitness to cover the denuded slip area while still being able to tumble down the legside for the loose delivery by the seamer. All very admirable, and, within the context of most cricket matches, that is all one asks of the modern wicket-keeper. You are only as good a performer as the structure of the game requires. Yet there is something wrong with a game when you consider that the last Englishman to be stumped in a Test Match in England was in August 1979, when Ian Botham's welcome aggression was ensnared by the wiles of Venkat, the Indian captain and off-spinner. In two entire series (England/West Indies and England/Australia) the square leg umpire never needed to raise his finger to confirm the presence of the cricketing equivalent of an eclipse.

The decline in Test stumpings in England has been consistent over the last decade. A total of 59 Tests have been played since Edgbaston 1971 through to the Oval 1981 – and a grand total of twelve

159

stumpings have been achieved. Only six wicket-keepers have succeeded – Knott, Taylor and Bairstow (England), Marsh (Australia) and
Engineer and Reddy (both India). Indeed the last time a wicket-keeper
from each side managed a stumping in the same series was the one
against India in 1971, coincidentally the last series to be decided by
spin bowling in England.

If ever confirmation was needed of the continuing irrelevance of
the slow bowler in the eyes of modern Test captains, the paucity of
stumpings provides it. The swift strike as the slow left-armer deliberately sends one down the legside with extra pace; the batsman using
his feet to drive who finds out that the ball has pitched in the rough to
beat him on the outside; and most difficult of all, the off break that the
wicket-keeper loses for a split second as it passes between the batsman
and his body. Conception and execution – the essence of that unique
empathy between slow bowler and wicket-keeper. An intuitive partnership that is now as relevant to Test cricket as the lob bowler.

In county cricket, the fingers of one hand can accommodate the
wicket-keepers who can rely on match practice to hone their all-round
skills. One is Andy Brassington of Gloucestershire – he is doubly lucky
in that he comes from the same part of Staffordshire as Bob Taylor and
had been coached by him for long periods, and also because his
county's spinners bowl more overs than most. In his short career, he
has kept regularly to a couple of left-handers – the classical skills of
John Childs, the flatter trajectory of David Graveney, plus the high
slow off-spin of Mike Procter and the optimistic yet underrated leg
spin of Sadiq Mohammad. As a result, Brassington looks like a throwback to the days when wicket-keepers did more than leap around like
salmon for the bouncer or make up for their inadequacies with a
thousand runs a season with the bat. Brassington relishes standing up
to the spinners: 'It's what I want all the time, it makes me concentrate
so much more. When the seamers are on, I switch off as they trudge back
and sometimes it's a real effort to screw up my concentration again'.

He is aware that stumpings are now almost a collector's item: 'I
always claim them before a catch. If there's any doubt, I go over to the
scorer's tent and tell them I stumped the batsman. As far as I'm
concerned, stumpings are one of the real tests of a keeper's ability.' If
he ever gets anywhere near the stumps, that is – and Brassington
worries about the modern trend: 'I don't think my education will be
anywhere near completion unless I stand up even more to the spinners,
but I'm luckier than most county keepers these days. I really feel for

the lads who go game after game standing back, then they find themselves on a turning wicket and they have to attune themselves to spin. That's hard enough as it is for me, although it's enjoyable and fascinating – but you have to get the chance to practise the particular type of skills needed.'

Those sentiments must make Les Ames delighted he played his cricket generations ago. If ever a current wicket-keeper wanted to know about the fun of keeping to slow bowling, he should sit down with Ames for a spell of reminiscence mercifully free from hyperbole, cant and bias. At 75, his cheerful presence at the Canterbury ground every match day is a welcome reminder that he still keeps in touch with the modern game – but also of the days when he would stand up all day to the leg-breaks of 'Tich' Freeman or Doug Wright. It is perhaps easy to forget that Les Ames was a good enough batsman to score over a hundred centuries, but his wicket-keeping is the more graphic example of the radical change that cricket has undergone. In 1932, he garnered 62 stumpings. In his career, more than a third of his 1,113 victims were stumpings – 'st. Ames b. Freeman' was as commonplace a dismissal as 'c. Marsh b. Lillee' is today.

'I loved keeping to the leg-spinners because there was always something happening,' he says. 'Tich and Doug were so different. Tich had accuracy, flight and was the best top spinner I've ever seen. Doug was very sharp indeed: he'd have you taking the ball up by your shoulder and because he spun it so much, so quickly, you really had to look out.' Like all great partnerships, the understanding was an instinctive one. 'If I'd been a batsman from another county who didn't keep wicket, I would never have known when Doug was going to bowl his googly. But with him and little Tich I somehow knew when it was coming. Tich would usually save it for the later batsmen while Doug's would often come after his quicker ball, but there was no set pattern.'

As Secretary/Manager of the successful Kent side of a decade ago, Les Ames considered it his duty to understand and sympathize with the trends of the modern game. He is realistic and unsentimental, yet for all that remains glad that he kept wicket when he did: 'Today, eighty per cent of the keeper's toil involves standing back. You don't have to be a great one to stand back all day to fast bowlers, you know. When the spinners came on in my day, I was doubly glad – it meant the fast bowlers wouldn't be knocking my hands about for a few hours, and I could then pit my wits against the batsman. The game suddenly became more absorbing.'

Les Ames' successor behind the stumps for Kent and England, Godfrey Evans, echoes this view: 'Anyone can catch them, but not many are good enough these days to stump them. They just don't get regular work up at the wicket.' An Evans stumping always seemed a pyrotechnic affair, compared to the diffident command of an Oldfield, an Andrew or a Taylor. Such masters would flick off a bail almost apologetically, inquiring politely of the square leg umpire if the batsman was out. With Evans, the stumps would be assaulted in a blur of arms and the exultant roar from Evans would be an affirmation of the dismissal, conviction rather than hope. Evans was the Liberace of wicket-keeping, and although the showman sometimes failed to deliver his best away from the glamour of the Test arena, nevertheless his flair for the big occasion brilliantly complemented his natural skills. For more than a decade, Evans dealt with a dazzling array of English slow bowlers – the spectacular leg-breaks of his county colleague Doug Wright, the more circumspect Eric Hollies, the off-breaks of Roy Tattersall and Jim Laker, the devastating left-arm changes of pace by Tony Lock and the talented Johnny Wardle's orthodox slow left-arm, supplemented by his chinaman and googly. A total of 46 stumpings underlines both Evans's expertise and the sheer quality and quantity of the England slow bowling in the 1950s. Evans unashamedly relished the persona of the extrovert: 'My aim was always to make my presence felt with the batsman. I always tried to be fair, but I saw nothing wrong in clearing my throat, stage-managing a little cough or a wisecrack while the bowler was walking back to his mark – that way I was letting the batsman know that if he lifted his foot outside a certain area, he was done for. I used to feel that if a man was caught at slip off a spin bowler, that was as much my catch, because I'd cramped the batter, sown seeds of doubt in his mind.

It was wonderful to stand up to someone like Jim Laker, to see that lovely looping flight and know that it was going to undo the batsman. I could tell that he wasn't going to get quite to the pitch of the ball and that he would be caught at short leg. It was exciting, engrossing. I really feel sorry for today's 'keepers.'

When Godfrey Evans retired in 1959, Alan Knott was already consolidating the progress that took him to the place previously occupied by Evans – in the Kent and England team. At the age of thirteen, Knott would attend the Eltham Cricket School, where the avuncular yet shrewd eyes of Les Ames picked out a natural cricketer.

Godfrey Evans, of Kent and England
– a keeper good enough to fathom
the wiles of spinners like Laker,
Lock, Wright, Hollies, Wardle
and Tattersall during his illustrious
career

Yet at that time, Knott bowled leg-breaks and off-spin at the indoor school; there was no room for him to keep wicket and Ames was astonished to be told by Knott that he was also a wicket-keeper. 'He was full of cricket even then', recalls Ames, 'I thought he was an all-rounder, so you can imagine my surprise when I next saw him keeping wicket for Kent School at Canterbury.' So the amazing chain of great Kent wicket-keepers was maintained; yet the wonderful skills of Alan Knott only serve to reaffirm the decline of slow bowling during his great Test career.

From 1967 until his defection to World Series Cricket in 1977, Knott was England's first-choice wicket-keeper, an acknowledged master of all the arts. Yet from a tally of 269 Test dismissals, only 19 of them were stumpings. Knott accepts he has been a product of his age and considers that his best years for England were between 1966–73, when he stood up to slow bowlers like Gifford, Underwood, Pocock, Birkenshaw, Illingworth and Hobbs. At that time with Kent, he would often be standing up at both ends after just half an hour's play – to Underwood and the off-spin of Alan Dixon. 'During that period, I felt

I was a true all-round 'keeper. I was using all the skills in the middle. Practice is all very well, but it's not easy when suddenly you have to do it out of the blue in a match and you know that you're rusty at keeping to slow bowling. Your body gets out of the habit of standing up to the stumps, you can forget the basic principles like getting the knees out of the way when you want to take the ball and remembering not to panic in the rare event of a possible stumping.'

Knott accepts that his career ratio of stumpings to catches (1:11) compares unfavourably with Evans (1:4) and Ames. He acknowledges that it would have been wonderful to stand up to Doug Wright or 'Tich' Freeman season after season, but sees little point in dwelling on an age where any class batsman would use his feet and most tail-enders would increase the prospect of stumpings by trying to slog. Knott maintains: 'All sports have got more professional and cricket is no different. We put in more effort now and as a result, the entertainment value decreases. I believe that all modern batsman prefer to play spin rather than four quick bowlers. That feeling comes down from Test level to the county scene and that's why spinners are going out of the game, I'm afraid. That trend will not be reversed until the wickets become browner, dryer and flatter. Until that happens, England's priority will be to find eight Michael Holdings, rather than class slow bowlers.'

While Alan Knott expects the all-round demands on the wicket-keeper to decrease, one of the greatest exponents of the art takes a more sanguine view. Keith Andrew adorned the Northants side for fifteen years and only the brilliance of Godfrey Evans restricted him to a couple of England caps. Season after season, Andrew was the acknowledged master-keeper in county cricket on all wickets. That same professionalism that made him such an effortless performer behind the stumps is now being channelled into his job with the National Cricket Association. He is director of coaching and from his office at Lord's, Andrew is responsible for the daily running of the Cricket Council's coaching schemes. He sees many talented spinners coming through between the ages of thirteen and sixteen, but they tend to disappear once they go into club cricket. 'That's when the overs limitation gets to the young spinner and he has to keep it tight and compromise a lot of principles we've tried to pass on to him. The main problem is hanging on to this promising array of young slow bowling talent as they get older. Make no mistake, they are around, but the modern game needs a slight restructuring to accommodate him.'

One hopes that the young spinners under Andrew's caring tutelage take the time to talk to him about their relationship with wicket-keepers. No one associated with the game is better qualified to expound on the joys of a partnership with an intelligent, attacking spinner. In Andrew's case, it was the Australian George Tribe, that high-class slow-left arm bowler of chinamen and googlies. Tribe and Andrew were a team, an extension of each other, and Andrew's ratio of stumpings to catches (1:5) reveals what a successful partnership they were. 'I used to spend a lot of time with George', recalls Andrew. 'I had a film made of him in the nets so I could study his technique. Every day before play started, we would go out onto the ground and examine the end George would operate from. We'd talk over the conditions, discuss the light and the opposition batsmen. As far as I was concerned, getting to know the man was getting to know the bowler.'

To Andrew, the art of slow bowling is to make batsman play

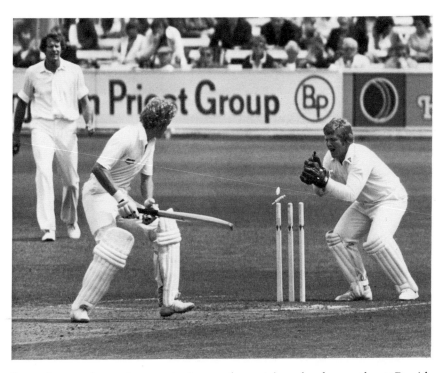

Stumpings are becoming a rarity in top-class cricket – but here, at least, David Gower's wicket falls to David Humphries off the bowling of Norman Gifford

forward, thereby increasing the chance of a stumping. 'George Tribe was a master at getting them playing across the line off the front foot. He gave them little time to adjust on the back foot. It sounds conceited, I know, but it was wonderful to be part of an understanding that threatened the batsman. Very often, he was tied to his crease when he shouldn't have been, but our combined pressure made him unsure of himself.'

Andrew and Tribe; Knott and Underwood; Ames and Freeman. Even these great parnerships pale in comparison with the uncanny understanding between Fred Titmus and his Middlesex colleague, John Murray. Warwickshire's David Brown, who played with and against them for many years, says: 'Their sixth sense was uncanny, an art form in itself. Murray always knew where Fred was going to bowl it.' Glenn Turner, Worcestershire's great batsman says he always knew when Titmus had bowled the 'arm' ball, the one that trapped umpteen batsmen LBW: 'As soon as he'd let it go, JT would have his arm up, ready with the appeal if I missed it. I don't know how he managed to spot it so early.'

Murray modestly plays it down: 'I was lucky, I played with a great slow bowler every day of my career, but Fred didn't give the ball all that much width. He bowled straight and we knew where the batsman's pads were, so we had a good idea about LBWs.' The Murray/Titmus combination flourished for twenty years with the elegant Murray responding effortlessly to Titmus's ceaseless probing and subtle variations in flight. The batsman may have thought that a ball pitching around middle stump was an ordinary off-break, yet there was that late drift in the air away from the bat – and there was Murray, perfectly positioned with his left leg in line with off-stump, waiting for the ball to take the edge of the bat or nick the off-bail. Such empathy was the product of hard work. Recalls Murray, 'Even when Fred was an established Test player, I'd get him in the nets and tell him what he was doing wrong. If he was bowling badly, he was being cut to the boundary; his arm would get a little lower and I'd do my sergeant-major bit and remind him of the basics. For a slow bowler, it's important to realise that the margin of error is just a few inches. To bowl at middle-and-off from 22 yards takes hard work and great skill and I'd point out to Fred that off-breaks on leg stump was a case of bad bowling.'

Murray initially kept to Titmus in the first team just two years after taking up wicket-keeping. 'It took me five full years in county cricket before I could even claim to be competent at standing up to Fred. I loved the challenge that slow bowling brought to the game – as a batsman, wicket-keeper and even as a spectator. I well remember my early days in the side when Denis Compton's battles with the great spinners were so entertaining. When he walked out to face someone like Bruce Dooland, we'd all make a point of watching, we'd think "this is going to be fun". And believe me, it always was.'

For Murray, one of the fascinations about keeping to Titmus came when the batsman somehow survived after being outwitted. 'Fred might turn a bloke inside out with an off-break when he was expecting the away floater. He'd be in a sort of French cricket position and just manage to get a bat on it. Fred and I would exchange a little grin, the batsman would do the same, the umpire at Fred's end would enjoy it too. We'd all enjoy the moment, even though it was a "dot" ball and perhaps to the spectators, a fairly mundane incident. But to those of us out there in the middle, the sheer enjoyment of such a battle was huge.'

Murray is too much of a gentleman to admit it, but he remains envious of Jim Parks's prolonged run in the England team as wicket-keeper to Titmus. Parks was the better batsman in an era that was becoming increasingly seam-orientated. So Murray had to content himself with a handful of appearances for England at the same time as his great friend. He would have been thrilled to establish an England partnership with Titmus that rivalled that of Knott and Underwood at both county and Test level, but Murray is a philosophical man. He is also a man of principle who was sufficiently worried about the decline in wicket-keeping standards to resign as England selector in protest at the selection of Roger Tolchard for the 1978–9 tour of Australia. Murray makes it quite clear that his assessment of Tolchard's abilities was not clouded by any personal animosities; he admired the Leicestershire man's combative skills, especially in one-day cricket. 'I just felt that the best two 'keepers pure and simple should have been picked. Bob Taylor, of course, was the best and I wanted Paul Downton. But Mike Brearley said he wished to consider every single member of the tour party for each Test, so Tolchard's utility qualities were decisive. I felt very unhappy about that. I believed – and still do – that the best 'keeper should be selected, whether or not he can bat.'

He is happy about the emerging talents of Surrey's Jack Richards and the evergreen skills of Bob Taylor – 'but there's only a handful of top-class keepers, the ones who look equally good standing up or back. Slow bowling and wicket-keeping are declining together; I've seen it happen in my career and now the seamer is the dominant influence. We must do something to reverse the trend.'

As John Murray admits, he was lucky to be associated with a great slow bowler for twenty years. Some wicket-keepers have a tantalising taste of the cup of quality, only to have it dashed from their lips after a maddeningly brief period. George Sharp of Northants is an example; he kept to the great Bishen Bedi for four full seasons before the Indian was sacked in 1977. That period remains for Sharp the greatest thrill of his professional career, the highlight being the 1973 season. That year Bedi's classical slow left-arm bowling and the leg-breaks of Mushtaq Mohammad picked up almost 150 wickets for Northants and a third of Sharp's victims were stumpings – the nearest to the Les Ames ratio in modern times. 'When those two were rolling them over, I really had to concentrate all the time', says Sharp. 'Apart from Mushy's googly, the ball would be leaving the right-hander so I had to get every ball. I was only 22 and they were both great to me – terrific if I missed a stumping and genuine encouragers.'

He became more and more confident and soon he was approaching that instinctive understanding achieved by the likes of Murray and Titmus. 'I got to the stage when I knew when Bish was going to bowl the orthodox one to leave the bat, or the "arm" ball that would come in to the right-hander. Mushy, on the other hand, had two googlies – one that he almost threw to the moon which a schoolboy could pick and another one that he rarely showed, which was good enough on its day for any class batsman. Eventually I could tell by his approach to the wicket which ball it would be. Luckily, the batsmen weren't so used to him and I was kept busy.'

George Sharp is both lucky and unfortunate. Unlike most modern county wicket-keepers, he has had experience of keeping to a couple of slow bowling artists at the same time. He still talks about those days with unaffected pride and relish, and yet he is too conscientious a professional to admit making comparisons with the current off-spinners in the Northants side, Richard Williams and Peter Willey, both of whom are predominantly batsmen. George Sharp will continue to keep wicket for Northants with his usual dedication and soundness, yet it is only when he talks about Bedi and Mushtaq that one realizes how much he gained, then lost.

# 8. Spin in Limited-Over Cricket

'In one-day cricket the onus is on the batsman – that favours the bowler and the faster he is, the less time a batsman has to get at him' – M. J. K. Smith.

'People tell me I wouldn't get to play in the one-day game but I think if you can bowl, you can do so in any type of cricket' – Richie Benaud.

The two opinions summarize the conflicting views of the efficiency of spin in limited-over cricket. There is no doubt that the cause of the slow bowler has been hampered since the one-day game began in 1963. Traditionally, the aim of slow bowling has been to bowl sides out, a philosophy epitomized by immortals from Blythe and Rhodes, through to Laker. In recent years, slow bowlers have needed to adapt to the exigencies of one-day cricket – those who survived have digested the painful lesson that the skill is in keeping the runs down, not in dissmissing a batsman by the classic virtues of flight, guile and pronounced spin. Spinners sacrificed their innate gifts in favour of firing the ball in on the leg-stump or following the batsmen's feet to stop him scoring easily. Genuine flight and turn is a rarity when overs are limited and the result is a negation of the slow bowler's art.

It makes like difficult for the spinner. A typical week's cricket might involve a county match on a Saturday, John Player League commitments the next day, followed by two more days of county cricket and on the Wednesday, a Nat-West Cup game. He will be expected to perform like an authentic spin bowler on the Saturday, Monday and Tuesday, while for eight overs on Sunday and for twelve overs on Wednesday, he must bowl flat at nearly medium pace. His art is difficult enough to develop in today's pragmatic cricketing age without the problems of adjusting his line and length from day to day. In Geoff Boycott's opinion, one-day cricket has ruined spin bowling: 'I've seen spinners run in and bowl leg-stump yorkers quicker than I can bowl medium pace. That's merely bowling to a plan designed to stop batsmen scoring. It's an art in a way, but it's not spinning.'

The conventional wisdom is that seam bowling short of a length is the correct attack for one-day cricket. Thus a moderate, inexperienced slow bowler has no chance of playing, while seam bowlers of similar mediocrity proliferate. Most captains feel safer with a full hand of seamers, even if they have to operate from reduced run-ups in the Sunday League. Two captains greatly influenced this attitude, simply by being successful. Mike Smith and Ted Dexter sorted out the technique of bowling in one-day cricket far quicker than other captains when the Gillette Cup was launched in 1963. While other sides played as if it was a truncated form of the county championship, both Warwickshire and Sussex defended their totals with fielders strung around the boundary and seamers tying down opposition batsmen. Geoff Boycott remembers how long it took Yorkshire to come to terms with the new game: 'Brian Close said no one would hit us for more than three an over and we kept on attacking with two short legs for Wilson and Illingworth. Then you had people like Jim Parks hitting our seamers over cover for six. We were the best side in the championship, yet poor at the one-day game.'

Both Dexter and Smith point out that the strength of their out-cricket at that time was based on seam bowling. They say they would have played class spinners if they were on their books. Smith asserts that all sides today imitate Warwickshire and Sussex of 1963–4 in the field and nobody criticizes modern captains for being as defensively-minded as Dexter and himself. As such, seam is more sensible and valuable in the one-day game.

Not surprisingly the good slow bowlers vehemently disagree. They say that a man who knows his craft can control one side of the pitch and frustrate batsmen; they generally agree that flight has to be sacrificed but intelligence is not jettisoned. John Emburey tries to stop a batsman driving him: 'I want to get them on the back foot, playing me away to mid-wicket. Apart from the speed of Wayne Daniel, Phil Edmonds and I are the most successful one-day bowlers for Middlesex. We often tighten things up when the seamers have been slogged.' Richie Benaud feels it is far too glib to assume that his leg-spin would be a luxury in the limited-overs context. From his position in the BBC TV commentary box, he sees many such games and his keen tactical eye can sum up a slow bowler's worth, without sentiment or partiality. 'I wouldn't alter my basic technique, only my field placing. Not many players used to get down the wicket to me anyway, so I wouldn't worry about that. Flippers, top-spinners and googlies are dangerous balls in any form of cricket. If you've got any brains, if you can spin the ball or flight it, I don't feel that it matters what type of cricket you play in – if the batsman has to slog, the bowler has an advantage.'

Don Wilson believes flight can be deadly when the batsmen are thrashing around. He cites no less an authority than Viv Richards. 'Viv told me that he found it a little tricky when the ball goes above eye level because he then has to make two decisions: to look up, then down again to get the length. When the spinners just fire it in, it's easy for a bloke like Viv because he judges the length so quickly.'

Norman Gifford is a quintessentially modern spin bowler in limited-over cricket. Unlike most of his breed, he thrives on it; he relishes the competitive edge involved in stopping a batsman from scoring runs and believes he would have retired a long time ago without such a regular stimulus. 'The great players can take any bowler apart, but a spinner can be invaluable when his line is good and the average batsman can't get him away. If one of those is trying to hit me through the offside, I'll follow him down legside and frustrate him. It's all a matter of bowling the right length at the right time. And for the last few overs, the right place is in the blockhole.'

David Graveney is a disciple of the Gifford style of bowling in limited-over games. He lacks the flight ability of his Gloucestershire team-mate, John Childs, and concentrates on leg-stump line. As captain of his county, he realizes that the crucial matter is when to bring on the spinner – 'ideally it's when two new batsmen are in. At the start, a new batsman is looking for ones and twos, rather than big, booming drives and if a spinner can get into a groove, he can whistle through his allotted overs and the pressure will get to the batters.'

The successful spinners have one main advantage in this form of cricket: the pace of the ball. A seamer can be played away easily off the edge of the bat and the speed of delivery will take the ball to the boundary if it eludes the fielder. With a spinner, the batsman has to force the pace; a little nick goes for one or two, no more. As Norman Gifford says: 'if a spinner is bowling properly, the batsman has to start taking risks because he can't play it away so calmly for boundaries. He'll start hitting the ball in the air and, all things being equal, the ball should be going near the fielders if the line is right.' David Brown agrees with Gifford: 'We all dread that part of the game where we have to make the play when the spinners are on. We can't rely on the pace of the ball anymore and our batsman have to take so many risks to get at them.'

The facts support the spinner's view that they are economical in limited-over cricket. Over the last three English seasons, only fast and fast-medium bowlers have gone for less runs per over than the left-arm spinner and the off-break bowler; the difference between the three types is minimal, but the medium-pacer is comfortably in fourth place. (See Appendix C). So the medium-pacer is a more expensive proposition than the spinner, yet the latter remains the bowler under threat.

So many games can be dragged up from the past to justify the view that spin can greatly influence a limited-over match. In 1979, Majid Khan's allegedly gentle off-spin accounted for Boycott, Gower and Botham in the Prudential World Cup quarter-final, and in the semi-final on a perfect Oval pitch against the powerful West Indies batsmen his figures were 0 for 26 off 12 overs while illustrious seamer like Sarfraz and Imran were hammered for six an over. I remember how Giles Cheatle tied down Viv Richards in the Sussex–Somerset Gillette Cup Final of 1978. Cheatle admittedly bowled flat on the leg-stump, but he so frustrated Richards that the great man fretted and fell to Barclay's off-spin at the other end. Sussex won the Final.

Keith Fletcher is still cursing himself that for once, he did not use Ray East in the Benson and Hedges Final of 1980. East did not bowl one over and Acfield was not selected. The all-seam attack of Essex was plundered by Allan Lamb in the Northants innings and then the off-spin of Peter Willey and Richard Williams teased out Gooch and McEwan when Essex batted. The ball turned and Fletcher admits he made a miscalculation: 'We thought the wicket would get flatter and flatter but it didn't. I almost brought Ray on about four times but Keith Pont kept getting a wicket and he stayed on. Eventually we ran out of overs.' Yet surely Northants deserved their victory because they played a balanced attack of three seamers and two spinners?

Anyone who believes the spinner is invariably thrashed out of sight should listen to Tom Graveney. In 1949, he was on the receiving end of a county championship record of consecutive scoreless deliveries from the spinner Horace Hazell of Somerset, who bowled slow left-arm with a canny relish. He sent down 105 balls in a row that yielded no run from the bat, and Tom Graveney faced most of them. 'In that spell, he bowled only a couple of loose ones. One I cracked hard and it hit Johnny Lawrence on the shin at gully. Apart from that, nothing. He was a wise old bird, with a little bit of swing and turn and the ball held up a bit. Don't tell me spinners can't keep a man quiet.' It should be pointed out, too, that the runner-up to Hazell is another slow left-armer, Don Wilson of Yorkshire – fifteen maidens in a row against Lancashire in 1969.

Despite overwhelming evidence on behalf of the spinner, some illustrious slow bowlers of the past feel the younger ones should be kept away from limited-over cricket. Ray Illingworth feels a young slow bowler has enough problems learning his trade today: 'An experienced one can cope with short boundaries and batsmen going for the slog. I don't want to see a good young spinner getting his line messed around from one day to the next. If he's good enough, he has a long career and it takes years to master his art.' Jim Laker remarks: 'I'd never play a young spinner in these slogging games. I'd have enjoyed it when I was about thirty, but not before. I feel sorry for the poor old spinner who has to pack up after eight, eleven or twelve overs just when he's getting into his rhythm. They introduced an overs limitation on individual bowlers because they were worried about killing off the art of spinning. So what do captains do? They play five seamers instead.'

Pleas for patience from master bowlers like Laker and Illingworth inevitably sit rather uneasily on the restless shoulders of inexperienced, promising slow bowlers like Nick Cook and John Childs. Leicestershire's Cook is a genuine prospect, yet his lot in the 1981 season was a regular place in the county games and rare appearances in limited-over matches. The day after he took 7 for 81 in a championship game, he found himself playing for the second team, while his county took on Northants in a Nat-West Cup tie. Cook finds it galling: 'It's wrong to assume I'd just bowl it faster in a one-day game. I'd simply bowl wide of the crease and aim on the leg-stump, rather than get close to the stumps and try to turn it away. I think I wouldn't need to alter my speed of delivery, so why would I get mucked up?' Gloucestershire's John Childs can commiserate: he lacks Cook's useful batting ability and quality as a fielder, and as a specialist, his place is invariable in danger for the one-day games. Yet in 1981, he took 1 for 4 off eleven overs in a Benson and Hedges match against Nottinghamshire, bowling beautifully at Rice, Randall and Birch. These strong players eventually blocked Childs and tried to score runs at the other end. It was a classical piece of slow bowling: the wicket turned a little, Childs pitched the ball up and invited the batsmen to call the tune. They failed. One would have thought that Childs had proved his point – yet he missed *10* of the 16 John Player League games. That fine slow-bowler, David Allen, finds it hard to believe: 'John Childs can bowl anywhere, at any time. I would only leave him out of Sunday matches if I felt it affected his bowling for the rest of the week, which it doesn't.'

Derek Underwood feels sorry for the young spinners who have to battle against entrenched attitudes towards one-day cricket. 'I learned my trade in the three-day game and I'm grateful for that. We have a fine young prospect in Kent called Lindsay Wood, but it's going to be a lot more difficult for him to develop into a left-arm spinner than it was for me. The game has changed so much and it's up to the spinner to adapt to the evolving scene. Stopping a batsman from scoring is a challenge, but it doesn't help the young slow bowler.'

That presents no problem to Dilip Doshi. The Indian left-arm spinner sums up his philosophy: 'runs are like oxygen to the batsman, you must cut off the supply'. He likes the battle of wits involved in keeping batsmen quiet – his main frustration during the 1981 season was in trying to get into the Warwickshire side for the one-day games. The previous season, his accuracy and experience had had much to do with his county's success in the John Player League but the pressure on the specialist slow bowler meant he was dropped in favour of Anton Ferreira. Revised regulations meant that only two overseas players could be selected and with Alvin Kallicharran's batting so invaluable, the choice was between Doshi's artistry and the all-round abilities of the South African, Anton Ferreira. Ferreira won – he would save a few runs in the field (Doshi could not), he could hit a fast thirty or so (Doshi could not), and bowl medium pace. With Warwickshire just missing out on the John Player title, the management policy could be said to have succeeded, yet they won it with Doshi's assistance in 1980. Moreover, poor Ferreira proved to be the most expensive bowler in all limited-over cricket in 1981. (See Appendix C).

Pat Pocock has managed to keep his place in the Surrey side by revising his technique for limited overs. A decade ago, he spent a winter in the nets learning how to bowl seamers; now, in the one-day games, he gets his head and shoulder pointing down the wicket, takes a shorter delivery stride and bowls open chested, so that his arm will be higher. He still spins the ball, which is a bonus. In the last five years, he has been the most economical bowler in the Surrey side in the one-day games. He says: 'The only reason why Derek Underwood and I are consistent in these games is that we bowl it fast. I don't hold the ball any differently – I bowl cutters more than anything. If the boundaries are big enough, I'll also bowl a ball that loops to tempt the batsman occasionally. In the one-day game, I look to take wickets by frustration, not the orthodox way.' For Pocock the essence of this type of bowling is to avoid being hit straight or across the line. In simple terms he is aiming either for the splice or the bottom of the bat; if he can extract bounce, that is even better, because he cannot be hit over his head.

To many fans of one-day cricket, 'Flat Jack' Simmons is the prime example of a spinner who bowls properly. Although Simmons can toss the ball up and even gets wickets occasionally with leg-breaks, he is fundamentally a mean, nagging bowler. The Simmons philosophy is simple and effective for the one-day game. For him, there are three principles:

You cannot defend two sides of the field; Concentrate for every ball; Bowl straight all the time.

Simmons sees the 'Flat Jack' nickname as a compliment; he admits he is a better bowler in limited overs than in the three-day game, where the more classical slow bowling facets are employed by the dwindling few. He was lucky that his career in the Northern League equipped him for one-day cricket; most of the League wickets were slow and he was used to firing the ball in at the blockhole. When the John Player League started in 1969, Lancashire adapted quicker than any other side; they had some brilliant fielders, fast-scoring batsmen, accurate seamers and in Jack Simmons, a man who baffled class batsmen by bowling yorkers every delivery. It took a few seasons before they worked him out – Barry Richards was the first to move back towards the legside and hit Simmons over the top of cover. In recent years, Simmons has varied his pace a little more, and he bowls short of a length sometimes. He thinks he is now a better bowler: 'I keep a diary in my head about the strengths of the great players. I never drop anything short to Gordon Greenidge; I'll go over and close to the wicket to bowl at men like Zaheer and Dennis Amiss who are so good at creaming you through the covers when the ball is going down legside.'

The most difficult batsman he has bowled at is Alan Knott: 'He's always fiddling away and getting you off line. He plays the lap shot well, his footwork is superb and his running between the wickets unbelievable.' For Simmons, getting a great player away from the

If you're going to appeal, make it a big one . . . Jack Simmons appeals successfully for LBW against M. J. K. Smith – not in a Championship game but in the 1972 Gillette Cup Final

strike is almost as vital as dismissing him. He remembers the occasion when Viv Richards nullified all his plans to keep him away from the bowling: 'I was bowling legstump yorkers at Viv, hoping to give him a single at the start of the over and keep the other fellow on strike for the remaining five balls. I bowled the right stuff, but Viv's so fast that he ran six two's in the over!'

If Simmons has prospered in this type of cricket, others have struggled to come to terms with the compromises needed. Ray East thinks it hampered his development: 'It's been the bugbear of my career. My action has been spoiled as I pack the legside on a Sunday and bowl flat, then try to cope with six fielders on the other side the following day. I lose rhythm and my arm gets loose.' Robin Hobbs is even more emphatic: 'I've never had any wish to play in the Sunday League, because of its negative aspect. It's not a proper game of cricket – how can a slow bowler bowl without close fielders?' Jack Birken-shaw considers it an affront to the purists who want variety in the game: 'You can watch the opening overs, go to sleep and then wake up for the last few overs and you've missed little of interest. It's so sad that many captains don't realize that a good spinner can whip through a few maiden overs while the new batsmen are settling – and the game looks better for that.'

Predictably, the old players feel the present breed of slow bowlers over-dramatize the effects of one-day cricket. Les Ames believes the leg-spin of 'Tich' Freeman would be devastating if he was pitched into the Sunday slog. 'He was a great bowler and they always bowl well, whatever the rules of the game. And he was so accurate and fast through the air when it suited him.' Johnny Wardle thinks that the ability to change the length of the delivery when the batsman has moved would be invaluable. 'Anyone who can sense what the batter's trying to do that little bit earlier has an advantage. And with all these marvellous fielders around, I'd have gone mad if I didn't get a bowl in the one-day stuff.' Sam Cook – who umpires in such games today – has no doubts that he would bowl the same way as in county cricket. 'I'd still pitch it outside off-stump and say "come and fetch it" to the batsmen. The ball that turns away from the bat is a good delivery.' Fred Titmus went through the whole gamut of bowling styles as he tried to come to terms with one-day cricket. 'In the end, I stayed with my usual style and was economical. It didn't muck me up for the longer games and I did what was needed.'

Perhaps the old-timers are being a little dogmatic. It may sound principle to keep to the same bowling style every day, but a captain will not be impressed by the sight of Viv Richards smashing slow off-spin through the covers. Ultimately it depends on the captain's tolerance and vision or how impressed he is by the factual proof that medium-pacers are more expensive than spinners in one-day cricket. Tunnel vision is not a rarity in county cricket.

# 9. Portents from the 1981 Season

A season that saw the departure of Robin Hobbs, Intikhab Alam, Dilip Doshi and Jack Birkenshaw could hardly be judged a vintage one for slow bowling. It was a vintage summer for cricket, thanks to a pulsating Test series against Australia, but from those Tests, there was little to comfort supporters of spin. Yet there were crumbs of comfort to be gleaned away from the Test arena.

The regular spinners bowled a greater number of overs in first-class cricket than in recent years. Norman Gifford bowled more than anyone and seven other spinners bowled more than the hardest-worked seamer, Richard Hadlee. Edmonds, Hemmings, Emburey, Underwood, Acfield and Childs all exceeded 70 wickets, demonstrating that ability and experience are invaluable assets whatever the speed of delivery.

The removal of the 100-overs restriction on first innings helped the slow bowler in 1981 – although the prospect of the second new ball after 85 overs cannot have helped. The introduction of covered wickets did not please Derek Underwood, even if he did bowl more than 200 overs than in 1980. We lost the fascination of watching batsmen struggling on rain-affected wickets against the spinners but, on the other hand, covered wickets seemed to indicate extra work for slow bowlers.

Nottinghamshire's championship win owed much to the off-spin of Eddie Hemmings. Rice and Hadlee were the sharp edge of their attack with splendidly incisive seam bowling, but Hemmings gave much-needed variety, bowling 250 overs more than Rice and nearly 50 ahead of Hadlee. The main ingredient in Hemmings' success at Trent Bridge was the wicket – it had bounce. It was usually very green, ideal conditions for Hadlee and Rice, but Hemmings proved the old adage that a good slow bowler can thrive on green wickets, provided there is some bounce. Says Hemmings, 'At Trent Bridge, if I manage to hit the top of the bat, the ball will carry to the close fielders. Quite a change from Edgbaston!!' The groundsman, Ron Allsop, admits to preparing pitches that encourage his county's three main bowlers and the manager Ken Taylor says the rationale was to make things happen in a match, to get positive results. Opposition batsmen may have resented such practices but there were no complaints from their spinners. John Emburey bowled Nottinghamshire to defeat at Trent Bridge in July and he thought it a good cricket wicket: 'It had bounce and the ball turned towards the end of the second day. I wish there were other wickets like Trent Bridge around the country.'

In the Ashes series of 1981, slow bowling took a back seat as a succession of unreliable pitches encouraged the seamers. Apart from the Oval, the wickets were generally unsatisfactory and although there was any amount of exciting cricket, the uniformity of the out-cricket was depressing. Australia refused to agree to a rate of 100 overs per day, even though England are fined if they do not reach 16.25 per hour. The tourists felt this was an unnecessary intrusion into the rules of the game and refused to budge. So the over rate hovered around the 14-an-hour mark and spin played a minor role until Emburey and Bright took important wickets in the Fourth Test at Edgbaston. At the start of the series, England bowled 187 consecutive overs of seam until Emburey's first over at Lord's – he proceeded to dismiss Kim Hughes first ball. Of 2,115 overs bowled in the six-Test series, 409 were by the spin of Emburey, Willey, Bright and Yallop. The antipathy towards spin in Tests was further underlined in September when the West Indies picked six fast bowlers for their tour to Australia and England selected just Emburey and Underwood for the trip to India. The England selectors admitted that they were gambling a little on the fitness of Emburey and Underwood, but recent experiences had shown that three slow bowlers were a luxury, pointing to the last Indian tour when Lever, Willis and Old took most of the wickets while at the same time ignoring that Underwood took more than anybody.

On the evidence of the Ashes series of 1981, slow bowling will struggle to recover any ground until the wickets alter in character and something punitive is done about over-rates. Away from the heady excitement of the Tests, slow bowlers concocted a subtler brew as the pitches dried out under the prolonged sunshine of July and August. At Canterbury in the Essex-Kent match, 35 of the 36 wickets to fall were taken by the spinners and it was absorbing to watch East, Acfield and Underwood ensnaring batsmen on a wicket that would only reward players with good footwork, a sound technique and the *nous* to hit a rare bad ball very hard indeed. The Sri Lankan tourists came to

England and showed a delightfully old-fashioned attitude to the game; they brought three high-class spinners with them, bowled their overs at nearly twenty an hour and, all in all, looked a refreshing addition to the ranks of Test-playing countries. Somachandra de Silva, a medium-pace leg-bowler à la Chandrasekhar, looked a superb bowler, surely the best of his type in the world. I saw him beat and bowl Wayne Larkins with a beautifully flighted leg-break at Trent Bridge in the game against a Test and County Cricket Board Eleven. De Silva was on as early as the seventeenth over and Mendis, Larkins, Love and Parker were all troubled by him. The Sri Lankans were reminiscent of the Indian side of a few years back, when men like Gavaskar and Solkar would open the bowling simply to get the shine off the ball and get the spinners on early. In 1981, such an attitude was a delightful antidote to the conformity of Test cricket and in every match against them, young county batsmen proved just how little they knew about playing top-class spin bowling that leaves the bat.

In September 1981, Surrey and Middlesex played a county match at Uxbridge that seemed to belong to a bygone age. In two-and-a-half days, over 1100 runs were scored on a hard, firm pitch that helped spin bowlers. Emburey and Edmonds took 15 wickets and Pocock and Intikhab 10 – out of 32 wickets to fall in the match. Pocock and Intikhab opened the bowling in the Middlesex first innings, and with their captain Roger Knight keeping faith in them, there was an air of challenge about the proceedings. Phil Edmonds enjoyed the match immensely: 'A magnificent wicket caused the ball to bounce. There was something in it for us *and* for the speed-of-light merchants, and nothing at all for the little phantom seamers. The outfield was fast, which meant we had to concentrate hard, but no reputable spin bowler will complain about that.'

Elsewhere it was good to see specialist slow bowlers getting some hard work in the county championship, the only real place to learn their trade. Leicestershire's Nick Cook bowled more than 800 overs – the third highest in the country – and John Childs of Gloucestershire more than doubled his tally of overs. He returned the best figures of the season in first-class cricket (9 for 56 against Somerset) and showed the strong Essex batting side how a good slow bowler can prosper in a limited-overs match. In a Nat-West Cup tie at Bristol he bowled his 12 overs for 29 runs, bowling Graham Gooch and Keith Pont in the process. He did not compromise his talent as a genuine slow bowler and exploited the conditions admirably. He also took 1 for 4 in 11 overs against Nottinghamshire earlier in the season in a Benson and Hedges game, so it can be said that he did his cause no harm in limited-over cricket as well as the championship.

Other cameos come flickering back to illustrate the charm of those days in 1981 when spin bowling played its part in the varied flow of the game: Johnson and Underwood bowling at Cheltenham to Zaheer Abbas on a glorious August day, Gifford proving far too wily for the frenetic young Yorkshire batsman at Worcester, the accuracy and shrewdness of Robin Hobbs at Hereford when Younis Ahmed was the only Worcestershire batsman to play him correctly with nimble foot-work and boldness. One dismissal lingers in the mind, and a mundane one it may seem. At Stourbridge, the Northants innings had become rather becalmed as the Worcestershire bowlers toiled on a good bat-ting wicket: Neil Mallender, the Northants tail-ender, had batted for an hour and a quarter with little difficulty, pushing down the line at the seamers. The game was stagnating and Glenn Turner brought on young Tim Curtis to try his leg-breaks. In his second over, he dismis-sed Mallender with the perfect leg-break, pitching middle-and-leg, turning sharply to have him caught in the gully. A classic example of the leg-spinner's value and full marks to Turner in trusting a twenty-one-year-old to do the job. It would have been instructive for fifteen other county captains to have seen that dismissal.

Stourbridge on the day after the Royal Wedding must seem an unlikely place to witness one delivery that stands out in a season of such excitement. Yet it symbolised the fact that cricket is still a game of subtlety, a quality that must stand alongside the big hitting, fast bowling and breathless finishes off the last ball.

# 10. How to Revive Spin Bowling

The panacea pages in any cricket book are always the least read. It is the same at cricket dinners – you can sense the incipient snores, the restlessness as someone delivers a well-meaning homily on how cricket can be improved. Rather like taking syrup of figs or bicarbonate of soda, the feeling is 'ah well, let's get it over with, I suppose it'll do some good'. All very understandable, but something must be done to flesh out the cadaver of the modern spin bowler. He will not return in profusion without the conditions of the game being altered to make life more difficult for the seamer.

'Gubby' Allen – England captain, chairman of the selectors and highly influential administrator in the past – summed up the modern attitude to slow bowling: 'Everybody pays lip service to helping them, but no one gets down to the problem. People tell me they'd play a spinner if they could find one good enough, but they won't appear out of thin air unless the conditions are right and they're given ample opportunities to play *and* to bowl.' He is right; many past and present players I talked to would agree that something must be done for the spinner while lamely concluding after thrashing around the subject that they could not think of positive solutions. Nor are they alone – the item has been on the agenda at countless meetings at Lord's in recent years, to little purpose. The revival of spin bowling is rather like the reduction of income tax – almost everyone wants it to happen, but few know how to achieve it.

I believe there are seven main areas to tackle:

1  The quality of wickets
2  The over-rate in Tests
3  Limiting the run-up of fast bowlers
4  Intimidation by fast bowlers
5  Revision of the LBW law
6  The type of cricket balls
7  The question of bonus points

## 1   The quality of wickets

At the start of the 1981 season, the Test and County Cricket Board issued directives to umpires and groundsmen on what constitutes a good cricket wicket – they should be dry at the start of the match, and turn progressively towards the end. Donald Carr, the TCCB Secretary, tried to reassure groundsmen; 'We didn't mind if the pitches broke up on the third day, all we were worried about was if they split open on the first day. Basically we didn't want juicy wickets that roll out slow after helping the seamer on the first morning.' The marking system has been changed in recent years, so that umpires file reports on the pitches to Lord's, not the captains, who could well be partial. Geoff Boycott feels that has come not a moment too soon: 'The marking system by captains inhibited groundsmen. After all, it's their jobs that are at stake and a captain who has lost a game may be unfair in his assessment. So the groundsman plays safe and produces a nothing wicket.'

The TCCB is actively encouraging faster, harder and dryer pitches, but the message still has not reached the ears of most county groundsmen. Bernard Flack is the Inspector of Pitches with responsibility to solve any problems associated with unsatisfactory county wickets; in his opinion, the Lord's directive has made little difference: 'Some groundsmen have even gone the other way by leaving too much grass on the wicket. Efforts to produce pitches on the Lord's model are still very much on the fringe at the moment. A lot of groundsmen are rather proud, they don't want to be reported for a pitch that helps spin early on, although it's alright in their eyes if the seamers prosper.'

Bernard Flack's forty years' experience as groundsman convinces him that the wickets are slower and less bouncy. That opinion is backed up by almost every player I interviewed during my research; some, such as Bob Willis and Alan Knott, say the problem is now a world-wide one – for every Perth flier there seem to be four Melbournes. In England, Hove is a popular ground with fast bowlers and spinners, because of the even bounce. At the Oval, Harry Brind's efforts in digging up the old wickets have helped to prolong Intikhab's career and brought a glowing tribute from the Australian captain, Kim Hughes, during the last Test of 1981. The Trent Bridge groundsman, Ron Allsop, has been criticized for preparing green wickets but at least they had bounce to help the slow bowlers. Nottinghamshire's manager, Ken Taylor – a member of the Pitches Committee at Lord's – justifies the new attitude at Trent Bridge by saying that results are surely better than spurious declarations: 'In the past, there've been games here when there's been no point in coming on the last day. The pitch was dead, the game lifeless and it was just a technical exercise for twenty-two players. We owe the public a lot more than that.'

It may be that the Trent Bridge philosophy will set a trend. For the moment, Ron Allsop's efforts are closer than most county grounds-men to the ideal set out by a sub-committee of twenty years ago that looked into methods of preparing faster pitches. The terms of reference were – 'To look into ways and means of producing pitches which are faster in pace and do not help one type of bowler only.' Bernard Flack was on that sub-committee, along with Bert Lock, Surrey's groundsman, Wilf Wooller, Glamorgan's secretary and two captains – Don Kenyon of Worcestershire and Keith Andrew of Northampton-shire. The chairman was Brian Castor and their conclusion was that three main factors were vital to produce the proper type of pitch:

(a) The right texture of soil;
(b) Pre-season consolidation of the square to a depth of approximately four inches;
(c) Complete dryness of the pitch at the commencement of the match.

All very admirable but wickets still got slower over the next twenty years. Keith Andrew says: 'It was a very interesting meeting but it's one thing to say something is wrong and another to get the grounds-men to do something about it. In the end, you just can't beat the climatic conditions – is there anybody alive who can produce a fast wicket to order in England?'

If there is, I know a lot of cricketers who would gladly pay him a small fortune to work the miracle. It is almost impossible to produce a fast wicket after a week of heavy rain but there are ways of lessening the deadening effect of rain. Bernard Flack believes groundsmen should revert to using marl to bind the surface, rather than loam which tends to anaesthetize the pitch. With marl as a sub-soil, the wicket can break up more and give extra bounce. Flack says, 'Many are afraid to use marl in case the pitch breaks up too drastically, but since loam came into fashion twenty-odd years ago, the wickets have got slower. That's not a coincidence.'

The players are resigned to the inadequacies of English wickets. Admittedly, professionals tend to be a little obsessional about a play-ing surface that affects their careers but it is difficult to disagree with the words of Bob Willis: 'Groundsmen haven't had enough stick for what they've done in recent years. At the start of the game, you should be able to put a pen-knife into the pitch as far as the handle and it should come up with no grass attached to it. It should then turn on the second day. Is that such an impossible task?' David Graveney thinks that county captains ought to press for an inquiry into groundsmanship: 'We should find out what are the best ingredients for making good cricket wickets. Loam just produces a neutral surface which is no good to anybody, yet enables you to play first-class cricket because it won't be reported. It's important that an edge carries to a close fielder – an incorrect shot must be punished correctly.' Derek Underwood cannot understand why scientific expertise has not been fully utilised: 'In recent seasons, I've hardly played a game in England without thinking how slow the wicket is. I see the ball pitch and the keeper takes it down by his toes and then I look forward to another day for the run accumulator, rather than the stroke player or the spinner.' The problem is not just confined to England. Richie Benaud has advocated seminars for groundsmen in Australia for the last five years – to no avail. He says: 'Pitches of uneven bounce where the ball moves off the seam are getting common in Australia as well. The spinner will continue to take a back seat until we get hard pitches with true bounce.'

The wickets are not the only problem concerning the ground itself. The outfields are too lush and green; they look like a bowling green on television and people say it all looks lovely, while forgetting that it means the shine stays much longer on the ball. Les Ames remembers how long the shine lasted in his day: 'After about twelve overs the ball would be roughed up by the outfield which was light brown and shaved. The medium pacers couldn't do a thing after that. Now one side of it is almost new after 85 overs. I never saw a spinner shine the ball in my day, yet they have to do it now – in the process ensuring that the seamer will soon be back bowling.'

Most current players believe that covered wickets will, in the long run, help the slow bowler. The feeling seems to be that a wicket unexposed to the elements is automatically drier and better, and the truer the pitch, then the more flight, guile and ability to impart spin is needed. Richard Hadlee, Nottinghamshire's world-class seam bowler, thinks the presence of overseas players in the county championship and covered wickets will eventually assist spin: 'The overseas batsmen score their runs at a fast rate and covered wickets mean more runs. A spinner will have to bowl more, because the seamers can't be expected to run up all day'. For the moment, though, it is impossible to predict what effect covered wickets will have on the variety of out-cricket.

## 2 The over-rate in Tests

This is a subject guaranteed to bring froth to the mouth of the mildest of old players. Every pejorative adjective is wheeled out and the rose-coloured spectacles are donned with unconscious irony. Modern county cricketers who will never know the pressures of playing for their country are derisive about the over-rates in Tests, compared to the fines county sides face if they fail to meet the TCCB requirement of nineteen an hour. The danger is the effect of Test Cricket on the public consciousness; they watch fast bowlers strolling back interminably and decide to imitate them. A whole generation is growing up under the mistaken belief that you have to run forty yards to bowl at fast-medium pace. The youngsters do not realize that long run-ups are generally tactical, to avoid delivering too many balls to a batsman in a day's play. No one would deny the glory of a Michael Holding in full throttle but when the dose is repeated constantly without the aesthetic beauty of a Holding, the process becomes very wearing. With no sanctions on the over rate, the fast men can bowl all day as a rotating quartet, with the spinner invariably lounging in the dressing-room, wondering if he can stay awake for the next drinks interval.

Peter May, England's new chairman of selectors, says the Test over-rate is the biggest problem in the game, while Richie Benaud accuses the players of being cynical. Their sentiments are so admirably frank that it would be churlish to remind them that they both played for their countries at a time when it became tactical to slow the game down on occasions. With typical honesty, Mike Smith admits: 'Hand on heart, I must confess I slowed the game down sometimes. You do things you're not proud of.' Smith puts his finger on the basic problem when he says: 'Bowlers have been allowed to come into the game and develop a very slow rhythm' – in other words, they do not slow things down on occasions, they are slow *all the time*. Fred Titmus noticed a subtle change when he returned to the Middlesex side: 'I was told to slow it down and I just couldn't, even if I wanted. No matter how hard I tried, I could never take longer than three minutes to bowl an over. I suppose I might be a luxury in a Test Match now, because I was so quick.'

The decline in Test Match over-rates has been astonishing. In

187

1930, Don Bradman took 330 minutes to score 254 at Lords and the average bowling rate was 22 overs an hour. In 1981, in the England first innings, it took Australia 357 minutes to bowl 85 overs, at 14 overs an hour. If Bradman had played on the same ground half a century later, he would have scored 162, not 254. Thus the tempo has been reduced by nearly 40 per cent over 50 years. 'Gubby' Allen played in that 1930 Test and he blames the absurd run-ups of the fast bowlers for the decline in balls per hours. He swears that the number of fast bowlers who ran more than twenty-five yards before the Second World War could be counted on the fingers of one hand – today the norm is about forty yards.

The West Indies are the worst offenders. In 1980 they averaged 12.3 overs an hour in the series in England, compared with 27 an hour in 1950, when both sides had many spinners. If the 1980 West Indians had been made to bowl at something nearer 20 overs an hour, they would have had to break up their speed quartet, make the surviving fast men cut down their run-ups and introduce some slow bowlers. No wonder Jack Fingleton wrote with feeling, 'Watching the 1980 West Indians in the field is the most boring experience I have had in Test cricket'.

Every year, the International Cricket Conference deplores the dwindling over-rate and does nothing more drastic than that. England is the only member country that wishes to introduce fines but the others will have none of it. The 1981 Australian tourists were asked to agree that a minimum of 100 overs a day should be bowled. They refused, saying such a startling suggestion would distort the true nature of Test cricket. Even 15 overs an hour was an unreasonable suggestion in their eyes – hardly surprising when one realizes that their strategy was built round the seam attack of Lillee, Lawson, Alderman and Hogg. Once again, England lost out in the over-rate wrangle, and the spinners and the public were the principal sufferers. Richie Benaud has an interesting suggestion: fine the players £10 a ball per man *below* a hundred balls per hour, which would lead to hefty payments under existing attitudes: 'You'd soon see an improvement and the spinner would be bound to get in'. For the moment, the only way we can expect 100 overs a day from Test Matches is by installing flood lights at every ground.

## 3    Limiting the run-up of fast bowlers

The corollary to declining over-rates is to stop the bowlers running so far. On the face of it, this seems doctrinaire and authoritarian, but not if the limitation is partial. For some years, Reg Simpson has been spreading this particular gospel at Trent Bridge – that no more than *three* bowlers can run up from more than *six yards*. When he first floated the idea, he was scorned, but after the visit of the West Indians, he received a more favourable response. He maintains: 'They can't bowl seamers from six yards and for most spinners, that's a perfectly reasonable run-up. You could still have the fine sight of a Holding or a Lillee running in, but it would curtail the influence of the seamers. Anyway, isn't three seamers enough for any side? If the rule applied at school and club level, then captains would also have to bowl the spinners and give them vital experience in match play.'

Keith Andrew likes the idea and in his captaincy as Director of Coaching for the National Cricket Association, he is pushing its claims through the corridors of Lord's. 'I see nothing wrong with the genuine fast bowler steaming in off a good run, but I'm all for bowlers having to learn how to use their fingers from a run-up of six yards or so. It would bring craft and variety back into the game.'

Ted Dexter has also campaigned against long run-ups for some time and he believes Simpson's idea is perfectly feasible: 'The only player who would suffer is the fourth seamer. I believe everybody else would approve. Why should a battery of fast bowlers get physical relief on their walk back without being told to hurry up?' Among the modern players, Dennis Amiss was the most enthusiastic supporter: 'If everybody had to do it, those with the best spinners would do well and it would speed up the game. Anyone can run up and bowl halfway down the wicket but the game is richer with slow bowlers around.'

I can imagine an almighty fuss if this proposal was put to all the Test playing countries at the next ICC meeting. Members would twitter about tampering with the game to no real purpose, Australia would splutter that the traditional aspects of cricket were being distorted (even though that country has cravenly adopted several of Kerry Packer's innovations), and the West Indies would simply refuse to co-operate, saying that England would not suggest such an idea if they had a battery of four fearsome quick bowlers. Perhaps the ICC members would like to sit on the popular side during a Test Match and ask the public's opinion of bowlers who meander back to their mark, fail to use the first third of their run up, then play 'statues' at the bowling crease, after the ball has been delivered.

## 4 Intimidation by fast bowlers

I believe that fast bowlers are getting away with too much short-pitched bowling in both Test and county cricket. The trend started in 1974–5 when Lillee and Thomson were terrifying against England on Australian wickets of uneven bounce; the following year, the West Indies came to Australia and suffered the same fate. Clive Lloyd decided to adopt the 'blood and thunder' policy and the West Indies have packed their sides with quick bowlers ever since. In 1977, World Series Cricket was formed and, for two years, it did nothing to halt the inclination of fast bowlers to bowl short, hoping for bounce at the batsmen's bodies and heads. Night-watchman, Iqbal Quasim, was hit a sickening blow on the head in the first Test against Pakistan at Edgbaston in 1978. The current West Indies attack contains only one bowler – Andy Roberts – who bowls a consistently full length and their fast bowlers are physically frightening propositions.

To combat this glut of short-pitched fast bowling, batsmen have had to take refuge behind helmets, visors and other impedimenta designed to cushion the blows. The result has been to increase the amount of intimidation. Bowlers are now let off with far too many short-pitched deliveries; it is very rare that an umpire shows his mettle and warns a fast bowler. Dennis Amiss and Glenn Turner, two prolific opening batsmen, have borne the brunt of such treatment in recent years. They are both fed up with it. Amiss: 'We must play the only sport where the ball is aimed at the head. Fast bowlers bang it in short more than at any stage of my career – some even whack it in at their own feet to get it near our heads! For me, the game is getting far too aggressive.' Turner believes the intimidation started just before helmets and visors were popularized and that umpires now feel batsman are sufficiently protected. 'But where will all the front foot shots go?' he asks, 'We'll soon be teaching kids to hold the bat like a baseball player.'

Turner feels particularly angry at the interpretation umpires place on a dangerous ball. At the moment in England, a bowler is allowed one delivery per over that goes *above* shoulder or head height *in the batsman's normal stance*. After that, he is warned by the umpire and he can be taken off for the rest of the innings. In a match against

Derbyshire in 1981, Turner was hit in the visor first ball by Paul Newman. Turner enquired of the umpire if that was the one for the over, only to be told that the delivery had to pass over the shoulder. So Turner realized with a grim fatalism that he could face six similar balls in a row and Newman would not be warned. Sylvester Clarke of Surrey was also allowed to get away with intimidation when bowling at Turner: 'Two went past my shoulder and I gloved the next one in front of my face. That made three in a row and nothing had been said. That shouldn't be allowed.'

Last summer, Turner met a young Pakistani whose attitude to fast bowling told him all he needed to know about the effects of intimidation by Test Match bowlers. 'He was a friend of Younis Ahmed, one of our batsmen, and he came and bowled in our nets. He bowled bouncers every ball and in the end, I had to say, 'pitch it up, son!'. He replied, 'what is *up*?', and continued to bowl bouncers. At sixteen, he wanted to bowl like Imran Khan!'

So it will continue until the umpires act more decisively. Too often the ball is not aimed at the stumps but at the *person* of the batsman – if he does not fend the ball off into the hands of the close fielder, he cannot score too freely against such an attack. The habits of the Test players percolate through the game and the result is a uniformity that is worrying those who want to see umpires do their job. Not for the first time, I wish Sid Buller was still alive and umpiring.

## 5  Revision of the LBW law

The existing LBW law favours those bowlers who bring the ball *into* the right hand bat. That means off spinners of course, but more relevantly, the medium-pace seamer who shines the ball well. The game has swung more towards the legside, with a decrease in offside shots and it has accelerated the demise of the wrist spinner, the man who can turn the ball away from the right hander.

The law was introduced experimentally in 1935 and adopted in 1937. The aim was to prevent the batsmen padding up to balls that pitched just outside off stump; it was argued that batsmen would have to play a shot and offside play would increase. Instead it caused many batsmen to push forward and play defensively to such deliveries, rather than taking a chance to play an attacking shot. 'Gubby' Allen supported the change in the LBW law back in 1935 but he now calls it: 'the most disastrous piece of legislation in my lifetime. I'm ashamed to

191

think that I voted for it, albeit in my infancy as a cricket administrator. I suppose I supported it, because I was fed up seeing Jack Hobbs, Herbert Sutcliffe and the others shouldering arms to me. Sutcliffe said it would mean he'd never get 2,000 runs again in a season and Frank Chester said the umpires wouldn't be able to interpret it, both of which were rubbish. It was argued that the revision would help all types of bowling equally. It has helped those who bring the ball into the batsman and this has contributed to the demise of the leg-spinner and the slow left armer. Surely it can't be a coincidence that they have faded out.

For thirty years, Allen's friend Sir Donald Bradman, has been campaigning for a revision of the LBW law to help the wrist-spinner. He thinks that balls pitched outside the *leg stump* should dismiss a batsman provided they would hit the stumps in line with the wickets. Jeff Stollmeyer tabled an amendment two years ago; the former West Indies captain suggested that the ball should be delivered *over* the wicket by right handers, and *around* the wicket by left handers, in both cases to a right-handed batsman. To a left-handed batsman the successful right-arm bowler would come from *round* the wicket and the left hander from *over* the wicket.

Some members of the ICC agreed to try the Bradman/Stollmeyer proposal for one season in Australia and New Zealand. It is not yet known how successful the experiment was, but Don Oslear, the English Test umpire, implemented it and thought it an excellent idea. He spent the 1980–1 season umpiring in New Zealand and gave two men out under the experimental law. 'I think it gives the wrist-spinner an advantage because usually the batsman can stand in front of his stumps and pad the ball away if it pitches outside leg-stump. The ball should be hit with the bat, not the pad and cricket laws should benefit all parts of the game in equal proportions.' Richard Hadlee hopes than an experiment in his country will soon be an official law: 'If a bowler has enough skill to turn the ball from leg to off, then he should be rewarded. At the moment, the LBW law favours the defensive batsman, who just kicks the ball away.'

Some umpires might say that the proposed law would be difficult to implement – but surely not if he sorted out the possibilities in his mind as the bowler handed him his sweater and told him if he was bowling from round or over the wicket? Ted Dexter believes it should be tried in England: 'The game slowed down the day it became effective to fire the ball in at the batsman. The LBW laws ought to be revised to benefit the guy who bowls straight and sends the ball away from the bat'. 'Gubby' Allen is strongly opposed to the Bradman/Stollmeyer plan. 'The help it will give the leg-spinner and slow left-armer will be negligible and it might encourage some of them to bowl at, or just outside the leg stump, which is the last thing that is wanted.' Allen believes the stumps should be widened by an inch and a half in conjunction with a return to the pre- 1935 LBW law. 'This would give the bowlers a bigger target to aim at and would provide some compensation for the ball pitching just outside that would have hit the wicket. But I would retain the "intent" clause, otherwise padding up would be back in a big way.'

The last time the stumps were altered was in 1931; the height and width were both increased by an inch. That is a gap of fifty years in which the balance of power has shifted back and forth from bowler to batsman. Some may think that widening the stumps would be a drastic move – but it is surely an innovation that is well worth considering.

## 6   The type of cricket balls

In the last decade cricket balls have become harder and kept their shine longer. Outfields that caress the ball mean the shine stays on for hours and many seamers have become expert shiners of the ball. When Alan Knott first played for Kent, things were different: 'The outer coating of the ball would go after about ten overs and then the spinners would be on. The balls were manufactured differently in those days and the dry, brown outfield soon roughed them up.'

The seam is more pronounced on the modern cricket ball, in Colin Cowdrey's opinion: 'I've noticed it in the last fifteen years and this trend, added to the increased shining, means that the ball is still tremendously alive in mid-afternoon. In my time, that was the period when you were finished with the seamers and were grappling with the spinners, but now the ball still continues to do all sorts of tricks. Once the spinner came on, no one was allowed to polish it. If we can somehow reduce the influence of the seamers so that they'd be meat and drink to the batsmen by mid-afternoon, then the captains would have to rely on slow bowling.'

Perhaps just one new ball per innings would be the answer. Current county captains like Bob Willis, Keith Fletcher and David Graveney support the idea in principle but remain worried about the lack of standardization in the manufacture of cricket balls. Colin

Cowdrey believes it is worth a try, pointing out that the slow bowlers of his time used to like to grip a fairly hard ball and often complained when it was too soft – 'but the modern ball seems much harder. I think that's why so much padding is needed by batsmen, the ball stays harder for longer periods'.

It would be wrong to penalize attacking fast bowlers by forbidding them to shine the ball, but surely there is room for a compromise. Perhaps a ban on polishing the ball after 30 overs? Or even to outlaw shining by anyone other than the bowler? Any variation on this theme could only help the slow bowler.

## 7   The question of bonus points

Under the present system in the county championship, bowlers can pick up bonus points by containment. They can push back the fielders, and batsmen have to sacrifice their wickets as they chase four bonus points in the first 100 overs. The abolition of the 100-overs limitation on first innings has done nothing to alter that fact. If batting bonus points were eliminated altogether, then bowlers who attacked could get due reward. It would pay captains to have men round the bat and that would in turn lead to more runs. Bonus points would be available only to bowlers who had the ability to bowl sides out rather than frustrate them in their quest for quick runs.

There are other revisions in the laws that might benefit the spinner – longer boundaries, four-day cricket and abolition of the 1981 regulation that allowed a new ball after 85 overs. It seemed a bizarre decision to encourage the spinner by scrapping the 100-overs limit on first innings, then dampen his optimism by making a new ball available just after the seamers had enjoyed a rest. Four-day cricket on covered wickets would surely mean more work for the slow bowler because not even fit young seamers can keep going all that time, with fines for slow over-rates always a threat. Boundaries should be at least eighty yards long to avoid occasions when a batsman mishits a spinner for six. The modern bats are now so heavy that a man like Graham Gooch can hit a slow bowler over a short boundary, even if he is not to the pitch of the ball. I feel for the spinner on Final Day at Lord's in any of the limited-over competitions; the authorities are so determined to cram in the crowds that the boundaries are shortened. Sometimes they can be as little as 65 yards – and the captain wonders why his slow bowler proves so expensive! Taunton is another spinner's nightmare; in 1980, Ian Botham made a superb double hundred there against Gloucestershire, with many of his boundaries coming as he hit David Graveney back over his head to the short straight boundary. Why should batsmen have such an advantage that has nothing to do with merit?

Perhaps the pitch should be lengthened. It has been 22 yards for more than a century now and in that time the height of the average man has greatly increased. If the pitch was a metre longer, then the intimidatory stuff would lose some of its impact because the batsman would have a fraction more time to see the ball. The distance of 22 yards seems ludicrous when set against the bounce that a towering man like Joel Garner can achieve – and for the spin bowler, the only adjustment needed to cope with a longer pitch would involve throwing the ball up a little more.

Most modern first-class cricketers react with dismay to suggestions that the pitch should be lengthened. They metamorphosize from being shrewd realists to conservatives in the best Colonel Blimp tradition, muttering darkly about 'tinkering with the laws' etc, etc. They ignore the fact that cricket must be evolutionary, that no set of regulations should favour or inhibit one particular style of bowler or batsman.

Whatever amendments are made to the laws of cricket in the next year or so, I hope they are slanted towards the slow bowler. We cannot wait for the captains to make gestures in their direction, they have to be encouraged to believe that it is in the best interests of the side to encourage spinners. If one accepts that the English climate will militate against many groundsmen's best intentions, then it is clear that spinners must be legislated back into the game. It is easy to state that the present obsession with victory is just a front for the pursuit of money that dogs most aspects of life. In that sense, the argument goes, cricket in the 1980s is just a manifestation of the society in which we live. Yet it is far easier to alter the rules of a game that has been affected by some of society's ills than it is to tell the human race how to structure their lives. Drab uniformity is the curse, variety the utopia; high-speed fast bowling is a wonderful spectacle and no lover of cricket would ever wish to nullify the ardour of the Holdings, Tysons, Lindwalls and Truemans, yet surely a wicket-keeper wants to stand up to the stumps as often as a batsman longs to play the off-drive without having his hair parted? At this time in cricket's history, the game is too important to be left to the players.

# Statistical Appendix

Appendix A

---

**Spin Bowling in County Cricket**
*By Charles Heward*

The following table gives the percentages of balls bowled by spinners.
Column A is the total percentage
Column B is the percentage bowled by RHOB and SLA
Column C is the percentage bowled by LBG

| Season | A | B | C |
|--------|-------|-------|------|
| 1953 | 45.91 | 37.36 | 8.55 |
| 1956 | 51.61 | 41.97 | 9.64 |
| 1957 | 48.00 | 40.19 | 7.81 |
| 1963 | 34.67 | 31.15 | 3.52 |
| 1968 | 32.88 | 28.91 | 3.97 |
| 1973 | 36.92 | 32.43 | 4.49 |
| 1975 | 37.37 | 33.47 | 3.90 |
| 1976 | 40.64 | 37.92 | 2.72 |
| 1977 | 39.25 | 37.41 | 1.84 |
| 1978 | 38.69 | 37.22 | 1.47 |
| 1979 | 37.66 | 36.06 | 1.60 |
| 1980 | 36.48 | 35.57 | 0.91 |
| 1981 | 36.49 | 34.17 | 2.32 |

## Appendix B

### Scoring and Striking Rates in County Championship
*By Charles Heward*

| Years | Balls bowled | Runs scored | Runs per 100 balls | Wickets taken | Striking rate |
|-------|--------------|-------------|--------------------|---------------|---------------|
| 1901 | 274302 | 131386 | 47.90 | 4872 | 56.30 |
| 1904 | 250166 | 118622 | 47.42 | 4525 | 55.28 |
| 1911 | 287607 | 146658 | 50.99 | 5752 | 50.00 |
| 1914 | 292130 | 139336 | 47.70 | 5864 | 49.82 |
| 1925 | 361698 | 154204 | 42.63 | 6837 | 52.90 |
| 1928 | 422253 | 184005 | 43.58 | 6194 | 68.17 |
| 1935 | 374745 | 167181 | 44.61 | 6999 | 53.54 |
| 1946 | 352770 | 149880 | 42.49 | 6392 | 55.19 |
| 1949 | 409640 | 178587 | 43.60 | 6581 | 62.25 |
| 1953 | 384757 | 162391 | 42.21 | 6377 | 60.34 |
| 1958 | 337552 | 134940 | 39.98 | 6429 | 52.50 |
| 1963 | 374571 | 151468 | 40.44 | 6522 | 57.43 |
| 1968 | 344824 | 141914 | 41.16 | 6145 | 56.11 |
| 1973 | 266524 | 117007 | 43.90 | 4466 | 59.68 |
| 1976 | 291530 | 138821 | 47.62 | 4835 | 60.30 |
| 1977 | 272964 | 121709 | 44.59 | 4516 | 60.44 |
| 1978 | 279571 | 124671 | 44.59 | 4555 | 61.38 |
| 1979 | 269806 | 121840 | 45.16 | 4264 | 63.28 |
| 1980 | 267472 | 126718 | 47.38 | 4372 | 61.18 |
| 1981 | 293736 | 140042 | 47.68 | 4742 | 61.94 |

## Appendix C

## A Comparison between Pace and Slow Bowlers in Domestic Limited Overs Cricket in Seasons 1979, 1980 and 1981
*By John Stockwell*

The following statistics relate to the performances of bowlers who played for the seventeen first-class counties in the Gillette/National Westminster Cup, Benson & Hedges Cup, and John Player Sunday League.

| | Type | No. bowlers | Overs | Runs | Wkts | Average | Runs per over |
|---|---|---|---|---|---|---|---|
| 1979 | Fast/Fast medium | 52 | 5,933.5 | 20,635 | 959 | 21.52 | 3.48 |
| | Slow left arm | 18 | 1,227.2 | 4,500 | 196 | 22.96 | 3.67 |
| | Off break | 24 | 1,983.5 | 7,443 | 285 | 26.12 | 3.75 |
| | Medium | 78 | 5,382.1 | 20,731 | 786 | 26.38 | 3.85 |
| | Leg break | 6 | 105.3 | 499 | 17 | 29.35 | 4.73 |
| | *Total* | 178 | 14,632.4 | 53,808 | 2,243 | 23.99 | 3.68 |
| 1980 | Fast/Fast medium | 63 | 6,814.5 | 24,614 | 1,107 | 22.23 | 3.61 |
| | Off break | 25 | 1,778.1 | 6,937 | 213 | 32.56 | 3.90 |
| | Slow left arm | 19 | 1,331.0 | 5,222 | 188 | 27.77 | 3.92 |
| | Medium | 83 | 5,864.4 | 23,666 | 859 | 27.55 | 4.03 |
| | Leg break | 3 | 17.2 | 81 | 0 | — | 4.67 |
| | *Total* | 193 | 15,806.0 | 60,520 | 2,367 | 25.56 | 3.82 |
| 1981 | Fast/Fast medium | 67 | 6,536.4 | 24,401 | 1.040 | 23.46 | 3.73 |
| | Off break | 25 | 1,753.5 | 6,585 | 249 | 26.44 | 3.75 |
| | Slow left arm | 17 | 1,074.1 | 4,196 | 148 | 28.35 | 3.90 |
| | Medium | 72 | 4,802.4 | 19,690 | 744 | 26.46 | 4.09 |
| | Leg break | 5 | 49.4 | 241 | 8 | 30.12 | 4.85 |
| | *Total* | 186 | 14,217.0 | 55,113 | 2,189 | 25.17 | 3.87 |

## Most Expensive Bowler (1981) *By John Stockwell*

|    |                   |     | **Runs per over** |
|----|-------------------|-----|------|
| 1  | A. M. Ferreira    | M   | 5.14 |
| 2  | G. C. Small       | FM  | 5.10 |
| 3  | J. M. Rice        | M   | 5.04 |
| 4  | S. M. Hartley     | M   | 4.86 |
| 5  | S. J. Malone      | M   | 4.80 |
| 6  | S. J. Rouse       | FM  | 4.77 |
| 7  | S. J. Dennis      | FM  | 4.70 |
| 8  | M. Johnson        | M   | 4.64 |
| 9  | S. Oldham         | FM  | 4.60 |
| 10 | N. F. M. Popplewell | M | 4.57 |
| 11 | C. S. Cowdrey     | M   | 4.53 |
| 12 | A. H. Wilkins     | M   | 4.44 |
| 13 | D. S. Steele      | SLA | 4.43 |

Out of 32 bowlers who averaged more than 4.00 per over 18 were medium, 10 were fast medium and **only** 4 were slow bowlers.

## Appendix D

### County Spinners with more than 1000 wickets in first-class cricket since 1939–45 war (Qualification at least 5 county seasons)
*By Robert Brooke*

| Player | Balls bowled | Runs conceded | Wkts taken | Runs per 100 balls | Av.balls per run | Av.balls per wkt | Av.runs per wkt |
|---|---|---|---|---|---|---|---|
| R. Tattersall | 70921 | 24704 | 1369 | 34.83 | 2.87 | 51.80 | 18.05 |
| J. C. Laker | 101980 | 35791 | 1944 | 35.10 | 2.85 | 52.46 | 18.41 |
| J. H. Wardle | 102367 | 35027 | 1846 | 34.22 | 2.92 | 55.45 | 18.98 |
| G. A. R. Lock | 150047 | 54710 | 2844 | 36.46 | 2.74 | 52.76 | 19.24 |
| M. J. Hilton | 55368 | 19536 | 1006 | 35.28 | 2.83 | 55.04 | 19.42 |
| J. A. Young* | 77600 | 26173 | 1343 | 33.73 | 2.97 | 57.78 | 19.49 |
| D. L. Underwood | 111036 | 39307 | 2004 | 35.40 | 2.82 | 55.41 | 19.16 |
| W. E. Hollies* | 91736 | 31445 | 1588 | 34.28 | 2.92 | 57.77 | 19.80 |
| R. Illingworth | 114052 | 40485 | 2031 | 35.50 | 2.82 | 56.16 | 19.93 |
| D. J. Shepherd† | 108506 | 36228 | 1803 | 33.39 | 3.00 | 60.18 | 20.09 |
| C. Cook | 106319 | 36578 | 1782 | 34.40 | 2.91 | 59.66 | 20.53 |
| G. E. Tribe | 64048 | 28321 | 1378 | 44.22 | 2.26 | 46.48 | 20.55 |
| D. Wilson | 69724 | 24977 | 1189 | 35.82 | 2.79 | 58.64 | 21.01 |
| B. S. Bedi | 90166 | 33438 | 1546 | 37.09 | 2.70 | 58.32 | 21.63 |
| B. Dooland | 52734 | 22332 | 1016 | 42.35 | 2.36 | 51.90 | 21.98 |
| F. J. Titmus | 173438 | 63221 | 2827 | 36.45 | 2.74 | 61.35 | 22.36 |
| N. Gifford | 101604 | 38164 | 1689 | 37.56 | 2.66 | 60.16 | 22.60 |
| J. B. Mortimore | 113478 | 41904 | 1807 | 36.93 | 2.71 | 62.80 | 23.19 |
| D. V. P. Wright* | 65638 | 34962 | 1486 | 53.27 | 1.88 | 44.17 | 23.53 |
| D. A. Allen | 77619 | 28585 | 1209 | 36.82 | 2.72 | 64.20 | 23.64 |
| P. J. Sainsbury | 89936 | 31777 | 1316 | 35.33 | 2.83 | 68.34 | 24.15 |
| J. E. Walsh* | 51533 | 27334 | 1119 | 53.04 | 1.89 | 46.05 | 24.43 |
| R. O. Jenkins* | 54600 | 28368 | 1153 | 51.96 | 1.92 | 47.35 | 24.60 |
| B. A. Langford | 89160 | 34964 | 1410 | 39.21 | 2.55 | 63.23 | 24.98 |
| P. I. Pocock | 83432 | 34962 | 1354 | 41.90 | 2.39 | 61.62 | 25.82 |
| E. Smith | 78440 | 31448 | 1217 | 40.09 | 2.49 | 64.45 | 25.84 |
| R. N. S. Hobbs | 61979 | 29776 | 1099 | 48.04 | 2.08 | 56.40 | 27.09 |
| L. R. Gibbs | 78157 | 27878 | 1024 | 35.67 | 2.80 | 76.33 | 27.22 |
| J. Birkenshaw | 69205 | 29276 | 1073 | 42.30 | 2.36 | 64.50 | 27.28 |
| Intikhab Alam | 91764 | 43455 | 1570 | 47.36 | 2.11 | 58.45 | 27.68 |

N.B. Raymond Smith (1112), D. B. Close (1167) and G. S. Sobers (1043) all obtained more than 1000 wickets while bowling a mixture of seam and spin. It is not possible to apportion the exact totals but all took less than 1000 wickets with spin.

* Indicates also played Pre-War (figures ignored)

† Indicates changed from seam to spin exclusively during career. Only wickets taken with spin are counted here.

## Appendix E

### More than 100 Wickets in Post-War Test Matches by Spin Bowlers
*By Robert Brooke*

| Player | Balls bowled | Runs conceded | Wkts taken | Runs per 100 balls | Av. balls per run | Av. balls per wkt | Av. runs per wkt |
|---|---|---|---|---|---|---|---|
| ENGLAND | | | | | | | |
| J. H. Wardle | 6597 | 2080 | 102 | 31.53 | 3.17 | 64.68 | 20.39 |
| J. C. Laker | 12027 | 4101 | 193 | 34.10 | 2.93 | 62.32 | 21.25 |
| G. A. R. Lock | 13147 | 4451 | 174 | 33.86 | 2.95 | 75.56 | 25.58 |
| D. L. Underwood | 20159 | 7141 | 279 | 35.42 | 2.82 | 72.26 | 25.60 |
| D. A. Allen | 11297 | 3779 | 122 | 33.45 | 2.99 | 92.60 | 30.98 |
| R. Illingworth | 11934 | 3807 | 122 | 31.90 | 3.13 | 97.82 | 31.21 |
| F. J. Titmus | 15118 | 4931 | 153 | 32.62 | 3.07 | 98.81 | 32.23 |
| AUSTRALIA | | | | | | | |
| R. Benaud | 19108 | 6704 | 248 | 35.09 | 2.85 | 77.05 | 27.03 |
| I. W. Johnson | 8780 | 3182 | 109 | 36.24 | 2.76 | 80.55 | 29.19 |
| A. A. Mallett | 9990 | 3940 | 132 | 39.44 | 2.54 | 75.68 | 29.85 |
| SOUTH AFRICA | | | | | | | |
| H. J. Tayfield | 13568 | 4405 | 170 | 32.47 | 3.08 | 79.81 | 25.91 |
| WEST INDIES | | | | | | | |
| S. Ramadhin | 13939 | 4579 | 158 | 32.85 | 3.04 | 88.22 | 28.98 |
| L. R. Gibbs | 27115 | 8989 | 309 | 33.15 | 3.02 | 87.75 | 29.09 |
| A. L. Valentine | 12953 | 4215 | 139 | 32.54 | 3.07 | 93.19 | 30.32 |
| INDIA | | | | | | | |
| B. S. Bedi | 21364 | 7637 | 266 | 35.75 | 2.80 | 80.32 | 28.71 |
| S. P. Gupte | 11284 | 4403 | 149 | 39.02 | 2.56 | 75.73 | 29.55 |
| B. S. Chandrasekhar | 15963 | 7199 | 242 | 45.10 | 2.22 | 65.96 | 29.75 |
| E. A. S. Prasanna | 14353 | 5742 | 189 | 40.01 | 2.80 | 75.94 | 30.38 |
| M. H. Mankad | 14686 | 5236 | 162 | 35.65 | 2.81 | 90.65 | 32.32 |
| S. Venkataraghavan | 13442 | 4944 | 145 | 36.78 | 2.72 | 92.70 | 34.10 |
| PAKISTAN | | | | | | | |
| Intikhab Alam | 10474 | 4494 | 125 | 42.91 | 2.33 | 83.79 | 35.95 |

N.B. G. O. S. Sobers took 235 wickets with a mixture of spin and speed bowling. It has proved to be impossible to apportion the exact totals with each method however.

# Index

## A

Acfield, D. L. 4, 95–6, 104, 112, 113, 152, 172, 179, 180
Adcock, N. A. T. 119
Aftab Gul 70
Aitchison, the Rev. J. K. 24
Alderman, T. 188
Allen, G. O. 3, 8–9, 124, 139–40, 183, 188, 191–3
Allen, D. A. 3, 10, 17, 22, 67–8, 95, 96, 98, 99, 111, 126–7, 130, 132, 150, 174
Alleyne, H. 7
Allin, A. W. 102
Ames, L. E. G. 6, 161, 163, 166, 177, 186
Amiss, D. L. 43, 70, 72, 74, 83, 114, 147, 151, 175, 189, 190
Andrew, K. V. 52, 62, 63, 108, 162, 164–6, 185, 189
Appleyard, R. 52, 58–9, 70, 78
Archer, R. G. 120, 122
Arlott, J. 46, 130
Atkinson, D. 140

## B

Barnett, C. J. 64
Barton, M. R. 25–6
Bailey, T. E. 28, 48, 119, 122, 140
Bainbridge, P. 151
Bairstow, D. L. 160
Balderstone, J. C. 115
Barnett, K. J. 108–9
Barrington, K. F. 130
Bedi, B. S. 70–6, 88, 103, 149, 157, 168

Benaud, R. 50, 87, 120, 122, 124, 126–33, 157, 169, 170–1, 186, 188
Birch, J. D. 173
Bird, H. D. ('Dickie') 43
Bird, R. E. 61–2
Birkenshaw, J. 87–9, 115, 163, 177, 179
Blythe, C. 169
Booth, A. 110
Border, A. R. 89, 118
Botham, I. T. 89, 107, 116–18, 149, 159, 172, 195
Bowes, W. E. 103
Boycott, G. 6–7, 88, 93, 169–70, 172, 184
Bradman, Sir D. G. 30–1, 54, 111–12, 128, 192–3
Brain, B. M. 97
Brassington, A. J. 49, 160
Brearley, J. M. 8, 72, 89, 103, 108–9, 113, 114, 118, 167
Bridge, W. B. 99–101, 103
Bright, R. J. 116–17, 155, 180
Broad, B. C. 151
Brown, A. S. 5, 8, 17, 19, 68, 151
Brown, D. J. 44, 49, 64, 84, 99–101, 107, 109–110, 114, 134, 136, 138, 166, 171
Burke, J. W. 121
Buse, H. T. F. 56

## C

Carr, D. B. 184
Chandrasekhar, B. S. 119, 181
Chappell, G. S. 78
Chappell, I. M. 78, 134

Cheatle, R. G. L. 172
Chester, F. 192
Childs, J. H. 4, 96–8, 160, 171, 173, 174, 179, 181–2
Clark, E. W. 20
Clarke, S. 191
Close, D. B. 38, 76, 116, 127, 129, 131, 132, 133, 139, 140, 170
Compton, D. C. S. 29, 58, 77–8, 148, 155, 167
Connolly, A. N. 137
Cook, C. ('Sam') 14, 16, 18–22, 30, 55, 67, 98, 177
Cook, G. 75
Cook, N. G. B. 4, 173, 181
Corrall, P. 61
Cowdrey, M. C. 2, 6, 54, 55–6, 58, 72, 122, 123, 133, 134, 135, 136, 137, 138, 140–5, 148, 150, 158, 193, 194
Craig, I. D. 121
Croft, C. E. H. 2
Curtis, T. S. 182

**D**

Davidson, A. K. 126–7, 128, 130, 131, 132
Daniel, W. W. 158, 170
De Silva, S. S. 181
Dexter, E. R. 40, 52, 127, 128, 131, 132, 136, 152, 170, 189, 192–3
Dilley, G. R. 116
Dixon, A. L. 163
D'Oliveira, B. L. 77, 134, 136
Dollery, H. E. 24–5, 29, 30, 31, 33, 116
Dooland, B. 10, 59–61, 88, 149, 167
Doshi, D. R. 107–8, 114–15, 174, 179
Downton, P. R. 167

**E**

East, R. E. 46–8, 95, 96, 104, 112, 113, 152, 172, 177

Edmonds, P. H. 5, 92–5, 103, 112, 118, 170, 179, 181
Edrich, G. A. 56
Edrich, J. H. 134, 136
Edwards, M. J. 46
Emburey, J. E. 4, 66, 67, 89–91, 92, 93, 112, 113, 118, 156, 158, 170, 179, 180, 181
Emmett, G. M. 13, 18, 20, 22–3
Engineer, F. M. 160
Evans, T. G. 7, 120, 123, 141, 143, 162, 164

**F**

Ferreira, A. M. 174
Fingleton, J. H. W. 188
Fishlock, L. B. 17, 62
Flack, Bernard 184, 185
Flack, Bert 124, 126
Flavell, J. 127, 130, 131
Fletcher, K. W. R. 47, 50, 52, 74, 95, 96, 112–13, 114, 151–2, 172, 193
Freeman, A. P. 25, 55, 161, 164, 166, 177

**G**

Garner, J. 2, 195
Gatting, M. W. 118, 155
Gavaskar, S. M. 181
Gibbs, L. R. 9, 108, 145
Gifford, N. 4, 7, 24, 42–6, 47, 70, 72, 75, 76, 79, 83, 90, 101, 106, 110, 116, 147, 148, 151, 163, 165, 171, 179, 182
Gilchrist, R. 140
Gladwin, C. 16, 27–8
Gleeson, J. W. 137
Goddard, J. D. C. 140, 141, 144, 145
Goddard, T. W. J. 14–15, 19, 21, 67, 158
Gooch, G. A. 109, 156–7, 172, 181, 194
Gover, A. R. 64

Gower, D. I. 71, 155, 157, 165, 172
Graveney, D. A. 49, 160, 171, 186, 193, 195
Graveney, T. W. 17, 18, 22, 25, 26, 39, 51, 58, 61, 77, 81, 84, 101, 124–5, 136, 148, 150, 157, 172–3
Greenidge, C. G. 175
Greig, A. W. 74
Grieves, K. J. 56
Griffith, C. C. 119
Grout, A. W. T. 126, 127, 128

# H

Hadlee, R. J. 179, 186, 192
Hall, W. W. 119
Hammond, W. R. 20, 21, 30, 128
Hampshire, J. H. 1, 40, 70, 76, 81, 86
Harman, R. 101, 103
Harvey, R. N. 51, 120, 121, 132
Harris, C. B. 28
Hassett, A. L. 32
Hazell, H. L. 28–9, 172–3
Heine, P. S. 119
Hemmings, E. E. 105, 106–7, 110, 112, 179
Higgs, J. D. 113–14
Hobbs, Sir J. B. 50, 148, 192
Hobbs, R. N. S. 4, 47, 48–50, 96, 163, 177, 179, 182
Hogg, R. M. 113, 188
Holding, M. A. 2, 10, 164, 187, 189, 195
Hollies, W. E. 27–33, 101, 116, 149, 162
Horner, N. F. 27–8
Hughes, D. P. 75
Hughes, K. J. 116–17, 118, 184
Humpage, G. 152
Humphries, D. J. 7, 165
Hutton, Sir L. 34, 35, 88, 148

# I

Ikin, J. T. 56

Illingworth, R. 3, 8, 10, 37, 38, 42, 46, 56, 59, 64, 69–71, 76, 77, 79, 84, 87, 88, 89, 110, 115, 116, 134, 135, 136, 163, 170, 173
Imran Khan 172, 191
Insole, D. J. 5–6, 37, 39, 59, 61, 139, 149–50
Intikhab Alam 84–6, 87, 179
Inverarity, R. J. 133, 134, 136, 137
Iqbal Quasim 190

# J

Jackson, V. E. 61
Jarman, B. N. 135, 136
Jenkins, R. O. 7, 22–7, 29, 33, 54, 59, 61–2, 149
Johnson, G. W. 8, 182
Johnson, I. W. 121, 124, 150
Jones, A. 10, 83, 102, 149, 158

# K

Kallicharran, A. I. 84, 174
Kanhai, R. B. 50, 84
Kent, M. F. 156
Kenyon, D. 185
Knight, R. D. V. 181
Knott, A. P. E. 7–8, 52, 69, 78–9, 134, 136, 138, 149, 155, 159, 160, 162–4, 166, 167, 175, 184, 193

# L

Laker, J. C. 2, 5, 9, 10, 39, 51–3, 56, 57, 64, 70, 83, 89, 90, 99, 101, 116, 119–25, 135, 144, 162, 173
Lamb, A. J. 147, 172
Lambert, G. E. 15, 24
Langridge, John 13–14, 15
Larkins, W. 181
Lawrence, J. 88, 89, 172
Lawry, W. M. 126, 132, 134
Lawson, G. F. 188

Lever, J. K. 46–7, 180
Lewis, B. 102
Leyland, M. 25
Lillee, D. K. 10, 34, 119, 161, 188, 189, 190
Lindwall, R. R. 31, 112, 119, 131, 195
Livingston, T. L. 63
Lloyd, C. H. 84, 190
Lock. G. A. R. 38, 39–42, 88, 101, 119, 120, 121, 122, 123, 125, 141, 162
Love, J. D. 181

# M

McConnon, J. 52
McDonald, C. C. 86, 121–3
McEwan, K. S. 172
McHugh, F. P. 60
McIntyre, A. J. W. 40, 101–2
McKenzie, G. D. 126–7, 128, 131, 132, 136, 138
Mackay, K. D. 120, 122, 126, 127, 130, 131
Maddocks, L. V. 119, 122, 130
Majid Khan 172
Makepeace, H. 56
Mallender, N. 182
Mallett, A. A. 136
Marlar, R. G. 125
Marsh, R. W. 7, 89, 160, 161
Martin, J. W. 27
May, P. B. H. 37, 58, 77, 116, 121, 123, 125, 126, 128, 132, 139–45, 148, 150, 157–8, 187
Mendis, G. D. 181
Milburn, C. 136, 138
Miller, G. 5, 89, 113
Miller, K. R. 31, 36, 112, 119, 122
Milton, C. A. 13, 18, 20, 68, 99, 150
Morgan, D. C. 16
Mortimore, J. B. 17, 60, 67–8, 97, 98, 151
Moss, A. E. 17
Murray, D. L. 84

Murray, J. T. 63, 64, 66, 68, 130, 132, 166–7, 168
Mushtaq Mohammad 86–7, 149, 168

# N

Neale, P. A. 151
Newman, P. 191

# O

O'Neill, N. C. 130
Oakman, A. S. M. 120, 122, 125
Old, C. M. 115–16, 180
Oldfield, W. A. S. 162
Oslear, D. O. 192

# P

Parfitt, P. H. 66
Parker, C. W. L. 14, 17, 68
Parker, P. W. G. 181
Parks, J. M. 16, 167, 170
Patel, D. 7, 151
Peel, R. 3, 36, 76
Pocock, P. I. 4, 8, 46, 81–4, 86, 92, 147, 149, 151, 163, 174–5, 181
Pollock, P. M. 119
Pont, K. R. 172, 181
Pritchard, T. L. 28
Procter, M. J. 97, 119, 160
Pullar, G. 127, 131

# R

Ramadhin, S. 139–45, 150
Randall, D. W. 45, 113–14, 154, 173
Reddy, B. 160
Redpath, I. R. 134
Rhodes, W. 3, 9, 36, 76, 169
Rice, C. E. B. 98, 106, 112, 173, 179
Richards, B. A. 75, 175

Richards, I. V. A. 86, 96, 107–8, 171, 172, 177, 178
Richards, C. J. 167
Richardson, P. E. 139
Roberts, A. M. E. 2, 190
Robertson, J. D. B. 26
Rowan, E. A. B. 57

## S

Sadiq Mohammad 160
Sarfraz Nawaz 172
Sharp, G. 76, 87, 168
Sheahan, A. P. 78, 135
Shepherd, D. J. 102
Sheppard, the Rt. Rev. D. S. 120, 125
Simmons, J. 175–6
Simpson, R. B. 128, 130, 131, 132
Simpson, R. T. 60, 144, 189
Sims, J. M. 64, 66, 90, 149
Skelding, A. 15
Smith, M. J. K. 40, 47–8, 72, 81, 111, 155–6, 169, 170, 176, 187
Smith, T. P. B. 47, 149
Snow, J. A. 69, 134, 136
Sobers, Sir G. St. A. 84
Spooner, R. T. 157
Statham, J. B. 2, 56, 119, 127, 130
Steele, J. F. 115
Stollmeyer, J. B. 192–3
Subba Row, R. 127, 128, 129, 130, 131
Sutcliffe, H. 192

## T

Tattersall, R. 52, 53, 56–8, 162
Taylor, B. 50
Taylor, D. D. 28
Taylor, K. A. 180, 184–5
Taylor, R. W. 159, 160, 162, 167
Thomson, J. R. 190
Tidy, W. N. 100–1, 102
Titmus, F. J. 10, 43, 63–7, 68, 81, 83, 89, 90, 92, 95, 112, 166–7, 177, 187

Tolchard, R. W. 69, 70, 88, 167
Toshack, E. R. H. 112
Townsend, C. L. 67
Tribe, G. E. 61–3, 77, 88, 165–6
Trueman, F. S. 11, 36, 38, 68, 119, 127, 128, 133, 195
Trumper, V. T. 128
Turner, G. M. 45, 72, 147, 151, 152, 153–4, 155, 166, 182, 190–1
Tyson, F. H. 20–1, 119, 195

## U

Underwood, D. L. 4, 5, 8, 22, 45–6, 76, 78–81, 92, 93, 103–4, 107–8, 119, 133–8, 147, 151, 163, 166, 167, 174, 179, 180, 182, 186

## V

Valentine, A. L. 139
Venkataraghavan, S. 74, 159
Verity, H. 3, 9, 76, 115

## W

Walcott, C. L. 2, 9
Walsh, J. E. 61–3, 88
Walters, K. D. 134
Wardle, J. H. 3, 5, 10, 33–9, 42, 46, 52, 60, 61, 69, 103, 110, 115, 143, 162, 177
Warner, Sir P. F. 32
Washbrook, C. 34, 62–3, 124
Wells, B. D. 11–18, 19, 20, 21, 22, 24, 43, 55, 60–1, 149, 156
Wharton, A. 36
Willey, P. 155, 168, 172, 180
Williams, R. G. 168, 172
Willis, R. G. D. 10, 112, 114, 117, 184, 185–96, 193
Wilson, D. 76–8, 104, 116, 155, 170, 171, 173
Wood, L. 174

Wooller, W. 185
Wright, D. V. P. 6, 20, 21, 22, 50,
    53–6, 59, 149, 161, 162, 164
Wyatt, R. E. S. 25–6

# Y

Yallop, G. N. 89, 113, 180
Yardley, N. W. D. 30
Yarnold, H. 7
Young, J. A. 64, 90
Younis Ahmed 182, 191

# Z

Zaheer Abbas 49, 70, 175, 182